OXFORD ENGLISH MONOGRAPHS

General Editors

CONRAD
AND
WOMEN

SUSAN JONES

CLARENDON PRESS · OXFORD

OXFORD

UNIVERSITY PRESS

Great Clarendon Street, Oxford OX2 6DP

Oxford University Press is a department of the University of Oxford.
It furthers the University's objective of excellence in research, scholarship,
and education by publishing worldwide in

Oxford New York

Athens Auckland Bangkok Bogotá Buenos Aires Calcutta
Cape Town Chennai Dar es Salaam Delhi Florence Hong Kong Istanbul
Karachi Kuala Lumpur Madrid Melbourne Mexico City Mumbai
Nairobi Paris São Paulo Singapore Taipei Tokyo Toronto Warsaw

and associated companies in Berlin Ibadan

Oxford is a registered trade mark of Oxford University Press
in the UK and certain other countries

Published in the United States
by Oxford University Press Inc., New York

© Susan Jones 1999

The moral rights of the author have been asserted
Database right Oxford University Press (maker)

First published 1999

British Library Cataloguing in Publication Data

Data available

Library of Congress Cataloging in Publication Data

Jones, Susan, 1952–
Conrad and women / Susan Jones.
Includes bibliographical references (p.   ) and index.
1. Conrad, Joseph, 1857–1924—Characters—Women.   2. Conrad,
Joseph, 1857–1924—Relations with women.   3. Authors, English—20th
century—Biography.   4. Women—Books and reading.   5. Women in
literature.   I. Title.
PR6005.04Z7494   1999
823'.912—dc21   99-20890

ISBN-0-19-818448-4

1 3 5 7 9 10 8 6 4 2

Typeset by Graphicraft Limited, Hong Kong
Printed in Great Britain
on acid-free paper by
Bookcraft Ltd.
Midsomer Norton, Somerset

Acknowledgements

I am grateful to The British Academy for an Award, and to St Hilda's College for supporting doctoral work that contributed to this book. My thanks go to The University of Glasgow for electing me to a Newlands Visitorship, which provided me with valuable research time and access to the University Library's Special Collections. Much of the manuscript was prepared while teaching at the National University of Ireland, Galway and I would like to thank my colleagues in the Department of English.

I would like to thank the Librarians of the Beinecke Library at Yale University, the Berg Collection of the New York Public Library, the Bodleian Library, Oxford, the British Library and the Newspaper Library, Colindale, the Rockefeller Library and the John Hay Library at Brown University, and the University of Glasgow Library. I also appreciate the support of Hugh Epstein, Keith Carabine, and The Joseph Conrad Society of Great Britain; and of Bette and James Carey, whose help and hospitality made research in New York possible as well as a delight. I would like to thank Lyndall Gordon for her generous support, encouragement, and friendship. I have been fortunate to receive advice and assistance from John Batchelor, D. F. McKenzie, Martha Vogeler, John H. Stape, Gene Moore, Owen Knowles, Sid Reid, Robert Hampson, and Cedric Watts. My special thanks to numerous friends, especially Sandra Dodson, Tamara Follini, Clare Morgan, Elizabeth Tilley, Kathy Laing, Allan Simmons, Eckhard Thiemann, Matt Carey, Judith Toms, Sherman Sam, and Dora Jones.

For permission to reproduce manuscript material I thank the Berg Collection of English and American Literature, The New York Public Library, Astor, Lenox and Tilden Foundations; the Joseph Conrad Collection, General Collection, Beinecke Library, Yale University; Glasgow University Library, Department of Special Collections.

For permission to reproduce the illustrations I would like to thank: for Fig. 2, front cover/spine from *Chance: A Tale in Two*

Parts by Joseph Conrad, 1913. Shelfmark = 25611 e 2560, the Bodleian Library, University of Oxford. For Figs. 1, 3, 4, the General Research Division, The New York Public Library, Astor, Lenox and Tilden Foundations. For permission to use material from parts of this book already published elsewhere I thank the editors of *The Review of English Studies*, Oxford University Press (Ch. 8); of *The Conradian* (Ch. 5) and *Editions Rodopi*; and Maria Curie Skłodowska University, Lublin (Ch. 2). For their hard work in producing the book I give warm thanks to Jason Freeman, Sophie Goldsworthy, Frances Whistler, and Tom Chandler of Oxford University Press.

This book is for Dan with thanks for his help, inspiration, and love.

Contents

Editorial Note

Unless otherwise stated, all references to the work of Joseph Conrad are taken from The Collected Edition of the Works of Joseph Conrad (London: Dent, 1946–55), and page numbers are quoted in the text.

Unless otherwise stated, all references to the letters of Joseph Conrad are taken from *The Collected Letters of Joseph Conrad* (ed. Frederick R. Karl and Laurence Davies (Cambridge: Cambridge University Press, 1983–   )) and abbreviated as *CL* followed by the volume number: vol. 1 (1861–97); vol. 2 (1898–1902); vol. 3 (1903–7); vol. 4 (1908–11); vol. 5 (1912–16).

Preamble

In a letter of 14 July 1923, written near the end of his life, Joseph Conrad reflected on the shape of his career and public reputation as a writer. Corresponding with Richard Curle, he worried that the prevailing image of him as an author of sea stories risked obscuring the full range of his work. He hoped to be 'freed from that infernal tail of ships', since, in reality, 'in the body of my work barely one tenth is what may be called sea stuff'.[1] Not only did the popular perception overstate his devotion to nautical tales, but he added the complaint that the mere presence of seamen in many of his books did not necessarily make them sea stories. Yet Conrad's objection to his public profile did little to prevent the survival of a reputation established during his lifetime. Even today Conrad is still most widely recognised as a writer of 'sea stuff', a man in a man's world, occupying an exclusively masculine tradition.

Nowhere is this bias more striking than in the received view of Conrad's relation to women. Ostensibly, as a man of the sea we assume that Conrad must have neglected women's themes and felt ill-prepared to engage in their concerns. But, as I argue in this book, the evidence of his biography, correspondence, and fiction suggests a very different conclusion, indicating a complex and intriguing relationship between Conrad, the women in his life, his female characters and readers of his work. This is not to deny that Conrad produced important representations of the male consciousness and male society, but rather to redress the imbalance in our perception of his widespread preoccupations. Although he explored the epistemological dilemmas of the male protagonists in the earlier part of his career and never relinquished these themes altogether, he began in the Malay fiction by producing prominent female figures whose position offered an important critique of imperialism, a role that women continued to fulfil in the political works of the middle years,

---

[1] G. Jean-Aubry, *Joseph Conrad: Life and Letters* (New York: Doubleday Page, 1927), ii. 316.

such as *Nostromo*, *The Secret Agent*, and *Under Western Eyes*. Later his work appeared in the highly visual contexts of popular magazines and journals, and he embarked on a new form of investigation, questioning the presentation of spectacle, outward appearances, and the framing of the aesthetic object.[2] Above all he increasingly turned to the issue of gender, female identity, and, in relation to romance, how women are invited to conform to its conventionalised gestures and plots.

Many critics have identified a decline in his shift towards the romance genre in the later work, but I argue that they miss the continuity in his career and neglect important aspects of his experimentation and social commentary. He was not altogether the lonely seaman uncomfortable in female company, but rather a sympathetic interpreter of women's contemporary situation. His relationship to women, to his women characters, and his women readers was at times difficult, challenging, but nevertheless one that initiated an astute, though largely unrecognised, exploration of female identity in the fiction.

In order to rehabilitate Conrad in relation to women, I investigate a host of issues, drawing on criticism of his novels, questions of biography, issues of marketing, textual scholarship, and visual theory. I take a historical perspective initially, and begin in Chapter 1 with a survey of critics' responses to the theme of Conrad and women, showing the way in which he has been traditionally associated with a predominantly male discourse. The reception of his work in modernist circles privileged a narrow band of texts that focused on male experience through the fragmentation of the text, the dislocation of consciousness, the undermining of realist ventures in fiction, the questioning of the nature and meaning of textuality. This trend of taste and critical evaluation neglected large portions of his work and overlooked important evidence, but it particularly inhibited any serious attention to his later work when he experimented with popular forms such as the romance, historical novel, and sensation fiction.

Biographical criticism has also co-operated with the male-oriented reading of his fiction, and Conrad emerges as someone

---

[2] Jean-Aubry, *Life and Letters*, ii. 317. In this letter to Curle, Conrad emphasised the continuity in his work in terms of its visual aspect, which, he claimed, was always 'fluid, depending on grouping (sequence) which shifts, and on the changing lights giving varied effects of perspective'.

who preferred the company of men and who looked to women only for domestic and moral support. In Chapters 2 and 3 I consider major female influences on his life and writing. First, I explore the female presence during his formative years in Poland, and illuminate the role played by female protagonists in Conrad's fiction by considering them in the context of the status and image of women in Polish romantic literature and culture. Second, I explore the role of his distant cousin by marriage, Marguerite Poradowska, as a creative influence on Conrad's career. Poradowska, herself a writer of French fiction, corresponded with Conrad during his transition from seaman to author, and the two frequently discussed each other's work. In the letters, Poradowska provided an audience for some of Conrad's earliest rehearsals of later fictional themes, and in the texts of her novels she offered valuable source material for his experimentation with romance forms.

In Chapter 4, challenging traditional notions of the Conrad canon, I introduce his novel *Chance* as the central focus of this book. Serialised in *The New York Herald* Sunday Magazine in 1912, and aimed at the women readers of the paper, the novel represented a turning-point in Conrad's career, his first economically successful venture in reaching a wider audience and addressing the themes of gender and romance that would occupy the later fiction. Conrad's creation of a central female protagonist has often been heralded as the moment when his artistic powers began to diminish. The novel has also received negative responses from those critics who see it as an unsuccessful attempt to emulate Henry James. Instead, I read *Chance* as a new direction in Conrad's fiction, one where he engages in a theoretical debate with 'The Master' on the relationship of vision and epistemology in the presentation of women in romance.

In Chapter 5 I look at the genesis of the novel in greater detail. By studying three texts of *Chance* (manuscript, serial, published novel) we gain a sense, not merely of the length of Conrad's commitment to the project but also the nature of the experiment he engaged in. This novel's history offers a paradigm for Conrad's artistic development from the early years of 'rites of passage' narratives of an exclusively male discourse, through to the responses to gender and genre in the late work, revealing a greater continuity in Conrad's career and establishing a serious alternative to the bifurcation of his fiction into 'achievement and decline' (established by Thomas Moser and followed by numerous other critics).

Chapters 6 and 7 place Conrad's work in a wider textual field. I explore Conrad's shift in methodology in the later fiction, showing how it arises partly from a response to the visual emphasis found in his new marketing contexts. In spite of the modernist emphasis on the fragmentation of vision, the new media of glossy magazines, photographs, and films ensured the endurance of hegemonic codes—of perspective, framing devices, and portraiture. Conrad examined the survival of these codes in a literal sense, looking at the ways in which traditional structures of vision contribute to the limitation of female identity, particularly within the popular genres. Conrad's unexpected contribution to an ongoing debate about female identity, in novels like *Chance*, *Victory*, *The Arrow of Gold*, *The Rover*, and *The Rescue*, puts him in a much closer relationship with his contemporaries, with the work of authors ranging from Wharton, James, Bennett, Galsworthy, Ford, to the inexpensive editions of neglected popular writers.

The final chapter explores the late works in relation to an earlier popular form of women's writing: the sensation novel of the 1860s and 1870s. By comparing Conrad's final, unfinished novel *Suspense* (published posthumously, 1925), and the sensation fiction of Mary Braddon and others (particularly Braddon's *Lady Audley's Secret* (1862)) I show the extent to which Conrad was indebted to the methods of sensationalism right up to the end of his life. The closing chapter demonstrates the importance of women's writing, women readers, female portraiture, and the relationship of text and illustration in the serialised novels in shaping Conrad's later fiction. It draws attention to the re-emergence of Poradowska's influence, and how, in the late work in particular, Conrad exploited the techniques of traditional forms in order to question the structures of romance which continued to confine and classify women.

I
Conrad, Women, and the Critics

Nothing is more familiar to readers of Joseph Conrad than the image of the author as a lonely seafarer, drawing on the memories of life on board ship to construct the tales that sustained his career as a writer. We can easily picture the sensitive, displaced individual fashioning modernist narratives of dislocation and despair upon the moral framework of a male community to which he gave priority, and from which, above all, women were excluded. The conventionalised view is highly selective, but it has nevertheless proved remarkably enduring, and has reduced the value of much of the work that fails to fit its frame of reference. My purpose is to challenge the prevailing image of Conrad and to offer an alternative to its tenacious hold on the critical tradition. But before such a powerful paradigm can be overturned, it needs to be understood in the light of its long history. This chapter focuses on the construction of Conrad's public image, beginning with an account of Conrad criticism (including the earliest notices of his published work), at the same time considering the marketing strategies used by various editors and friends to promote his fiction. Subsequently, I explore the ways in which his biography has been understood and disseminated in the light of the received critical tradition.

Conrad's association with the sea established his reputation as an author of exotic adventure told from within a predominantly male discourse. The marketing of his early novels capitalised on the portrait of the sailor turned writer, a gentleman of the Polish 'szlachta'[1] who transformed the voyages of his youth into tales expressing nostalgia for the male seafaring community (as in 'Youth' and 'Typhoon'). For example, in 1904, *T.P.'s Weekly* published an unsigned biographical article to promote

---

[1] The term 'szlachta' has no equivalent in English. It refers to a hereditary class of landowning gentry established initially in medieval Poland, and to which Conrad's father belonged. See Ch. 2 n. 5.

the serialisation of *Nostromo*, drawing attention to the masculine tone of the writer's former life and its compatibility with his current authorial intention. His unnamed biographer observed that he 'wanted things always to be shipshape, in his writings as at sea'. While Conrad had previously endeavoured 'to turn his Conway boys into fine seamen', he now applied the moral incentives of the 'ancient and honourable craft' of seamanship to his new career as a writer.[2] Advertisements in the journal complemented the masculine image, with instalments of *Nostromo* sandwiched between notices for 'Three Nun's Tobacco' and ' "Citizen", the World's Best Boot for Men'. Prior to the serialisation of *Nostromo*, the tone of male exclusivity associated with the initial representation of Conrad had also been supported by the contexts in which his early works appeared. *Heart of Darkness* (1898–9), *Lord Jim* (1899–1900), 'Youth' (1898) and other short stories were published in *Blackwood's Magazine*, a literary journal suffused with the character of the gentleman's club, often imperialist in perspective and at times jingoistic in tone.[3]

The popular impression of Conrad as a male-oriented author of nautical tales coincided with his reputation for awkwardness with women. When Lady Ottoline Morrell expressed a desire to meet Conrad, the writer Henry James deterred her: 'But, dear Lady . . . he has lived his life at sea . . . he has never met "civilised" women.'[4] Lady Ottoline's later comments on Jessie Conrad corroborated this line of thinking. She saw Conrad's relationship with his wife not as one of compatibility, but one where Jessie merely represented 'a good and reposeful mattress for this hypersensitive, nerve-wrecked man, who did not ask from his wife high intelligence, only an assuagement of life's vibrations'.[5] The undignified description of Jessie, emphasising her passive role

---

[2] *T.P.'s Weekly*, 22 January 1904, 113. The Conway was a naval training ship of the time, of the type represented in *Lord Jim*.

[3] *Blackwood's* had initially developed out of a Tory response to the Whig *Edinburgh Review* in 1817. Thomas Power O'Connor founded *T.P's Weekly* in 1902. Designed to reach a wide audience, it was nevertheless sober in presentation. O'Connor was also well known in turn-of-the century journalism for his establishment of the *Star* and the *Sun*.

[4] Lady Ottoline Morrell, *Ottoline: The Early Memoirs of Lady Ottoline Morrell*, ed. Robert Gathorne-Hardy (London: Faber and Faber, 1963), 240.

[5] Ibid. 241.

and lack of sophistication, confirmed a popular image of the author's indifference to female companionship.

This reductive view of Conrad shows considerable persistence. With varying degrees of subtlety, the popular image still reflects the isolated sailor of exotic Polish origins transformed into a man of letters, who married beneath him to provide himself with a housekeeper, but who still preferred male camaraderie to the society of women. In 1960, Graham Hough extended the argument to include Conrad's literary audience. He insisted on Conrad's inaccessibility to women readers, locating the author's work in a 'male world':

In my experience very few women really enjoy Conrad, and this is not only because the feminine sensibility so often ceases to function at the mere mention of a topsail halyard, but because the characteristic concerns and occupations of the woman's world play such a very small part in Conrad's work.[6]

The presence of women characters in Conrad's novels has caused the greatest difficulties for such critics. Even by the 1980s some commentators could only account for Conrad's inclusion of female roles in his novels by referring to the author's commodification of them. Edward Said identified a list of 'substances' occupying Conrad's imagination, which the author drew upon as organising materials for his narratives: 'Lingard's gold, Kurtz's ivory, the ships of sailors, Gould's silver, the women that drew men to chance and romance'.[7] Meanwhile, some feminist critics continue to interpret Conrad's narratives as unremittingly patriarchal, reading into his presentation of women a blatant and uncomplicated misogyny. Joyce Carol Oates, for example, is convinced that Conrad's 'quite serious idea of a "heroine"' is always someone 'who effaces herself completely, who is eager to sacrifice herself in an ecstasy of love for her man'.[8] Drawn in by his lasting reputation, critics have dismissed the possibility that women have had any positive impact on Conrad's creative

[6] Graham Hough, *Image and Experience: Studies in a Literary Revolution* (London: Duckworth, 1960), 214.

[7] Edward Said, *The World, The Text and the Critic* (London: Faber and Faber, 1984), 106.

[8] Joyce Carol Oates, *Contraries: Essays* (New York: Oxford University Press, 1981), 84.

life, that they have taken a valid position in his fiction, or that
Conrad spoke to women readers.

Yet the evidence of his letters and essays suggests a much more
complex relationship between Conrad, the women in his life, and
the female characters of his narratives. While biographers and
scholars have privileged Conrad's correspondence with his many
male literary friends, his letters to Marguerite Poradowska,
Emilie Briquel, Constance Garnett, his wife Jessie, and others
reveal an identification with women that has gone largely unnoticed. One preliminary reference will serve as an example of
the material that has been neglected or dismissed. Early in his
career as a writer Conrad made a remarkable confession to his
close friend Mrs Helen Sanderson, in a letter congratulating
her on the birth of a daughter. The tone of the letter frankly
expressed his anxieties as a father, and his somewhat bewildered
and rather distanced early relationship to his son Borys (who
had been born the year before, on 15 January 1898). Most arresting in this letter is the following remark: 'I do not mind own-
ing I wished for a daughter. I can't help feeling she would have
resembled me more and would have been perhaps easier to
understand.'[9] This statement so baffled one commentator that
he dismissed it with an air of disbelief: 'His explanation for his
preference is to say the least, extraordinary, for it carries the
implication that he viewed himself as having more in common
with girls than with boys.'[10]

Conrad's identification with the female sex in this letter offers
a starting point for a critical re-evaluation. If, similarly, Conrad
identified with the daughters of his fiction, how might we reread
the roles of Nina, Aïssa, Winnie Verloc, Freya, Alice Jacobus,
Flora de Barral, Adèle de Montevesso, whose sense of exclusion
from the central narratives of men often match Conrad's self-
confessed feelings of dislocation and despair?

In order to address this issue we need first to gain a historical perspective on the formation of critical attitudes to the
subject of Conrad and women, showing the ways in which the
expectations of the market place (set against Conrad's ambiguous

---

[9] Letter to Mrs Helen Sanderson, 26 February 1899, *CL* 2, 173.
[10] Bernard C. Meyer, *Joseph Conrad: A Psychoanalytic Biography* (Princeton:
Princeton University Press, 1967).

attitude to the marketing of his novels), the early reception of his fiction, and the construction of the author's public persona created a precedent for a lasting view of his artistic incentives. Attempts were underway early on to deconstruct the prevailing image after Conrad's death, but they were soon overshadowed by the influence of critics of the 1940s and 1950s who recovered Conrad's work for modernist studies. These critics promoted the conventionalised view because it fitted with their particular agenda, and they often dismissed the material that failed to accommodate their themes.

I

In the light of subsequent criticism, it is something of a paradox that the earliest critical responses to Conrad's women characters were favourable. Following the publication of *Almayer's Folly* (1895), several critics considered that the *only* merit of his first novel resided in his presentation of female figures. *Literary World* (Boston) described the novel as 'a rather dull and dreary story', but one in which the scenes between Mrs Almayer and her daughter Nina show 'remarkable insight into the point of view of the Eastern woman'.[11] The London *Daily News* praised the characterisation of Nina Almayer,[12] while the New York *Bookman* described her presentation as 'masterly'.[13] Conrad's early Malay novels gained a limited reputation for the author, not for the rigorous intellectual component for which the works of the middle period became associated, but for their qualities as exotic 'romances'. H. G. Wells considered that the 'gloom' of *Almayer's Folly* was only relieved by the 'rare beauty' of the love story, and that *An Outcast of the Islands* (1896) showed great authenticity as 'real romance'.[14]

In fact, contrary to the reviewers' assumptions, even at this early stage of his career Conrad was writing against rather than aligning himself with popular or conventional generic forms.

[11] Unsigned review, 'Fiction: *Almayer's Folly*', *Literary World* 27 (18 May 1895), 155.　　　　[12] Unsigned Review, *Daily News*, 25 April 1895, 6.
[13] James MacArthur, 'New Books: Romance in Malaya', *Bookman* 2 (Aug.–Sept. 1895), 39–41.
[14] H. G. Wells, review, *The Saturday Review*, 16 May 1896, 509–10.

He brings the influence of French realism (from his reading of Flaubert, Maupassant, and Pierre Loti) to the genre of exotic romance, where his protagonists operate, not in a fantasy world of adventure, an 'empire of the imagination',[15] but in a bleak world of colonial opportunism. Nina Almayer's conflict of identity—split as she is between the influences of her Europhile father and native mother—disturbs the harmony of the romance closure. And the shifting narratorial perspectives of *Outcast* allow the reader to question the function of Aïssa's role as *femme fatale* of a tale of imperialist adventure. As Aïssa's presence increasingly disrupts political negotiations (between white and native factions), Conrad comments on the way in which women are denied access to the action in the masculine world of the adventure novel, while the female presence represents both the (white European male's) romantic desire for oblivion, and the threat of 'the other' whom he wishes to overpower and colonise. To the male protagonist Willems, the eroticism of Aïssa's enticing gaze represents the palpability of a weapon: 'he felt the touch of a look darted at him' (68–9)—'hard, keen, and narrow, like the gleam of sharp steel' (71). Willems's experience complies with the trope of male abandonment of identity to the enchanting but deadly threat of the *femme fatale*. But Aïssa's sense of Willems's alterity is presented with equal force, complicating the notion of a fixed imperial subject embodied in the white European male. To her, Willems also represents the exotic 'other' and from her perspective, his sense of colonialist superiority is enduring. He fails to concede any real autonomy to her. Instead, he takes exception to her cultural and religious customs, 'tearing off her face-veil' and trampling on it 'as though it had been a mortal enemy' (39), expecting her to abandon her people

---

[15] Reference to H. Rider Haggard, *She* (1887; Harmondsworth: Penguin, 1994). Conrad may have been alluding to the name of Haggard's protagonist, Ayesha, in his novel. Haggard's male protagonists explore 'the heart of the darkness' of Ayesha's Africa (261). See also a further allusion to Haggard's novel in Conrad's 'The Lagoon', *Tales of Unrest* (1898; London: Dent, 1947), 187–9, in the sense of dislocation experienced by the white man on entering the lagoon. Haggard also remarked how 'three modern Englishmen . . . seemed . . . out of tone with that measureless desolation' during their river journey in Africa (70). See also Andrea White, *Joseph Conrad and the Adventure Tradition* (Cambridge: Cambridge University Press, 1993), 99. White compares Haggard to Captain Marryat or Charles Kingsley: 'Haggard initiated a certain shift in the genre of adventure fiction that subverted some of its most traditional claims concerning the imperial subject.'

without offering her either Christian compassion or honesty in return, but concealing from her instead the fact that he is married. Conrad allows Aïssa a moment of clarity as she realises Willems's moral weakness and 'the tremendous fact of our isolation' (250)—the kind of recognition we usually associate with the Conradian hero. Yet her tragedy, like Willems's, emerges from a failure of vision. She is unable to acknowledge that she provides only temporary consolation for Willems, a transitory appeal in the face of his loss of identity and exile from the white man's world. When Willems's wife and son arrive at Aïssa's encampment and Aïssa shoots her lover from grief and despair, Conrad to some extent presents her role sympathetically, from the perspective of the native woman habitually betrayed by the white man. Aïssa's crime of passion, which will be repeated by two of Conrad's later heroines, Mme Levaille ('The Idiots') and Winnie Verloc in *The Secret Agent*, initiates a recurring theme in the fiction in which women play an important role in the critique of imperialism (both in colonialist and European settings).

The early critics' praise of Conrad's female characters reflects the substantiality of their roles in the plots of the Malay fiction rather than the ambiguity of their position within a critique of imperialism. But these views also reflect the expectations of critics testing a new arrival to the market for fiction. Just as the publisher William Blackwood, who initially gave Conrad an opening in *Blackwood's Magazine*, anticipated that he might develop into another Stevenson or a Kipling, reviewers of this period probably felt that he would go on producing exotic romances, maturing as a narrator of patriotic tales or adventure stories.

However, Conrad's reputation for the invention of romance roles for female characters would soon be eclipsed by the publication of *The Nigger of the 'Narcissus'* in 1897. Review after review regretted that 'the only female in the book is the ship herself'.[16] While *Literature* and *The Academy* both found Conrad's dismissal of 'hackneyed themes'[17] more challenging than most, the publications with a wider and less strictly literary readership

[16] Unsigned review, *Daily Mail*, 7 Dec. 1897, 3. There are women in *The Nigger*—the master's wife and Archie's mother—but these hardly count as substantial roles.

[17] Unsigned review, *Literature*, 26 March 1898, 354; and unsigned review, *The Academy* 1 January 1898, 1.

felt otherwise. James Payn, in *The Illustrated London News*, regarded Conrad's omission of the romance plot as something of an affront to the reader, comparing Conrad with the then famous writer of the sea, Clark Russell, who 'is so far complaisant to his readers as to admit a petticoat on board, even at the risk of the Queen's Regulations'. He warned the author of *The Nigger* that his readers, 'not content with ships and his ships' crews . . . may land and leave him'.[18]

With the publication of *The Nigger* a critical pattern begins to emerge in relation to Conrad's work. Reviewers of the more popular publications indicated that a steady diet of popular romance, aimed at a wide female readership, was Conrad's safest guarantee of sales. But at the same time his reputation was deliberately being fostered in a different way, first by W. E. Henley, who serialised *The Nigger* in *The New Review* (1897),[19] and then by William Blackwood, who soon realised that Conrad's work would be unlikely to reach the audiences commanded by Captain Marryat or Rider Haggard. These publishers promoted the image of the author as a writer for a somewhat select, coterie audience, thus initiating his reputation as what would later be termed 'modernist'. Their aim (one that coincided to some extent with Conrad's intellectual preference), was to avoid capitulating to the stale plots and characters required by the popular market.

Conrad desired popularity, yet shunned the writing of a 'popular novel'. He refused to send 'The Return' to *Pearson's Magazine*, even though this popular journal had expressed interest in his early work, and he informed T. Fisher Unwin that the piece was 'too good for any blamed magazine'.[20] In 1902 he

[18] James Payn, *Illustrated London News*, 5 Feb. 1898, 172. It is interesting to note that Rider Haggard had gained great success with *King Solomon's Mines* (1885; Oxford: Oxford University Press, 1989) in spite of the narrator's admission that 'there is not a *petticoat* in the whole history' (9). But Haggard adhered to the genre of 'boy's own' adventure, whereas Conrad's more overtly philosophical style in *Nigger* broke the conventions of the adventure tradition.

[19] See Peter D. McDonald, *British Literary Culture and Publishing Practice 1880–1914* (Cambridge: Cambridge University Press, 1997), 22–67, for a discussion of Conrad's shaping of the *Nigger of the 'Narcissus'* for the audience of the 'Henley circle'.

[20] Letter to T. Fisher Unwin, 5 Nov. 1897, *CL* I, 405. Conrad later thought less of 'The Return' (published in *Tales of Unrest*, 1898). In the Author's Note he referred to this story as 'a left-handed production' (viii).

wrote to George Blackwood (William's nephew) that 'it is an unspeakable relief to write for *Maga* [*Blackwood's*] instead of for "the market"—confound it and all its snipperty works'.[21]

In his discussion of the commercial background to the modernist novel, David Trotter outlines the circumstances in which the literary market of this period facilitated the somewhat ambiguous position of a writer like Conrad. The marketing of fiction underwent a significant change by the end of the 1880s. The demise of the 'three-decker' novel that had supplied circulating libraries like Smith's and Mudie's since the 1820s made room for the marketing of single novels at competitive prices. This climate gave rise to the bestseller, supplying publishers with the bulk of their revenue. But the single-volume novels simultaneously established a different sort of market. Publishers also produced higher-priced volumes for little profit, appealing to readers of literary taste in order to foster their reputation for supporting 'good' literature.[22] They soon realised that Conrad could be marketed in single volumes in this way (although, as Conrad discovered, the financial rewards for the writer were slight).[23]

Experimental writers like Conrad struggled to establish themselves financially in the new system, but, as Peter Keating has remarked, the advent of the single volume at least enabled them to make contact with a minority readership that was sympathetic to their work.[24] Garnett, Henley, and others all encouraged Conrad in his writing of sea stories whose philosophical tone prevented their assimilation into the genre of conventional

[21] Letter to George Blackwood, 28 Jan. 1902, *CL* 2, 375. Many of Conrad's early short stories were published in literary journals rather than popular magazines: 'The Idiots' in *The Savoy* (1896); 'An Outpost of Progress' in *Cosmopolis* (1897); 'The Lagoon' in *The Cornhill* (1897).

[22] David Trotter, *The English Novel in History* (London: Routledge, 1993), 64. Trotter argues that this situation in the marketplace gives rise to the modernist novel.

[23] See also Linda K. Hughes and Michael Lund, *The Victorian Serial* (Charlottesville and London: University of Virginia Press, 1991), 243–5, who remark on the modernist characteristics, even of the serial version of *Lord Jim: A Sketch*, published in *Blackwood's*. The plot fails to advance in the traditional manner by adding new episodes to Jim's life in a directly linear fashion. Instead the narrative goes on 'circling back to report again and again' a single important moment (the jump from *The Patna*).

[24] Peter Keating, *The Haunted Study: A Social History of the English Novel 1875–1914* (London: Secker and Warburg, 1989), 405.

adventure fiction. The image of Conrad as the lonely sailor-turned-writer, dedicated to truth and authenticity, resistant to the pull of the marketplace, fitted well with the redirection of his work towards an intellectual élite. To some extent his failure to supply the endless heroines of popular romance accommodated the image of Conrad cultivated by the publishers of 'good' literature for a marginal readership.[25] His movement away from the subject of romance after the early Malay fiction (however sceptical the treatment) precipitated an enduring dismissal of his abilities and even desire to write about or for women.

II

In fact, relatively few Conrad novels and short stories contain no women characters, but by 1903 his reputation (fostered partly by literary friends and editors) had been firmly established on the strength of a series of narratives associated with the masculine world of the sea. This theme reached the status of a commonplace in Conrad criticism after the publication of *Tales of Unrest* (1898), and *Lord Jim* (1900), narratives that contained only limited female roles. The earlier praise for the women of the Malay fiction was replaced by references to the few 'subsidiary sketches of savage womanhood' used 'as figures to fill a space in the background of his painting'.[26]

Jewel's role in *Lord Jim* may be slight, but she fulfils an important function in Conrad's critique of romanticism in this novel. For Jewel, Jim's 'suicidal' act questions the validity of *her* status as 'heroine'. His decision to face death at the hands of Doramin, rather than escape with her, signifies his renunciation of the life she offers him and constitutes the habitual betrayal of the woman of indigenous or mixed race by the white man. Her accusation to Marlow and Stein, that 'you always leave

[25] See Alan Judd, *Ford Madox Ford* (Cambridge, Mass.: Harvard University Press, 1990), 77. Conrad discussed at length the problem of genre and popularity in the context of his collaborations with Ford Madox Ford. They set themselves an 'exercise' in writing for the market with *Romance* (1903), in which they aimed not to achieve 'great literature', but to write instead 'an exotic thriller that would be as successful as R. L. Stevenson's books'.

[26] Unsigned review, *Glasgow Evening News*, 30 April 1903, 2.

us—for your own ends' (348) disturbs the male narrators' empathetic view of Jim. Marlow fails adequately to justify Jim's
actions to Jewell, and Stein offers her his weakest defence of Jim's
action, retreating to a position of patronising moral superiority
over the woman by claiming that she simply fails to understand
him. Marlow's subsequent account of Jewel's courageous and
practical expression of loyalty to Jim, right up to his death, serves
only to strengthen *her* moral position.

The publication of *Nostromo* in 1904 elicited further disappointment from the *Daily Telegraph*, specifically for Conrad's
'disinclination to concern himself with the delineation of feminine nature'. The reviewer found promise in the figure of Mrs
Gould, but, he lamented, 'it is only a sketch' that is 'never per-
mitted to develop'.[27] Yet Emilia Gould's function in the narrative is not merely a symbolic one. Her growing self-consciousness
of the 'plaster-cast' pose of the colonialist women shows a
development in characterisation.[28] Initially she glides gracefully
between the elegant spaces of her husband's residence, occupying the role of benevolent colonialist. However, her increasingly
strained relations with a distant husband suggest her emerging
disillusionment with Charles Gould's ambitions. Towards the
end of the novel Conrad identifies the full extent of her insight,
her recognition of a hollow sacrifice to her husband's obsessive
enterprise in acquiring the San Tomé silver:

An immense desolation, the dread of her own continued life, descended
upon the first lady of Sulaco . . . lying passive in the grip of a merci-
less nightmare, she stammered out aimlessly the words—
   'Material interests.'   (522)

The physical manifestation of Mrs Gould's painful inward
vision transforms her formerly optimistic pose. Though sparingly
drawn, the figure of Mrs Gould plays a fundamental part in generating the critique of capitalist venture central to the novel.[29]

[27] Unsigned review, *Daily Telegraph*, 9 Nov. 1904, 4.
[28] Jim Reilly, *Shadowtime: History and Representation in Hardy, Conrad and
George Eliot* (London and New York: Routledge, 1993), 35. Reilly observes that
the Sulacan women, whom Conrad presents as powdered 'till they looked like white
plaster casts' (73) dramatically symbolise the effect of political stasis in *Nostromo*.
[29] In fact Conrad will return repeatedly to the presentation of gender to explore
the way in which imperialism manifests itself in acts of individual consciousness
as much as in relationships between nations. His presentation of the relationship

But Conrad again failed to accommodate popular tastes. One reason lay partly in critics' response to the newsworthiness of women at this time. In the rise of public interest generally in the 'Woman Question', and in the wake of increased activity in the Suffragist Movement, as well as the publication of the New Woman novelists, Conrad's immediate male contemporaries were all producing galleries of women characters from a variety of social classes and backgrounds.[30] Henry James is perhaps the most obvious comparison, along with H. G. Wells, J. M. Barrie, Arnold Bennett, and John Galsworthy.[31] Indeed, Bennett had identified the new 'democratising' principles of popular fiction that called for the representation of the 'mystery' of the ordinary woman, rather than that of the idealised woman of romance (Mrs Gould to some extent occupies the latter category, at least initially). In his Preface to *The Old Wives' Tale* (1908) Bennett remarked that he knew he must choose for his heroine 'the sort of woman who would pass unnoticed in a crowd'.[32]

As Conrad attempted to alter his marketing strategies and reach a wider audience at this time, he began to work on a novel that emphasised the role of a working-class female protagonist. He later insisted that in *The Secret Agent* (1907) he had originally intended to convey 'the history of Winnie Verloc'.[33] But as he developed the narrative he expanded the roles of Verloc and the anarchists. While Winnie's actions are fundamental to the outcome of the story, some critics felt that the larger social theme of the novel obscured her central role in the domestic plot. Again in *Under Western Eyes* (1911), Conrad's striking

---

between Almayer and his daughter Nina, Aïssa and Willems, Charles and Emilia Gould, Peter Ivanovitch and Tekla, de Barral and Flora, Zangiacomo and Lena, de Montevesso and Adèle, all demonstrate that imperialism may be expressed as a complex interaction, not just between races and nations, but between the private and public domain.

[30] See Scott McCracken, 'Postmodernism, a *Chance* to Reread?', in Scott McCracken and Sally Ledger (eds.), *Cultural Politics at the Fin de Siècle* (Cambridge: Cambridge University Press, 1995) for a discussion of Conrad's response to the New Woman Novel.

[31] See Alfred Habegger, *Henry James and the 'Woman Business'* (Cambridge: Cambridge University Press, 1989), for a discussion of James's relationship to the popular traditions.

[32] Arnold Bennett, *The Old Wives Tale* (1908; London: Grosset and Dunlap, 1911), vi.

[33] Letter to Ambrose Barker, 1 Sept. 1923, in Jean-Aubry, *Life and Letters*, ii. 322.

representation of women caught up in Russian political struggles failed to alter the popular view of Conrad's texts as male-oriented narratives lacking in a heroine acceptable to contemporary, popular tastes.

Paradoxically, when Conrad did produce his romance for women, with its 'ordinary' female protagonist in *Chance* (1913),[34] the old critical legacy prevailed in spite of the outstanding economic success of this novel. It is true that Sydney Colvin's favourable review in *The Observer* precipitated a run of critical congratulations.[35] But when the late romances finally brought Conrad the longed-for popularity and financial reward, and despite his emphasis on the themes of gender and the role of women in some of the later novels, the now well-established assumptions about Conrad and women were never entirely dispelled. In 1914, the year of *Chance*'s publication in the United States, for example, a highly disparaging account of 'Conrad's Women' appeared in the New York *Bookman*. The reviewer, herself a woman, complained of a lack of complexity in the presentation of Conrad's female characters: 'it is not *their* development, *their* psychology which matters in Joseph Conrad's books'. They sustained an unconvincing two-dimensionality, she remarked, in which they remained 'always the passive factor, never the active or positive force.'[36]

Colbron's assessment was in fact inaccurate given the number of 'active' female roles in the fiction. Nina follows an individual path against her father's will. Aïssa, Mme Levaille, and Winnie Verloc resort to murder, Antonia Avellanos, Winnie Verloc's mother, Sophia Antonovna, the governess in *Chance*, all act autonomously and independently of the male protagonists of the novels. Colbron's chief objections amounted to what she regarded as the lack of interiority of Conrad's women characters, a reservation to be echoed by Henry James in his critique of *Chance* in *The Times Literary Supplement* in the same year,

---

[34] See Owen Knowles, *A Conrad Chronology* (Basingstoke and London: Macmillan, 1989), 89. The appearance of *Chance* in book form on 18 Sept. 1913 was delayed by a binder's strike at Methuen. About fifty copies survive with the original 1913 title page.

[35] From W. L. Courtney and others in *The Daily Telegraph*, *The Daily Chronicle*, and *The Manchester Guardian*.

[36] Grace Isabel Colbron, 'Joseph Conrad's Women', *The Bookman* 38 (Jan. 1914), 476–9.

when he suggested that the narrative convolutions somewhat obfuscated the portrait of the female protagonist.[37] Edward Garnett's review of *Chance* was also less than favourable, perhaps because he made the mistake of many subsequent critics, that of conflating narratorial and authorial voices in this novel. When he remarked that 'perhaps in Marlow's dislike of feminism the author's shadow is projected too obtrusively on the curtain', he failed to identify Conrad's use of Marlow as an unreliable narrator.[38] In fact, in this novel Conrad gives a deliberately oblique presentation of the central female protagonist, one in which he distances himself from a complex narratorial web of definitions and assumptions about women.[39]

What characterises most critics' responses in this period is a rhetoric that masked the lack of objectivity in their readings.[40] Complaints veered between a critique of Conrad's idealisation of women, and a sense that he failed to idealise them adequately. We hear far more, from both male and female critics, of what *they* felt about women than of how Conrad actually presented them, and they often expressed a curious sense of strain in discussing the subject. They ceased to apply critical distance and frequently reshaped Conrad's characterisation of women according to lingering Victorian platitudes privileging the role of 'Angel in the House'.[41] According to one reviewer of *The Rescue* (unsigned, but probably Garnett), Conrad 'has none of Turgenev's faith in women as a self-sacrificing redeemer of man' when writing about 'love'.[42] This says more about the reviewer's perspective on women than Turgenev's. Conrad himself had praised Turgenev for his female characters, not for their

---

[37] Henry James, 'The Younger Generation', *Times Literary Supplement* (2 April 1914), 158; part one of this review was published in the issue for 19 March 1914, 133–4. Revised and enlarged as 'The New Novel' in *Notes on Novelists with Some Other Notes* (London: Dent, 1914), 249–87. See Ch. 4 for a discussion of this review.

[38] Edward Garnett, *Nation*, 24 Jan. 1914, 720–2.   [39] See Ch. 4.

[40] See Richard Curle, *Joseph Conrad: A Study* (London: Kegan Paul, Trench, Trübner, 1914), 145–51: Curle disagreed with prevailing views of Conrad's indifference to creating women in the fiction, but his eulogies are overdone. As another critic comments, Curle protests too much (Robert Lynd, 'Mr Conrad's Fame', *New Statesman*, 4 July 1914). Today Curle merely sounds patronising to women: 'Winnie Verloc is tragic because her devotion has the unconscious grandeur of a real woman's lack of an ordered sense of proportion.'

[41] Poem by Coventry Patmore (1854–63).

[42] Unsigned review, *Nation*, 17 July 1920, 503–4.

salvation of men, but because the author 'understood them' on their own terms.[43]

Garnett was far from isolated in his attitude. Right up to Conrad's death, critics display their discomfort with his presentation of women while offering their own highly conventional preferences. Arthur Symons recapitulated the prevailing critical line in his 1925 retrospective, in which he presents the familiar rhetoric on Conrad and women as an unanswerable question: 'Why is it that no woman has ever been the centre of these stories? . . . unlike every other great novelist, his women are for the most part nameless shadows.'[44] Critics failed either to resist or to address this searching question, but continued to assert that Conrad's lasting voice arose from within what they considered to be a predominantly masculine milieu.

III

I have suggested that the marketing of the early fiction for a coterie audience contributed towards the formation of critical assumptions about Conrad and women. But marketing alone cannot bear the responsibility for critical tastes. One possibility, then, is that so much critical disapproval must surely indicate a serious flaw in the fiction. However, a body of counter-evidence shows that a minority of earlier critics approved of Conrad's presentation of women, or remained unperturbed by the elusiveness that provoked Arthur Symons's remarks.

Polish criticism of the same period found no such difficulty with Conrad's work. In her review of the 1904 Polish translation of *Lord Jim*, Emilia Wesławska noted that in spite of the marginal presence of the female character, the love plot 'is permeated by romanticism; only a Slav could have written it'.[45] There may be an element of partisanship in her desire to appropriate

---

[43] Joseph Conrad, 'Turgenev: 1917', in *Notes on Life and Letters* (1921; London: Dent, 1949), 46.

[44] Arthur Symons, *Notes on Joseph Conrad With Some Unpublished Letters* (London: Myers, 1925), 8.

[45] Emilia Wesławska, 'Przedmowa do *Lorda Jima* w przekladzie z 1904 t', (Preface to *Lord Jim* in the 1904 translation), *Lorda Jima* (Warsaw: Silorski, 1904). Excerpts trans. by Bruce Teets in *Joseph Conrad: An Annotated Bibliography*, ed. Bruce Teets (New York and London: Garland, 1990), 33.

Conrad's achievement for the homeland, yet Wesławska un-
consciously located a distinction between English and Polish
readings of Conrad's women at that time. The Polish writer
Wincenty Lutosławski reiterated her view in 1930, when he
detected the 'Polishness' of Conrad's presentation of the female
role and the romantic situation in *Outcast*.[46] It is worth emphasising that many turn-of-the-century English reviewers were
reading Conrad in the context of the British nineteenth-century
novel, or the romanticism of Wordsworth and Coleridge.[47]
While Conrad undoubtedly drew on this tradition (he frequently
alluded to Dickens and Thackeray[48]), the Polish critics recognised in his interpretation of romanticism a distinctly national
character that derived from a quite different form: the Polish
romantics of the 1820s and 1830s. The romanticism of Adam
Mickiewicz (1798–1855) and Juliusz Słowacki (1809–49), with
its highly politicised and self-reflexive content, emphasised
themes of loyalty, betrayal and self-doubt. Drawing on this context, the Polish critics perceived, in the early Conrad novels, a
romanticism in which the expression of the dilemma of male
heroes did not necessarily deny the presence of a 'female' voice.
The emphasis in Wesławska's review lay not so much on the gendering of the characters, rather on the gendering of the text.[49]

[46] Wincenty Lutosławski, 'A Visit to Conrad in 1897,' *Blue Peter* 10 (Dec. 1930),
638–40.

[47] For discussions of Conrad in relation to Wordsworth and Coleridge see Ian
Watt, *Conrad in the Nineteenth Century* (Berkeley: University of California Press,
1979), 78–81. Watt sees in the Preface to *The Nigger of the Narcissus* a continuity
with Wordsworth's Preface to *The Lyrical Ballads*. See also Michael P. Jones,
Conrad's Heroism: A Paradise Lost (Ann Arbor: UMI Research Press, 1985), 30–7;
David Thorburn, *Conrad's Romanticism* (New Haven: Yale University Press, 1974),
149–52; Sandra Dodson, '*Lord Jim* and the Modern Sublime,' *The Conradian* 18
(Autumn 1994), 77–101.

[48] See Frederick R. Karl, *Joseph Conrad: The Three Lives* (New York: Farrar, Straus,
and Giroux, 1979), 187, 272.

[49] See Hélène Cixous, 'Sorties: Out and Out: Attacks/Ways Out/Forays,' in *The
Newly Born Woman*, eds. Hélène Cixous and Catherine Clément, trans. Betsy Wing
(Manchester: Manchester University Press, 1986), 63–4, 83–8, 91–7. Cixous's well-
known notion of 'écriture feminine' has some relevance for understanding Polish
critics' early responses to Conrad's work. Many feminists have rightly argued that
Cixous propagates biological essentialism by reversing the gender status of Lacanian
psychoanalytic thought and denoting the fragmentation of texts as their 'feminine'
component. Nevertheless her description is useful here as it helps to dismantle conventional notions of Conrad's texts as unreservedly 'masculine'. In *Heart of Darkness*, for example, Marlow constantly interrupts the linear pattern of his narrative,

The Polish allusions in Conrad's writing are particularly important in the context of his representation of women, a theme I shall discuss fully in the next chapter. While passive heroines appear frequently throughout nineteenth- and twentieth-century European fiction, I believe Conrad borrowed the striking, somewhat gothic image of the silent woman (Arsat's lover in 'The Lagoon', Mrs Gould, Hermann's niece in 'Falk'), directly from the Polish romantics. The figure of the hermitess in Mickiewicz's *Konrad Wallenrod* (1823), for example, provides one such model for Mrs Gould in *Nostromo*. Mickiewicz's hermitess, deserted by her husband when he chooses to follow nationalist duties over domestic happiness, languishes in self-imposed isolation and silence in her tower. Likewise, Mrs Gould, described as 'the lady of the medieval castle' (68), characterised by her silent placatory gestures towards an uncommunicative husband, represents the figure of the abandoned wife, victim of her spouse's obsession with his professional life.

George Gissing, one of the few British critics to comment on Conrad's distinctive treatment of this trope in his fiction, wrote to Conrad in 1903: 'Wonderful, I say, your mute or all but mute women. How, in Satan's name, do you make their souls speak through their silence?'[50] Gissing was perhaps more perceptive than most, but we must accept the degree to which the initial reception of Conrad's work in Britain and America was influenced by a somewhat different literary tradition from that of his Polish romantic heritage. Conrad's often schematic mode of representation, emphasising the exteriority of the woman, must have been quite alien to those who admired the lively 'realism' of Thackeray and Trollope, the psychological interiority of the Brontës' and George Eliot's heroines and, amongst his contemporaries, Henry James; or even the sensationalism of Mary Braddon and Mrs Wood, Rhoda Broughton and Marie Corelli,

his final words trailing off inconclusively into a series of dots. See Watt on 'delayed decoding' in *Conrad in the Nineteenth Century*, 169–79. See also Jane Ford, 'James Joyce and the Conrad Connection: The Anxiety of Influence,' *Conradiana* 17:1 (1985), 3–17. See also Ch. 2. Conrad's use of 'defamiliarisation' techniques found their roots to some extent in the work of the Polish Romantics, who experimented with form, subverting generic expectations and patterns of linear narrative.

[50] George Gissing, letter of 1903, quoted in R. L. Mégroz, *Joseph Conrad's Mind and Method: A Study of Personality in Art* (London: Faber and Faber, 1931), 94.

whose daring or desperate heroines formed the central focus of their texts. Moreover, his highly sceptical treatment, although sympathetic to the social marginalisation of women, would be unlikely to attract those readers of the New Woman novels who might prefer something more directly polemical.[51] However, a greater sympathy for Conrad's presentation of women did begin to emerge during the two decades following his death. Although his work suffered a period of relative obscurity during the 1930s, a few, often sensitive, but now neglected critical studies offered greater insights than had appeared during his lifetime. Gustav Morf, following the theme of earlier Polish critics, associated the shadowy quality of many of Conrad's female figures with his memory of a powerful mother-figure lost in early childhood.[52] And R. L. Mégroz unequivocally addressed the critics' doubts:

The question has often been asked, why *Chance* should have turned the commercial tide for its author, and indubitably the right answer is that it appeals to the intelligence and feelings of women readers.[53]

He is the first critic not to be baffled by the favourable reception of *Chance*, nor by the response of women readers. Neither does he confuse authorial intention with the misogynistic tone of the narrator's voice: 'Marlow's half-facetious generalizations must not be taken too seriously, of course.'[54] He considered that *Chance* alone established Conrad as a successful creator of female characters, and, like Morf, placed them in a wider European context. In spite of the predominance of male figures who 'hold the stage' in Conrad, Mégroz argued that 'it should not be concluded that women play a small part in the Conradian world'.[55]

Chance was again recognised as a major novel in 1948. F. R. Leavis included it, along with *Victory* (1915), amongst the canonised works of *The Great Tradition*.[56] Leavis paid greater attention to the male protagonists of the novel than the female,

---

[51] See Ch. 4 n. 5.
[52] Gustav Morf, *The Polish Heritage of Joseph Conrad* (London: Sampson, Low, Marston, 1930).   [53] Mégroz, *Joseph Conrad's Mind and Method*, 193.
[54] Ibid. 193.   [55] Ibid. 191–2.
[56] F. R. Leavis, *The Great Tradition* (1948; Harmondsworth: Penguin, 1962), 222–47.

but his definition of the canon at least left an opening for subsequent studies of those Conrad novels emphasising women's roles
and exploring issues of gender.

But such possibilities were soon to be foreclosed by a much
more influential critical model. The idea of a decline in Conrad's
work began to take shape, emerging ultimately with greatest prominence in the pantheon of modernist studies in the 1940s and
1950s. Under this paradigm Conrad's modernism constituted
his major phase, where his male heroes offer a critique of European colonialism and capitalist venture. Literary commentators
recognised in the philosophical dilemmas of Conrad's earlier male
protagonists their own disillusionment with a modern indus-
trial Europe and its imperialist drives.[57] The popular press had
welcomed the publication of the late romances, but reviewers who
represented the more self-consciously literary journals began to
develop a nostalgia for the abstraction of the early works. There
is no necessary connection between modernism and the absence
of female characters, but in Conrad's case, his supporters promoted those works as modernist in which women feature less
prominently, making these texts paradigmatic of his 'genius'.[58]
This bias was misleading in the sense that he did develop female
characters whose experiences resemble those of his male (modernist) protagonists, and it was also selective because it neglected to appreciate different forms of experimentation. Conrad's
confrontation with the challenge of writing about women in
the latter part of his career was regarded as a denial of his aesthetic principles. His alleged inability and lack of desire to write
for and about women was now, paradoxically, turned to the
advantage of those who wished to promote his modernism.

---

[57] See David Daiches, 'Joseph Conrad', in *The Novel and the Modern World*
(Chicago: University of Chicago Press, 1939; rev. edn., 1960), 25–62. The distinction between the pre- and post-Second World War editions of David Daiches's essay
on Conrad in *The Novel and the Modern World* exemplifies the shift in the critical
reception of Conrad at this time. Whereas Daiches's 1939 edition focused on the
picturesque locations of the Malay novels and described Conrad as a writer of
situations rather than of individuals, the revised 1960 text emphasised Conrad's
'despairing politics' and the conflict of male individual and society.

[58] See also Bonnie Kime Scott (ed.), *The Gender of Modernism: A Critical
Anthology* (Bloomington: Indiana University Press, 1990), for discussions of the position of women and women's writing in modernism.

The 'decline' paradigm is initially put forward after his death by John Galsworthy[59] and Edward Garnett,[60] and echoed most notably by Virginia Woolf, who was one of the first to privilege the middle over the late works for their strong links with the modernist agenda. Woolf claimed that 'he never believed in his later and more sophisticated characters as he had believed in his early seamen' and, that 'the world of Conrad's later period has about it an involuntary obscurity, an inconclusiveness, almost a disillusionment which baffles and fatigues'.[61] Woolf uses the words 'involuntary' and 'disillusionment' as if Conrad were somehow writing against his will in this later period. She failed to acknowledge any merit in the later novels, dismissing them because she felt they no longer stimulated the rigorously confrontational relationship of text and reader characterised by the earlier sea stories. If we accept that Woolf's experiments with stream-of-consciousness deliberately aimed at an investigation of the interior workings of the minds of her characters, then we can see why she would not privilege Conrad's late novels.

But in 1918, Conrad announced that 'the angles of my vision, my methods of composition will, within limits, be always changing'.[62] In the late work Conrad explored more fully the formal structures of popular genres such as sensation novels, the historical novel, and melodrama. He also investigated the relationship of gender and genre, responding more specifically to the role of women in popular forms. He reversed the patterns of his formerly passive heroines, to some extent liberating his female protagonists from the constraints of inactivity and stasis on the periphery of the text. In both *The Arrow of Gold* (1919) and *The Rover* (1923), for example, he destabilises the conventional 'boy's own' plot by offering the heroine the active role. Unfortunately these later experiments have gone unrecognised because they do not resemble the more obviously 'modernist' explorations of language and strenuously philosophical issues addressed in his earlier phase.

[59] John Galsworthy, 'Reminiscences of Conrad' (1924) in *Castles in Spain and Other Screeds* (London: Heinemann, 1927), 74–95.

[60] Edward Garnett (ed.), *Conrad's Prefaces to his Works* (London: Dent, 1937), 34. Garnett expressed his disappointment that Conrad's greatest success should have arrived with his 'weakest work'.

[61] Virginia Woolf, *The Common Reader* (London: Hogarth Press, 1925), 289–90.

[62] Letter to Barrett H. Clark, 4 May 1918, in Jean-Aubry, *Life and Letters*, ii. 204.

Thus Woolf prefigured the most enduring tone of later Conrad criticism. She claimed for the early works the privilege of moral integrity. She suggested a lasting respect for the author's use of those narrative methods which aligned themselves most appropriately with her own modernist themes. Without attempting to address the nature of Conrad's later experiments, she saw in the late fiction a decline in Conrad's powers, associating his 'disillusionment' and 'fatigue' with a revisionist preoccupation with the romance genre.

A nostalgia for the predominantly male-oriented texts was never entirely dismantled in intellectual circles. Even Leavis's inclusion of *Chance* and *Victory* in the canon was heavily qualified by a dismissal of the very last novels: 'Conrad enjoyed a vogue in the early nineteen-twenties, when he was bringing out a series of inferior novels.'[63] Leavis expressed the by now conventional nostalgia for the early work, claiming that Conrad 'had too good reason to feel that he was regarded as the author of *Lord Jim*; the writer of stories about the sea, the jungle, and the islands, who had made some curious ventures outside his beat, but would yet, one hoped, return to it'.[64] Moreover, Leavis sustained the reductive assumptions about Conrad and women as the weakest aspect of the work, associating the famous utterance about 'adjectival insistence'[65] (initially used to describe the exposition of 'the darkness' and 'the horror' in *Heart of Darkness*) with Conrad's presentation of 'The Intended' and other female roles. Following E. M. Forster,[66] Leavis believed that Conrad's failure to find expression for 'the unknown', whether represented by the experience in the Congo, or the character of women, revealed his inability to objectify his subject with adequate clarity: 'he is intent on making a virtue out of not knowing what he means.'[67] Leavis's interpretation suggests the mistrust of an empiricist for the phenomenological aspects of Conrad's writing. His criticisms anticipate Wayne Booth's distinction between 'showing' and 'telling',[68] a distinction that owes much to Henry

---

[63] Leavis, *The Great Tradition*, 247.   [64] Ibid. 247–8.   [65] Ibid. 198.

[66] E. M. Forster, *Abinger Harvest* (1936; London: Edward Arnold, 1940), 135: 'the secret casket of his genius contains a vapour rather than a jewel'.

[67] Leavis, *The Great Tradition*, 199.

[68] Wayne Booth, *The Rhetoric of Fiction* (1961; Harmondsworth: Penguin, 1987), Ch. 1, 'Telling and Showing', 3–20.

James's theory of narrative outlined in 'The Art of Fiction' (1884). Leavis objected to Conrad's tendency to 'tell' rather than 'to show'. He saw in his account of the 'mystery' an imprecision, a failure to provide an 'objective correlative', to use T. S. Eliot's term. The endurance of empiricist thought in British and North American criticism might well account for much of the adverse interpretation of women in Conrad, since their characterisations so often seem 'mysterious' and incomplete.

Thomas Moser consolidated dominant opinions in 1957 when he published his influential thesis of *Achievement and Decline*.[69] He clinched the prevailing tone by dismissing the later work: 'any reader making a resolute effort to forget who wrote these books will immediately perceive that they are failures'.[70] Ultimately Moser's theory amounts to a judgement of taste, but it is also one that codifies the increasingly pervasive tendency in Conrad criticism to bifurcate the canon, even more thoroughly than Woolf and Leavis, into middle and late works. The Malay novels were relegated to the status of 'apprentice work'.[71] Conrad's strengths (based on his modernist strategies) were recognised in the work from *Heart of Darkness* to *Under Western Eyes*, failure and decline exemplified (except for *The Shadow-Line* (1917), which has no female characters) by the novels published between the years of *Chance* and *Suspense* (the latter, unfinished and published posthumously in 1925, is usually ignored altogether). Moser's theory depends above all on his assertion that Conrad's decline was rooted in an inability to write about women and sexual relationships. He reinforced Garnett's view that 'we are not sure that we like Mr Conrad best as a novelist of love',[72] with a repetition of the familiar note of regret, as he asked: 'Why did Conrad cease those explorations into moral failure in

[69] Thomas Moser, *Joseph Conrad: Achievement and Decline* (Cambridge, Mass.: Harvard University Press, 1957). For foreunners of Moser's thesis see M. C. Bradbrook, *Joseph Conrad: Poland's English Genius* (Cambridge: Cambridge University Press, 1941), 11. Bradbrook registered the falling away of Conrad's abilities during his 'relaxed old age'. See also, Douglas Hewitt, *Conrad: A Reassessment* (Cambridge: Bowes and Bowes, 1952), 89. Hewitt identified 'a retreat' from the complexities of the early novels. Paul Wiley, in *Conrad's Measure of Man* (Madison: University of Wisconsin Press, 1954) was one of the few critics to offer an alternative to this theme.   [70] *Achievement and Decline*, 180.

[71] Ibid. 50.

[72] Unsigned review (probably Garnett), *Nation*, 17 July 1920, 503–4.

the masculine world that had enabled him to achieve artistic success?'[73]

The persistence of this theory is marked by the number of critical works still devoted to a very small portion of the Conrad canon,[74] while studies of Conrad's romanticism that ostensibly oppose Moser's thesis ultimately avail of his themes.[75] In fact, most of the major responses to Moser draw attention, by their titles alone, to the continuing influence of his bifurcation of Conrad's work.[76] The privileging, almost exclusively, of the 'modernist' middle work still prevails in Conrad studies.[77] Most of the important recent additions to Conrad criticism, while often questioning the hegemony of 'achievement and decline', continue to favour modernist themes—scepticism, existentialism, 'the modern temper'.[78] Some take issue with Moser, but almost none takes account of *Suspense*, a novel that reveals some of Conrad's most striking responses to the presentation of gender in popular fiction.[79]

[73] Moser, *Achievement and Decline*, 102. See also Albert J. Guerard, *Conrad The Novelist* (Cambridge, Mass.: Harvard University Press, 1958) who adumbrated Moser's theories.

[74] See Jacques Berthoud, *Joseph Conrad: The Major Phase* (Cambridge: Cambridge University Press, 1978); Watt, *Conrad in the Nineteenth Century*; Arnold E. Davidson, *Conrad's Endings: A Study of the Five Major Novels* (Ann Arbor: UMI Research Press, 1984).

[75] See e.g. George Thomson, 'Conrad's Later Fiction', *English Literature in Transition* 12:4 (1969), 174; Thorburn, *Conrad's Romanticism*, p. xiv: 'after 1907 . . . Conrad deserted his best instincts', and returned to 'the debased Romantic mode'.

[76] Gary Geddes, *Conrad's Later Novels* (Montreal: McGill-Queen's University Press, 1980); Daniel R. Schwarz, *Conrad: The Later Fiction* (London: Macmillan, 1982).

[77] See Jeffrey Meyers, *Joseph Conrad: A Biography* (London: John Murray, 1991), 269. Meyers sums up this view when he speaks of the irony of Conrad's artistic career—'poor sales for his greatest books and popular acclaim for his late, inferior work'.

[78] See Mark Wollaeger, *Joseph Conrad and The Fictions of Skepticism* (Stanford: Stanford University Press, 1990); Otto Bohlman, *Conrad's Existentialism* (London and Basingstoke: Macmillan, 1991); Daphna Erdinast-Vulcan, *Joseph Conrad and the Modern Temper* (Oxford: Clarendon Press, 1991). Erdinast-Vulcan, 139–47, 172–85, for example, argues against the more reductive aspects of the 'achievement and decline' theory, but nevertheless believes in a form of 'decline'. She suggests that Conrad's later work, in its attention to the 'unreality of the world', constitutes a 'surrender' to the Nietzschean outlook that he had so far resisted throughout his career.

[79] Robert Hampson, *Joseph Conrad: Betrayal and Identity* (Basingstoke: Macmillan, 1992), takes issue with 'achievement and decline'. See also Richard Ambrosini, *Conrad's Fiction as Critical Discourse* (Cambridge: Cambridge University Press, 1991); see Ch. 8 for bibliography of critical work on *Suspense*.

Feminist and postcolonialist theory has at last recovered some of Conrad's neglected early and late novels and new perspectives on the canon are beginning to emerge.[80] Even so, surprisingly few thoroughly contest 'achievement and decline' as a measure of Conrad's work. Rather than exploring the complexity of Conrad's position in relation to the marketplace, they continue instead to advance the assumption that Conrad himself felt degraded by his later connection with 'the popular, the romantic, and the feminine'.[81] And while alternatives to the enduring theory continue to emerge with greater frequency, we have to admit that two of the most influential feminist essays on Conrad deal with *Heart of Darkness* and *Lord Jim*, and only two book-length feminist studies currently exist.[82]

[80] See e.g. Christopher GoGwilt, *The Invention of the West: Joseph Conrad and the Double-Mapping of Europe and Empire* (Stanford, Calif.: Stanford University Press, 1995), 103, on Conrad's displacement of 'patriarchal assumptions of imperialism'; see also, Gail Fincham and Myrtle Hooper (eds.), *Under Postcolonial Eyes: Joseph Conrad After Empire* (Rondesbosch: University of Cape Town Press, 1996).

[81] Robin Truth Goodman, 'Conrad's Closet', *Conradiana* 30:2 (1998), 86. See also, Geoffrey Galt Harpham, *One of Us: The Mastery of Joseph Conrad* (Chicago: the University of Chicago Press, 1996), 186. Harpham observes that there are strong and weak moments throughout Conrad's oeuvre, but he nevertheless concedes: 'There does seem to be a consensus that *The Nigger of "The Narcissus"*, "The Secret Sharer", *Heart of Darkness*, *Nostromo*, and *Lord Jim* stand on one side of the great divide, and *An [sic] Arrow of Gold*, *The Rover*, and *An Outcast of the Islands*, on the other.'

[82] Heliéna Krenn, *Conrad's Lingard Trilogy: Empire, Race, and Women in the Malay Novels* (New York and London: Garland, 1990); Ruth Nadelhaft, *Joseph Conrad: A Feminist Reading* (Hemel Hempstead: Harvester Wheatsheaf, 1991); Nina Pelikan Straus, 'The Exclusion of the Intended from Secret Sharing in Conrad's *Heart of Darkness*', *Novel: A Forum on Fiction* 20:2 (Winter 1987), 123–7; Padmini Mongia, '"Ghosts of the Gothic": Spectral Women and Colonized Spaces in *Lord Jim*', in Andrew Michael Roberts (ed.), *Conrad and Gender* (Amsterdam: Rodopi, 1993), 1–16. Other essays on Conrad and women include Gordon Thomson, 'Conrad's Women', *Nineteenth-Century Fiction* 32 (1978), 442–65; Karen Klein, 'The Feminist Predicament in Conrad's *Nostromo*', in *Brandeis Essays in Literature*, ed. John Hazel Smith (Waltham, Mass.: Department of English and American Literature, Brandeis University, 1983), 101–16; Susan Lundvall Brodie, 'Conrad's Feminine Perspective', *Conradiana* 16 (1984), 141–54; Monika Elbert, 'Possession and Self-Possession: The "Dialect of Desire" in *'Twixt Land and Sea*, in *Conrad and Gender*, 75–146; Heliéna Krenn, 'The Beautiful World of Women: Women as Reflections of Colonial Issues in Conrad's Malay Novels'; Padmini Mongia, 'Empire, Narrative and the Feminine in *Lord Jim* and *Heart of Darkness*', in Keith Carabine, Owen Knowles, Wiesław Krajka (eds.), *Contexts for Conrad* (Boulder, Colo.: East European Monographs, 1993). For discussions of *Chance* see Ch. 4.

Andrew Michael Roberts, a champion of 'alternative' readings of Conrad, identifies the current problem. In spite of expanding critical possibilities, in practice Roberts finds that still only a small section of the 'earlier' canon is studied in schools and universities and represented by theorists of Conrad's fiction. Making his selection for the Longman Critical Reader, Roberts's choice was ultimately governed by this enduring fact: 'I decided, with some regret, that I could not dedicate much space . . . to Conrad's late work.'[83] With the advent of feminism, postmodernism, and postcolonialism we have ostensibly left the value judgements of the New Criticism far behind. Yet the hegemony of 'achievement and decline' theory still hovers tenaciously, however well disguised, over Conrad criticism of the last five years, and over what is presumed to be worthy of study.

The barrage of criticism levelled against Conrad's treatment of women in general, and against the late fiction in particular, has thus far obscured any serious discussion of *why* he may have encountered difficulty in this area of his work, and what he *did* achieve in spite of his self-confessed anxieties about producing popular romances. After *Chance*, with its elusive portrait of an ordinary woman attempting to form an autonomous identity, Conrad went on to give us Lena, who achieves the 'real' victory of the novel;[84] Rita da Lastaola, who resists the conventional closure of romance fiction and chooses an independent existence without the hero; Arlette, who actively determines the outcome of her romance plot; and Adèle de Montevesso, whom Conrad finally gives a voice and who directly confesses to a male auditor the narrative of her failed marriage. It is therefore a great paradox of Conrad criticism that the early image of Conrad as writer for men, initially used by the reviewers of the popular press to attack the sea stories, ultimately sanctioned the neglect of the *late* works, and the privileging of Conrad as a model of modernist principles. The extent of the influence and power of this critical paradigm has left little room for alternative perspectives of Conrad's complex relationship to his women characters, and his confrontation with the issues of gender throughout the fiction.

---

[83] Andrew Michael Roberts, Preface, *Joseph Conrad* (London and New York: Longman, 1998), p. ix.

[84] John Batchelor, *The Life of Joseph Conrad: A Critical Biography* (Oxford: Basil Blackwell, 1994), 235.

IV

A succession of biographies similarly play down the importance of women in Conrad's life. The infrequency of his association with women during his career at sea represents only one area of emphasis. Supported by the 'achievement and decline' model, biographers repeatedly associate the failure of Conrad's late work with an inability to relate to women in his private life.[85]

A subtle marginalisation of the position of women in the biography begins with the tendency to emphasise Conrad's relationship with his father, Apollo Korzeniowski, the writer, rather than exploring the energetic figure of his mother Ewa. Marguerite Poradowska, a French writer who played a fundamental part in Conrad's transformation from seaman to writer occupies a subsidiary role as 'moral support' rather than that of creative influence.[86] And Jessie Conrad, penalised for her lack of sophistication and literary ability, is pictured as a passive drudge who could offer Conrad little more than domestic comforts. The ultimate effect is to promote the image of Conrad as a man in a man's world, a portrait which Frederick Karl wryly admits makes him into a 'rough-hewn sailor who preferred male-bonding to female companionship'.[87]

The impact of Conrad's mother on his development as a writer has yet to be thoroughly explored. Although Zdizław Najder undoubtedly admires Ewa Bobrowska, his biography of Conrad devotes only a page and a half of the first chapter to detailed comment on her life (while Apollo Korzeniowski's background, education, and political interests are described at length over twenty pages).[88] Yet in *Conrad's Polish Background*, Najder reveals that a considerable number of her letters and

---

[85] See Meyer, *A Psychoanalytic Biography*; Zdisław Najder, *Joseph Conrad: A Chronicle* (Cambridge: Cambridge University Press, 1983), 363; Cedric Watts, *Joseph Conrad: A Literary Life* (London: Macmillan, 1989), 125.   [86] See Ch. 3.

[87] Karl, *Three Lives*, 279. It is interesting to note that the association of Conrad with a male world extends even to photographs and paintings of the writer. None of the biographers record the fact that the last painting of Conrad was executed by an Irish female artist, Alice Sarah Kinkead (d. 1926) in 1924 (see letter from Edith Oenone Somerville to A. S. Kinkead, 27 June, 1924, Somerville Archive, Drishane House, West Cork. See also Otto Rauchbauer, *The Edith Oenone Somerville Archive in Drishane* (Dublin: Irish Manuscripts Commission: 1995)).

[88] Najder, *A Chronicle*, 3–32.

documents survive, offering suggestive insights into her character and ambitions, her strong attachment to husband and son, and her impact on Conrad as a child.[89] Perhaps because Ewa died young, and because Conrad's father was himself a writer and translator of considerable ability, as well as a substantial political figure, some biographers have been tempted to focus on Apollo's role in Conrad's early childhood. But Ewa was herself an educated woman who read widely and completed many translations.[90]

Bernard Meyer's psychoanalytic biography of 1967 does in fact attach great significance to the relationship of mother and son. However, he uses the fact to reduce the positions of Marguerite Poradowska and Jessie Conrad, implying that Conrad constantly shunned deep relationships with women, rejecting them as a means of revenge for the loss of his mother as a young child. Ignoring the complex rhetorical strategies of Conrad's letters to Poradowska suggesting a relationship of empathy and equality residing beneath their highly formal surface patterns, Meyer insists that Conrad addressed Poradowska with the love of a 'weeping child for a compassionate mother',[91] and that he ultimately kept her at a distance (in spite of the fact that he asked her to translate his first novel and take full credit as author). Meyer assumes that the break in the extant correspondence (between 1896 and 1900) can be explained by 'the pique of a woman scorned' when Conrad withdrew his attentions.[92] Yet there is no proof that *Conrad* had not been refused in an offer of marriage. Whatever actually did happen during those years, Conrad and Poradowska subsequently resumed their correspondence. She visited Conrad and Jessie in England and helped to finance Jessie's sisters' education.[93] But according to Meyer, Conrad emerges as a man who avoided relationships with women, from whom he constantly contemplated escape, preferring the isolation of bachelor life and the company of close male friends.

---

[89] Zdzisław Najder (ed.), *Conrad's Polish Background* (London: Oxford University Press, 1964), Ch. 1.   [90] See Ch. 2.
[91] Meyer, *A Psychoanalytic Biography*, 101.   [92] Ibid. 107 n. p.
[93] Letter to Marguerite Poradowska, 10 May 1900, *CL* 2, 266 n. 4. On this occasion Jessie included a note to Conrad's letter: 'I can never thank you enough for all you have done for the girls.'

The image of Conrad's wife Jessie plays into the established view in most biographies, often leaving the reader with the sense that Conrad would have preferred to remain single, marrying solely to acquire a housekeeper and typist.[94] Her 'unsuitability' for the role of partner for the great writer emerges as a prominent theme, as critics feel compelled to list her shortcomings, ranging from a lower-class background to a mind 'too undeveloped for her ever to be able to give Conrad proper companionship'.[95] Fortunately, a few biographers have granted that 'there was a kind of instinctive affinity'[96] between Conrad and Jessie, in spite of intellectual and social differences, or that Jessie's loyalty 'was more valuable to him than intellectual equality would have been'.[97]

However, a perception of Jessie's intellectual inequality prevails. Jeffrey Meyers cites Dame Veronica Wedgwood, whose parents 'found her a bore',[98] and T. S. Eliot's review of Jessie's first book of memoirs disqualifies her as a potential biographer of Conrad:

Mrs Conrad must have buried in her mind much that would be interesting and important in the world of letters. If this had been exhumed and dealt with by an experienced biographer the reminiscences might have been really vital.[99]

Jessie's so-called intellectual failures have been underscored by an unfavourable account of her physical size.[100] The attention

---

[94] Karl, *Three Lives*, 341: 'she possessed emotional and psychological qualities which fitted exactly into what he needed . . . a straightforward, devoted, quite competent young woman.'

[95] Jocelyn Baines, *Joseph Conrad: A Critical Biography* (London: Weidenfield and Nicolson, 1969), 6.

[96] Roger Tennant, *Joseph Conrad: A Biography* (New York: Atheneum, 1981), 104.   [97] Batchelor, *Life*, 57.

[98] Meyers, *Joseph Conrad*, 144.

[99] T. S. Eliot, 'Short Reviews: Jessie Conrad, *Joseph Conrad As I Knew Him* (London: Heinemann, 1926)', *Criterion* 5 (Jan. 1927), 159.

[100] Biographers have frequently drawn attention, in more or less inappropriate terms, to her stately figure. See Baines, *A Critical Biography*, 171, who talks of her 'tendency to become fat'; Meyer, *A Psychoanalytic Biography*, 167 n. b, who, drawing on Ford and Woolf's disparaging remarks about Jessie, speculates that 'her progressive obesity was at least partly the result of her utilizing overeating as a means of warding off depression and anger'; and Meyers, *Joseph Conrad*, 237, whose caption to a late photograph reads 'Jessie Conrad, 1926: Grotesquely obese and loaded, like a gypsy fortune-teller, with heavy beads'.

given to Jessie's physique seems gratuitous, since this material sheds no light on the Conrads' actual relationship. The positive elements of this long-lasting marriage are mostly played down: the affection, the loyalty, the friendship and devotion on both sides are obscured by the emphasis on Jessie's lack of sophistication, intellectual ability, or a slim figure. Instead, the hackneyed images of woman as distraction or burden on the creative male confirm the view that Conrad's misfortune lay in his apparently spontaneous decision to marry, and his immediate sense of entrapment after the ceremony.

Without accounting for the narratorial distance between author and protagonist, Meyer alleges that Conrad reproduced his horror of domesticity in his fiction. He remarks of *Outcast*: 'Like Willems, Conrad's behaviour invokes the image of a trapped man constantly plotting his escape.'[101] When in April 1897 Conrad began writing 'The Return', Meyer concludes that Conrad's problems with the story reflect his disgust with Jessie's pregnancy at that time: 'his comment "I hated while I wrote", referred no less to Jessie's creation than his own.'[102]

Meyer identifies Conrad's position with that of Alvan Hervey in 'The Return'. But Conrad's self-confessed difficulties with the writing of this story ('the only instance in my life when I made an attempt to write with both hands at once', p. viii) could equally well have referred to his failure to produce a satisfactory heroine in *Mrs* Hervey. *Her* disillusionment with an empty middle-class marriage of convenience constitutes one of Conrad's earliest attempts to present the painful despair of female isolation within a domestic situation. Taken in the context of Conrad's later heroines (Bessie in the play *One Day More*, Winnie Verloc, Flora de Barral, Rita de Lastaola, Adèle de Montevesso), Conrad's 'Ibsenian' heroine Mrs Hervey could be seen as the first of a line in Conrad's exploration of *female* entrapment.

Biographers have been swift to cast Jessie in a pejorative role in relation to Conrad's creativity. But they never really address the issue of what might have become of him *without* her. There

---

[101] Meyer, *A Psychoanalytic Biography*, 119.

[102] Ibid. 128. See also Karl, *Three Lives*, 591. As if Conrad bore no responsibility for these events, Karl likewise explains Jessie's second pregnancy as her 'means of maintaining some place in Conrad's life' since she could not hope to attract him on equal terms intellectually.

is a tendency to emphasise his achievements in the light of his sense of terrible isolation within marriage, rather than speculating on what he might not have achieved without the support of a devoted wife.[103] His self-awareness of his 'idiosyncrasies, strange moods, and unusual behaviour' was acute.[104] His psychological make-up had been shaped by the frequency of traumatic events in his life. The exile from Poland in early childhood, the loss of his parents, the sense of displacement and guilt at leaving the homeland, the instability and uncertainty of the life at sea had all contributed towards a habitual pattern of depression and recurring periods of inhibition in his creative life. These patterns had been established well before his marriage to Jessie (his letters to Poradowska refer frequently to his sense of psychological instability). Inevitably Conrad would never have been an easy partner, and marriage required considerable adjustments from both parties. In his letters to Garnett, Conrad empathised with his young wife's situation. The inexperienced Jessie had been forced abruptly to come to terms with Conrad's habitual depressions, 'the darkness and bitterness' that was 'beyond expression'. Absorbed by the intensity of his pain, Conrad was unable to lighten his wife's anxieties. 'Poor Jess feels it all,' he remarked, 'I must be a perfect fiend to live with.'[105]

The short story 'Amy Foster' (1901) has often been interpreted as an expression of isolation in his marriage.[106] It tells of an exile 'washed up' on a foreign shore, taken in by an empathetic woman. But she is eventually coerced by the weight of public opinion that has alienated him and she too becomes estranged from him. Conrad's presentation of Amy reminds us of Jessie's description of her own sense of dislocation on her honeymoon as she listened to her husband, during a bout of illness, speaking deliriously in an incomprehensible language:

To see him lying in the white canopied bed, dark-faced, with gleaming teeth and shining eyes, was sufficiently alarming, but to hear him muttering to himself in a strange tongue (he must have been speaking

---

[103] In *A Personal Record* (1912) Conrad acknowledged that 'I had never been made aware of the even flow of daily life, made easy and noiseless for me by a silent, watchful, tireless affection' (101).   [104] Najder, *A Chronicle*, 200–1.

[105] Quoted in Najder, *A Chronicle*, 201.

[106] 'Amy Foster', first published in *Illustrated London News*, later in *Typhoon and Other Stories* (1903).

Polish), to be unable to penetrate the clouded mind or catch one intelligible word, was for a young, inexperienced girl truly awful.[107]

Seen from the perspective of a man who identified with Jessie's position as well as his own, and who *sought* a family in England rather than shunned it, the tragic closure of Conrad's story expressed a real fear of losing his new-found security. Conrad's recollections in *A Personal Record* express only too well the extraordinary intensity of his attachment to a lost family. His need to rebuild that sense of belonging through friends and family in England was a matter of survival, perhaps the only compensation for the traumas of his youth. Richard Curle remarked on the importance for Conrad of a secure domestic environment:

Like so many sailors Conrad was never so happy as when he was in his own home. His dynamic spirit required the familiar atmosphere of well-known faces and accustomed objects for its peace.[108]

There is no evidence to suggest that the marriage in itself exacerbated Conrad's depressive illness or his long-term sense of isolation, and his sons' memoirs illustrate the way in which their devoted and affectionate father enjoyed a close family life, often seeking relaxation by joining in their childhood games.[109]

Jessie's health was far from perfect, and although she suffered considerable pain from severe knee injuries, she diligently nursed Conrad through countless depressions, and his severe breakdown in 1910. John Conrad presents a striking image of his mother's sacrifice, as she stood over the stove, leaning against the doorjamb, wearied by continuous discomfort, 'a candlestick in one hand while she stirred a saucepan with the other'. He remarks that there were times when she had been typing all day 'and her stoicism gave way in a flood of tears', but that 'it was not in her nature to fly off the handle' or storm out of the house.[110]

[107] Jessie Conrad, *Joseph Conrad As I Knew Him* (London: Heinemann, 1926), 35. The extract also provides a little counter-evidence for those who emphasise her inability to write.

[108] Richard Curle, *The Last Twelve Years of Joseph Conrad* (London: Sampson, Low, Marston, 1928), 134.

[109] Borys Conrad, *My Father, Joseph Conrad* (London: Calder and Boyars, 1970), 54, recalls his father reading to him frequently as a child from Kingsley, Fenimore Cooper, and Captain Marryat. John Conrad, *Joseph Conrad: Times Remembered* (Cambridge: Cambridge University Press, 1981), 165, remembers midnight chess games with his father.　　[110] John Conrad, *Times Remembered*, 78.

Indeed, little reflection has been given to *her* needs in the relationship, to the nature of her sacrifices, her input into Conrad's creative life, or to her considerable enjoyment of her role as 'the writer's wife'. Whatever trials this marriage brought for both parties, and whatever the discrepancies in their background and education, there can be no doubt that the relationship sustained Conrad's career as a writer. Conrad never expressed in writing anything but admiration for and devotion to Jessie.[111] Both Borys's and John's memoirs convey the sense of their mother's extraordinary ability to cultivate an atmosphere of domestic well-being, which Conrad also continually recognised. One frequent visitor to the household acknowledged that 'to [Jessie], too, was due much of Conrad's success, as he has been heard to say again and again'.[112] Jessie's talents as organiser and nurturer gave him a sense of security after a life of dislocation and displacement, and her tireless contribution gave him the space in which to pursue his literary career.

We are now in a position to evaluate Edward Garnett's response to Jessie's second volume of memoirs, published in 1935.[113] He wrote to Jessie accusing her of damaging her husband's reputation with her 'vindictiveness', 'jealous' nature, and use of a 'common' tone. He added insult to injury by suggesting she had 'very little critical sense', so could not possibly understand 'what an outrage' her book was 'on good taste and good feeling'.[114] Jessie dismissed Garnett's vitriolic attack with a few succinct and well-turned phrases, expressing her pride in producing a faithful portrait of Conrad and rightly adding: 'He has made his mark, and made it my dear Edward with no *inconsiderable* help from me.'[115]

---

[111] See letter to Galsworthy, 5 March 1907, Jean-Aubry, *Life and Letters*, i. 44. Conrad describes how Jessie 'heroically' devoted herself to their sons' care during a harrowing period when Borys had contracted the measles, followed by pneumonia: 'Jessie is wholly admirable, sharing herself between the two boys with the utmost sincerity . . . Nothing is right, good or even possible unless the mother is there.'

[112] Grace Willard, 'Conrad the Man', *New York Evening Post Literary Review*, 9 Aug. 1924, 952, in *Joseph Conrad: Interviews and Recollections*, ed. Martin Ray (London: Macmillan, 1990).

[113] Jessie Conrad, *Joseph Conrad and His Circle* (London: Jarrolds, 1935).

[114] Letter from Edward Garnett to Jessie Conrad, 11 July 1935, in *The Conradian* 19: 1 and 2 (1995), J. H. Stape and Owen Knowles (eds.), *A Portrait in Letters: Correspondence To and About Conrad* (Amsterdam: Rodopi, 1996), 256.

[115] Letter from Jessie Conrad to Edward Garnett, 14 July 1935, *A Portrait in Letters*, 257.

The biographical material shows the cumulative effect of a particular mode of presenting women in relation to Conrad. The traditional image of Conrad as author for men prevails, strengthened by the conventionalised view of his infrequent associations with women, his indifference to them, his strange choice of a wife, and his security in a predominantly male milieu. We might begin to dismantle reductive assumptions about Conrad's writing by first rehabilitating the role of women in his life.[116]

Throughout his career Conrad refuted his categorisation as writer, exclusively, of the sea. He complained to Richard Curle, 'I do wish that all these ships of mine were given a rest.'[117] But critical assumptions become traditionalised by constant repetition, authorised by prevailing critical practices. At the end of the twentieth century the lasting image of Conrad as writer for men has been sustained by a reductive theory, ensuring that his later investigations into the representation of women have been largely neglected. Only by rethinking aspects of the biography, reinstating the importance of female influences on Conrad, and exploring the fiction from the perspective of his confessed identification with the female sex, can the place of women be recovered from the predominantly masculinist tendency of Conrad criticism.

---

[116] For references to some of Conrad's important friendships with women see Karl, *Three Lives*: Harriet Capes, 532, 690; on Jane Anderson, 784–5, 790–1; on Agnes Tobin, 701, 706; on Aniela Zagórska, 496–7, 881–2.
[117] 14 July 1923, Jean-Aubry, *Life and Letters*, ii. 316.

2

Woman as Hero: Conrad and the Polish Romantic Tradition

In his reminiscences of a literary friendship with Joseph Conrad, Ford Madox Ford took occasion to remark on Conrad's distinctive evocation of the memory of his mother. He noted that, while 'it really pained him to think that his father had been a revolutionary', he spoke with great enthusiasm of his mother's contribution to the insurrectionists' cause. For Conrad, he claimed, 'the Polish national spirit had been kept alive by such women as his mother'.[1]

Ford's observation calls into question some traditional associations in Conrad criticism in which a greater emphasis has fallen on the influence of the father figure, Apollo Korzeniowski (1820–69). References to a strong male presence in Conrad's early life in Poland have enabled critics to support his traditional image as author of a man's world. The early death of Conrad's mother in 1865, when he was only seven, has precipitated much commentary on his close ties, first with his father, Apollo Korzeniowski, and later with his uncle Tadeusz Bobrowski, who became his guardian and father-figure after Apollo's death in 1869.[2] The evidence of Apollo's letters, which describe Conrad's brief but intensely emotional years spent with his father, as well as Conrad's intimate correspondence with

---

[1] Ford Madox Ford, *Joseph Conrad: A Personal Remembrance* (1924; New York: The Ecco Press, 1989), 76–7.

[2] See 'Introduction' Zdzisław Najder (ed.), *Conrad's Polish Background: Letters to and from Polish Friends* (London: Oxford University Press, 1964); Czesław Miłosz, 'Joseph Conrad in Polish Eyes', *Atlantic Monthly* 200:5 (1957), 219–28; Andrzej Busza, 'Conrad's Polish Literary Background and Some Illustrations of the Influence of Polish Literature on his Work', *Antemurale* 10 (Rome and London: Institutum Historicum Polonicum/Societas Polonica Scientarium et Litterarum in Exteris, 1966), 109–255; Adam Gillon, 'Conrad in Poland', *Polish Review* 19: 3–4 (1974), 3–28; Gustav Morf, *The Polish Heritage of Joseph Conrad* (London: Sampson, Low, Marston and Co., 1930).

his uncle, has prompted an examination of the paternal influences on Conrad's life and writing.[3]

The prevailing view is that Conrad inherited opposing moral values from his father and his uncle, a conflict that reappears in his novels as the dilemmas of conscience associated with his male protagonists.[4] In this school of thought Conrad's romanticism originates in the lessons of his father; his scepticism shows the influence of his uncle. Apollo Korzeniowski, the nationalist writer, deeply indebted to the Polish romantic literary tradition, taught his son high standards of loyalty to the homeland, an ethic steeped in the chivalry and patriotism of the 'szlachta'.[5] Conrad's *Lord Jim* demonstrates Apollo's unattainable belief in the ideals of a romantic, self-sacrificial hero. But Najder traces Conrad's presentation of doubt in Jim's ideals to the influence of Uncle Tadeusz, who deeply mistrusted a tradition that led only to a futile and illusory idealism. According to Najder, Bobrowski's philosophy of life was 'by no means a gospel of resignation', but he tried to persuade his nephew 'to take reality as it is, without complaining too much and without wanting to change it radically'. Najder concludes that Conrad had been influenced both by the Polish romantic tradition inherited from his father, through the work of national poets, Adam Mickiewicz (1798–1855) and Juliusz Słowacki (1809–1849), and by the more sceptical attitude of his uncle: 'believing in the necessity for "dreams"

---

[3] Zdzisław Najder, *Joseph Conrad: A Chronicle* (Cambridge: Cambridge University Press, 1983), 9. Najder claims that 'we may detect an echo in Joseph Conrad's *The Nigger of the "Narcissus"* [1897]' of Apollo's translation of Vigny's *Chatterton* (1856). See also 6–13, for Apollo's development as a writer. Apollo's first work of any significance, *Czyscowe piesni* [Purgatorial Songs] (1849–55), consisted of 'semireligious, semipatriotic poems' (7). His earliest play, *Komedia* (1854) earned him the reputation as a radical for its 'astonishingly sharp' presentation of social problems. Apart from *Chatterton*, he also translated Dickens's *Hard Times*, Hugo's *Les Travailleurs de la mer*, and Shakespeare's *A Comedy of Errors*. See also Conrad, letter to Edward Garnett, 20 January 1900, *CL* 2, 246. See also Najder, *A Chronicle*, 19, for a letter of 9 Nov. 1891 from Tadeusz Bobrowski to Conrad, expressing a view of life that presents an interesting parallel to the memorable conversation between Stein and Marlow in *Lord Jim*.

[4] Najder, *Conrad's Polish Background*, 19.

[5] See Najder, *Conrad's Polish Background*, 2 n. 2: 'The term cannot be adequately rendered in English because there was no difference in Poland between nobility and gentry . . . any member of the *szlachta* could theoretically become a member of the *Sejm* (Polish parliament, established in 1493) or even be elected a king. Belonging to the *szlachta* was marked by possessing a coat of arms.' Conrad's coat of arms was signified by the name 'Nałecz'.

and ideals, and knowing them to be illusions, Conrad seems to have listened both to Mickiewicz and to Bobrowski.'[6]

Najder's arguments are persuasive, but they do not fully account for the complexities suggested by Ford's perception of the female influence on Conrad's early life. Although Najder records the presence of women in Conrad's years in Poland, critics have not thoroughly examined their impact on the writer, nor, except for a few passing references, have they fully considered the genesis of his female protagonists from within the Polish tradition. The suggestive analogies between Conrad's presentation of women in the fiction, and those of the Polish romantics, have hardly been noticed.

Yet women played a vital role during Conrad's formative years in Poland. Without the sacrifice of a devoted mother during the initial period of the Korzeniowskis' exile it is doubtful whether the sickly infant Conrad would have survived.[7] Then, after Ewa Korzeniowska's death in 1865, his father Apollo relied heavily on the support of Conrad's maternal grandmother, Teofila Bobrowska (described by her son and Conrad's Uncle Tadeusz, in his memoirs, as a proud, intelligent, open-minded, warm-hearted woman[8]). When Apollo died in 1869, she was appointed one of Conrad's legal guardians. But her part in his upbringing extended to that of nurturer. Always anxious about his health, she stayed with the orphaned Conrad in Cracow for long periods after his father's death.[9]

In a letter of 1900 to Garnett, Conrad himself remarked on the benefit he had received from the close bond established amongst the Bobrowski women: 'There was an extraordinary sister-cult in that family, from which I profited when left an orphan at the age of ten.'[10] Although Conrad spent a relatively isolated childhood, a youth 'familiar with long silences',[11] he spoke affectionately of his intermittent female companionship during those early years. In *A Personal Record* (1912) he vividly remembers bidding farewell to a French governess, Mlle. Durand,

    [6] Najder, *Polish Background*, 19.
    [7] Ewa Korzeniowska (née Bobrowska, 1833–65).
    [8] The Bobrowski *Memoirs*, i. 11–12, in Busza, 'Conrad's Polish Literary Background', 153.   [9] Najder, *Conrad's Polish Background*, 11–12.
    [10] Jean-Aubry, *Life and Letters*, i. 291.
    [11] 'A Familiar Preface' to *A Personal Record* (1919), p. xx.

who had taught him to speak her language simply by being 'an excellent playmate' (65). He was very close to his cousin Józefa, his Uncle Tadeusz's daughter, a 'delightful, quick-tempered little girl', who 'died [in 1871] when she was only fifteen', but with whom Conrad claims to have spent 'the very happiest period of my existence' (24). Najder tells us that other childhood friends included Janina and Karolina le Taube, whom he met between 1870 and 1873, when he was sent to the Georgeon pension in Cracow. He established a lasting friendship with Janina, with whom he corresponded (as Baroness de Brunnow) later in life. When Uncle Tadeusz sent him to Lvov in August 1873, under the care of his cousin Antoni Syroczyński, he supposedly came into conflict with his new guardian by flirting with his daughter Tekla Syronczyńska.[12]

Najder shows us that women occupy prominent roles in Conrad's earliest years, yet he attaches little significance to their presence. Above all other memories of the period, Conrad poignantly recalled the intensity of feeling for his mother, however dimly remembered. His brief sketch of her in *A Personal Record* itself provides the basis for a re-evaluation of an elusive but compelling resonance in his writing. In the Author's Note (1919), he described the memory of her loving presence as one that dominated his recollections of the many people who wandered through the Korzeniowski household at number 45, Nowy Swiat, in Warsaw in 1861:

Amongst them I remember my mother, a more familiar figure than the others, dressed in the black of the national mourning worn in defiance of ferocious police regulations. I have also preserved from that particular time the awe of her mysterious gravity which, indeed, was by no means smileless. For I remember her smiles, too. Perhaps for me she could always find a smile. She was young then, certainly not thirty yet. She died four years later in exile. (p. x)

Conrad's relationship to his mother, along with the evidence of his early experiences and reading, shows that his childhood recollections, both personal and literary, offered a fundamental source for his later presentation of women in the fiction.

---

[12] Najder, *A Chronicle*, 32–6.

I

In 1930 Gustav Morf, an early critic of Conrad's Polish heritage, was one of the few who drew a brief analogy between Conrad's memory of his mother and his fictional women:

Most critics of Conrad have remarked that his women have something unfinished, something shadowy, something elusive about them. It is, indeed, as if the memory of her that flitted like a shadow through his infant life prevented him from drawing his women with the same sure stroke which characterizes his portraits of men.[13]

Certainly Conrad's portrait of his mother in *A Personal Record* stands out as 'elusive' and 'shadowy', reminding us of Edward Said's allusion to the 'fiction of autobiography' in relation to Conrad's work.[14] For not only did Conrad draw closely on personal experience to create his novels, he presented his autobiographical writing, conversely, as a form of partially fictionalised narrative. He claimed in 'A Familiar Preface' to this work that a novelist's writing is always to some extent autobiographical, but that 'the disclosure is not complete' (p. xiii).[15] In *A Personal Record*, he produced a highly selective account of his early life, characterised throughout by its episodic nature, by its omissions as much as its inclusion of personal detail.

Relying to some extent on the Bobrowski memoirs in re-creating the Polish episodes, his presentation of an enigmatic sketch of his mother appropriately illustrates his remarks about 'disclosure'. Conrad remembers a noble-spirited, gentle figure, habitually dressed in the black that signified mourning for Poland, most clearly remembered from the time of their three months' leave from the exile imposed on the Korzeniowskis by the Russians in the summer of 1863. In his description of Ewa, Conrad uses the same gestures and statuesque poses so often associated with the female characters of his novels. She initially appears as a quiet observer, captured in a moment of stillness, framed by the architectural features of his uncle's house in the Ukraine:

---

[13] Morf, *Polish Heritage*, 41.

[14] A reference to the title of Edward Said's *Joseph Conrad and the Fiction of Autobiography* (Cambridge, Mass.: Harvard University Press, 1966).

[15] 'A Familiar Preface' was published in 1919, added to later editions of *A Personal Record* (first published as *Some Reminiscences* in 1912).

'I seem to remember my mother looking on from a colonnade in front of the dining-room windows as I was lifted upon the pony' (23). The image calls to mind the gaze of Captain Whalley's daughter, at the close of 'The End of the Tether', whom we see finally in her plain black bodice, 'leaning her forehead against a window-pane', as 'the image of her husband and her children seemed to glide away from her in the gray twilight' (339).

Equally, Mrs Gould in *Nostromo* resembles Conrad's portrait of his mother. He describes the time at his uncle's house as the year in which 'I first begin to remember my mother with more distinctness than a mere loving, wide-browed, silent, protecting presence, whose eyes had a sort of commanding sweetness' (23–4). The image of 'the grey heads of the family friends paying her the homage of respect and love' (24) echoes the nurturing qualities of the benevolent Mrs Gould and her 'humanizing influence' as 'the European hostess' of Sulaco (45).

Conrad's most striking reference to Ewa, however, shows her taking leave of her relations for the last time on the steps of her brother's property in the Ukraine. He relates the poignant details of this departure, as she was forced by the Russian authorities to undertake the gruelling journey back into exile with her young son, even though she was barely fit to travel. He only briefly mentions Ewa by name here: 'my grandmother all in black gazing stoically, my uncle giving his arm to my mother down to the carriage' (64). The rest of the passage consists of a report (given in direct speech), of the Russian orders to escort Ewa and her son from Tadeusz's house. As if Conrad were scarcely able to recount this most painful of memories, he avoids any direct comment or interpretation of his mother's place in the scene (64–7). Indeed, the tragic memory of his mother's bravery, as she embarked on her last journey into exile, must surely account for some of Conrad's difficulty in finding comic resolution to the plots of his self-sacrificing, but ill-fated heroines.

Although Conrad allotted little space to anecdotes of his mother in his autobiographical work, she nevertheless constituted a steadfast presence, suggesting an intensity of character that belied her physical frailty. Conrad's unqualified praise of his mother as 'the ideal of Polish womanhood' (29), in her embodiment of noble self-sacrifice and loyalty to family and nation, indicates that her image exerted an enduring influence on him throughout his life, one that discretely entered the fiction by way of a number of cameo roles of considerable impact. Mrs Verloc's mother, Mrs de Barral, Mrs Haldin, sustain an unflinching poise in the face of Conrad's predominantly sceptical mode of presentation, offering the only measure of moral certitude within his narratives of pessimism and doubt. Conrad's shadowy memories of his mother may have suggested a model for the self-sacrificing mother-figures of the fiction.

Conrad's relationship to his mother also needs to be understood in the context of an enduring Polish tradition that idealised and sanctified the mother-figure socially, politically, and theologically. Indeed, the importance of the role of the mother in both the history of Polish nationalism and within the Polish family dynamic cannot be underestimated. Polish Catholicism privileges the image of the 'Mother of God' rather than that of the Virgin Mary, thus emphasising her nurturing qualities rather than her chastity.[16] A famous hymn of 1407 *Bogurodzica* (Mother of God) sustains a legendary history dating back to the tenth century, when it was presumed to have been written by St Wojciech. One small surviving fragment of the original manuscript provided a notable influence on Poland's subsequent political and literary history, as the Mother of God now becomes the Mother of the State. The hymn was transformed into a battle song, and was adopted as the national anthem in 1506.[17] In the seventeenth century it was translated into other languages by a Jesuit (Maciej Kazimierz Sararbiewskia) and in the nineteenth century it entered the Polish romantic tradition, when Juliusz Słowacki adapted it for his cycle of lyric poems connected with the November Rising of 1830.[18] Słowacki's *Hymn* merges the chivalric tradition associated with *Bogurodzica* with the revolutionary traditions of contemporary nineteenth-century Poland. The great piety

---

[16] Although Conrad's highly sceptical view of religious faith is frequently represented in his fiction, it is interesting to note that at a very early age he had learned to identify himself as, among other things, a Catholic. His oldest existing autograph (now in the Beinecke Library, Yale University) is inscribed on the back of a photograph: 'To my beloved Grandma who helped me to send cakes to my poor Daddy in prison—grandson, Pole, Catholic, nobleman—6 July 1863—Konrad'.

[17] See Julian Kryżanowski, *The History of Polish Literature* (1972; Warsaw: PWN-Polish Scientific Publishers, 1978), 16.

[18] See Juliusz Słowacki, in *Collected Works*, 2 vols., ed. Antoni Malecki (Lwów, 1866–7).

associated with the presentation of the 'Mother of God' perhaps accounts for the pathos and sincerity of the sacrificing mother-figures of Polish romantic literature.

While biographers have pointed out that Conrad's father—a writer dedicated to the second-generation revolutionary politics of partitioned Poland[19]—cut something of a romantic literary figure, Conrad's later recollections of his mother remind us that Ewa herself represented precisely the image of integrity and noble self-sacrifice that had been idealised throughout Polish national history. Judging by Ewa's surviving letters to her husband during the time of their separation in 1861, her fervent and practical devotion to her family constituted the same exemplary sacrifice that can be found in the presentation of the Polish mother in the previous generation's literature.

Apollo left his wife and young son in the Ukraine in 1861 to join a group of intellectuals in Warsaw, hoping to incite the longed-for insurrection against the Russian hegemony. During this period of separation Conrad was growing up in a fraught and tragic atmosphere, marked by images of an almost Gothic darkness, as, one by one, the Korzeniowskis' neighbours lost their loved ones in the fight against Russian domination—'everyone is in black here, *even the children*'—his mother once wrote during a protracted period of mourning.[20]

Ewa corresponded frequently with Apollo during his absence, although many of her letters were intercepted by the Russians, and later provided evidence for his arrest. Her surviving letters overflow with lavish affection and eagerly express her desire for domestic and intellectual activity. Conrad's literary interests clearly stemmed from both parents, not just from his father: 'Give me something to do while we are separated . . . Make me do some translations. Find something new and readable. I should so like to carry at least a small proportion of the cost of living.'[21] She constantly offered assistance: 'I do not want *to make things difficult*, I shall arrange everything as you would.'[22]

---

[19] See Frederick R. Karl, *Joseph Conrad: The Three Lives* (New York: Farrar, Straus and Giroux, 1979), 38–40.

[20] Zdzisław Najder (ed.), *Conrad Under Familial Eyes*, trans. Halina Carroll-Najder (Cambridge: Cambridge University Press, 1983), 51; 20 June/2 July. All references to Ewa Korzeniowska's letters to her husband are from this edition. Date and page number are quoted.   [21] 19 June/1 July 1861, 48.

[22] 21 June 1861, 46.

At the same time, she conveyed a sense of anxiety and isolation while suffering under the ubiquitous threat of the Russian
authorities. She often referred to a sense of her inability to communicate her feelings: 'How we miss you at home, you cannot
imagine and I should probably be unable to express it.' Nevertheless she wrote with a graceful, romantic style: 'You miss me;
and I do not want to speak of my longing for I know that even
without words you must feel it. Besides, what is longing in comparison with the constant fear of danger that, they say, threatens
you?'[23] Even through the medium of translation we can recognise a similar tone and sensitivity in Conrad's letters to Jessie.
Whilst travelling to, and visiting the United States in 1923 he
wrote to her: 'I miss you more and more . . . it seems ages since
I left you . . . [Borys] is very near to my heart—in which your
dear image dwells constantly commanding all my thoughts and
all my love.'[24] On another occasion he wrote to 'My dearest
Chica': 'There is not a moment when you are not in my thoughts.
I long to be back.'[25]

Ewa's capacity for intense emotional response was combined
with the Bobrowski pragmatism (most frequently attributed to
her brother Tadeusz). Her fears are often masked in the letters
by a sense of spirited optimism and self-reliance in her unfail-
ing support of Apollo: 'Several women's homes have been
searched. I am prepared for it, rest assured.'[26] She was also prepared to engineer, single-handedly, the hazardous trip to join her
husband in Warsaw (with the young Conrad): 'I shall manage
the travel expenses', she announced confidently, 'I shall carry out
all your instructions and shall bear in mind *the warnings*. I have
matured a great deal during the several weeks of our separation
and of constant longing combined with anxiety.'[27] Despite her
extraordinary courage and integrity, Ewa's sacrifices were ultimately futile. Apollo was arrested in October 1861 and Ewa later
accused of 'unlawful revolutionary activity'.[28] The 1863 insurrection failed miserably, and the Korzeniowskis were exiled to

[23] 20 June/2 July 1861, 51; 19 June/1 July 1861, 48.
[24] Letter of 30 April 1923 to Jessie Conrad, in Jean-Aubry, *Life and Letters*,
ii. 307.   [25] 6 May 1923, in Jean-Aubry, *Life and Letters*, ii. 309.
[26] 9/21 June 1861, 46.   [27] 20 June/2 July 1861, 50; undated, 52.
[28] Owen Knowles, *A Conrad Chronology* (London and Basingstoke: Macmillan,
1989), 2.

northern Russia, where the harsh winters precipitated Ewa's premature death.

We can only speculate on the effect of Ewa's letters on Conrad the writer, especially since we do not know if he read the ones that have survived. Those he did read he claimed to have destroyed, and was reluctant to discuss them. Yet we cannot overlook the importance of the date at which he read them and at which he became fully conscious of his appreciation of his mother. In a letter to Edward Garnett he recalled:

> my mother was certainly no ordinary woman. Her correspondence with my father and with her brothers which in the year 1890 I have read and afterwards destroyed was a revelation to me; I shall never forget my delight, admiration and unutterable regret at my loss (before I could appreciate her), which only then I fully understood.[29]

The date is significant, since according to *A Personal Record* Conrad began writing *Almayer's Folly* late in 1889.[30] He had taken the manuscript of his first novel with him to the Ukraine when he visited his uncle early in 1890, and it was there that he first read his mother's letters. At the turning-point in his life, as he initiated the transformation from seaman to writer, he directly relived, through his mother's letters, the events preceding his painful loss.

We should consider the impact of Conrad's memories of his mother as he wrote his first novel. Ewa would seem to be an unlikely model for Conrad's portrait of the slovenly Mrs Almayer.[31] However, it is more plausible that Conrad thought of his mother as he formed the character of Nina Almayer. As he relived the loss of a mother who had sacrificed herself for her

---

[29] 20 January 1900, *CL* 2, 245.

[30] See *A Personal Record* (9) and Zdzisław Najder, Notes to the World's Classics edition (Oxford: Oxford University Press, 1988), 157 n. 9. Conrad was living in London at Bessborough Gardens, Pimlico, London, at the time when he recalls beginning *Almayer's Folly*.

[31] However, there is an early reference to her unrecognised heroism as a young native girl, before she was 'rescued' and given a Christian education by the conquering white adventurer, Tom Lingard. See *Almayer's Folly*, The Cambridge Edition of the Works of Joseph Conrad, ed. David Leon Higdon and Floyd Eugene Eddleman with an Introduction by Ian Watt (Cambridge: Cambridge University Press, 1994), 18: 'on the day when the interesting young convert had lost all her natural relations and found a white father, she had been fighting desperately like the rest of them on board the prau.'

husband's political cause, it is quite possible that the assertive, active role of Nina in *Almayer's Folly* could be interpreted as a desire to reinvent his mother's life in his fiction. Ewa's father had considered Apollo an unsuitable match and had forbidden her marriage, and, in Conrad's novel, Almayer responds to Nina's attachment to Dain Maroola in a similar fashion. Like Dain, who offered Nina what Jocelyn Baines calls 'glamour', Apollo must have cut something of an exotic figure in the eyes of the young Ewa.[32] Ewa's mother only allowed her to marry the man she loved after her father's death. But Conrad gives his female protagonist greater powers of self-assertion. Nina defies her father and takes responsibility for her own life and choice of partner.

Biographers experience a certain difficulty in explaining the prominence of the father–daughter relationship in Conrad's early novels. Baines avoids a direct confrontation with the issue, suggesting that the father–*son* relationship 'was doubtless far too charged emotionally for Conrad to be able to represent it directly'. Instead, he found 'a disguised expression through a portrayal of the father–daughter relationship'.[33] Karl also implies an 'exchange' of gender roles in the early fiction. He remarks that when writing of his past, Conrad 'naturally' substitutes daughter for son, creating 'a dying, broken Almayer, with a daughter, not a son, anxious to survive a breaking away', while at the same time privileging the role of his father, not his mother, in the reconstruction of memories of Poland: 'Conrad may have been writing of Malayans, but his memories are also of Poles, of his father and of his home in those last days.'[34]

But Conrad's 'disguises'—as the daughters of his early work —warrant further attention, since they suggest the author's close identification with the women of his fiction. Almayer's relationship to Nina might not exclusively reproduce Conrad's conflict with his father. Conrad was also commenting on a longer tradition of familial discord between patriarchal values and conflicting 'female' responses to the father-figure.

Indeed, Conrad's earliest experiences had been dominated by Ewa's devotion, and after her death, by his father's intense

---

[32] Jocelyn Baines, *Joseph Conrad: A Critical Biography* (London: Weidenfield and Nicholson, 1960), 155.

[33] Ibid. 154–5.   [34] Karl, *Three Lives*, 76.

idealisation of her memory. The following account of Apollo's grief at the death of his wife encapsulates the spirit of high romanticism that the young Conrad (Konradek) must have perceived surrounding the memory of his mother. Stanisław Czosnowski wrote in 1929 of a visit to the Korzeniowskis a few years after Ewa's death:

I found Apollo sitting motionless in front of his wife's portrait. He never stirred on seeing us and Konradek who was accompanying me put his finger to his lips and said: 'Let us cross the room quietly. Father spends every anniversary of Mother's death sitting all day and looking at her portrait; he does not speak or eat.'[35]

Combined with his painful and distant memories of a self-sacrificing mother, Conrad had, at an early age, witnessed, during his father's vigil, a spectacle reminiscent of his later fictional idealisations of women, characterised, as they often are, by a sense of detachment, distance, and a passive, iconographic element. Something of this aestheticisation of women as paintings or artefacts survives in Conrad's habitual mode of presentation in the late romances, where Conrad emphasises the gap between what a woman 'is' and how she is represented. Drawing on his habitual mode of seeing, Conrad recalled, in his Author's Note (1920) to *Victory* (1915), the moment when he had first observed the woman who served as model for Lena. She had been playing in a café orchestra in the south of France: 'The shape of her dark head inclined over the violin was fascinating, and . . . she was, in her white dress and with her brown hands reposing in her lap, the very image of dreamy innocence' (p. xli). In the novel itself, however, Conrad ultimately transformed his passive portrait into an active role (in which Lena courageously dies for Heyst). Likewise Davidson describes Mrs Schomberg as if she were 'behaving like a painted image rather than a live woman' (44), yet the woman actively assists Lena in her escape from Schomberg's hotel. In *The Arrow of Gold* (1919), Rita da Lastaola's face was 'like some ideal conception of art' (222), but Rita herself resists all attempts to idealise her. Moreover, she evades the traditional closure of the romance heroine, ultimately choosing a solitary path.

[35] Stanisław Czosnowski, 'Conradiana', *Epoka* 136 (Warsaw, 1929), repr. in Najder, *Under Familial Eyes*, 136.

Apollo had been anxious that Conrad should retain a romantic, idealised view of his mother. He wrote to Kazimierz Kaszewski in 1865: 'He [Conrad] is all that remains of her [Ewa] on this earth and I want him to be a worthy witness of her to those hearts who will not forget her.'[36] Conrad often bore witness to his mother's memory in his minor fictional portraits of women. While the initial image of Mrs Verloc's mother in *The Secret Agent* is not particularly dignified, Conrad later provides her with a gesture of self-sacrifice in leaving the Verloc household because she feels her presence may irritate her son-in-law and weaken the success of her daughter's marriage. Her sensitive action sets her integrity against Verloc's pose of lazy self-absorption. Mrs de Barral in *Chance* selflessly supports her husband's entrepreneurial ventures, then languishes in 'exile' as de Barral's business claims his attention: 'she died . . . from neglect, absolutely from neglect, rather unexpectedly and without any fuss' (71–2). Like Ewa, she dies in isolation, leaving behind a grief-stricken husband and child.

II

While Conrad's limited memories of his mother echo in his briefly sketched fictional mothers, his presentation of women also alluded to the much longer tradition of idealised motherhood and female heroism that permeated Polish culture. In this respect Conrad's biography complements the nationalist literary tradition that he inherited from his father. This tradition consisted of the work of the great romantic male writers such as Adam Mickiewicz, Juliusz Słowacki, and Zygmunt Krasiński (1812–59), who wrote of the quests of Polish heroes, but in whose works women nevertheless occupied significant roles. In fact Conrad's romantic literary heritage expressed an uneasy ambivalence towards the role of the self-sacrificial heroine. The extent to which this literature informed the context of Conrad's upbringing helps us to understand not only the romantic element of Conrad's work, but also the impact on him of the female component of Polish romanticism.

[36] 10 June 1865, quoted in Baines, 17.

'*This is my Polishness*', Conrad once remarked, referring to the influence of Polish romantic literature on his novels. He concluded that it was his early reading of the work of Adam Mickiewicz and Juliusz Słowacki that accounted for 'something incomprehensible, impalpable, ungraspable' detected by English critics in his writing. Apollo Korzeniowski had passed on the traditions of Polish romanticism to his son:

My father read *Pan Tadeusz* aloud to me and made me read it aloud. Not just once or twice. I used to prefer *Konrad Wallenrod*, *Grażyna*. Later I liked Słowacki better. You know why Słowacki? Il est l'âme de toute la Pologne, lui.[37]

Jadwiga Kałuska, who knew Conrad in Lwów in 1867, confirmed Conrad's familiarity with the literature of this period. In an article appearing in *Czas* in Cracow, 1927, Roman Dyboski quoted Kałuska's observation that the young Conrad 'astonished everyone by reciting whole passages of *Pan Tadeusz* as well as Mickiewicz's ballads from memory'.[38]

We should not underestimate the extent to which Polish literary traditions were closely aligned with the national identity. The Polish romantics were associated with the Western European tradition through their reading of Schiller, Goethe, and Byron, but they were also strongly affiliated to the politics of partition that gave impetus to the nationalist risings of 1832, 1848, and 1863 (Conrad's father being involved in the latter).[39] The themes of this literature heavily metaphorised the struggle of Poland and Russia. Yet the romantics of 'The Great Emigration', exiled from home, compensated for their physical absence from the scene of political conflict by producing literature concerned primarily with the topics of loyalty and betrayal. They may have provided the impetus for insurrection, yet, as Nina Witoszek has pointed out, their attitude to what form this rebellion should take, and what the likely outcome would be, was ambiguous. Witoszek

[37] Conrad, Interview with Marian Dąbrowski (*Tygodnik Illustrowany*, 1917, in Najder (ed.), *Under Familial Eyes*, 199. Conrad referred to three patriotic poems by Adam Mickiewicz, *Pan Tadeusz* (1827), *Konrad Wallenrod* (1823), and *Grażyna* (1823).

[38] See Busza, 'Conrad's Polish Literary Background', 171, who cites Roman Dyboski, 'Z Młodoski Jozefa Conrada', *Czas* (Cracow, Dec. 1927).

[39] Mickiewicz also owed something to Walter Scott's ambivalent presentation of nationalism.

identifies 'two currents running through the national literature'. The first she calls 'messianic–optimistic', associated (amongst others) with the writing of Mickiewicz (whose work encompasses a vision of Poland as a 'chosen nation', led by a poet–seer). This perspective was taken up in the late nineteenth and early twentieth centuries by writers such as Eliza Orzeszkowa (who accused Conrad of deserting the homeland in 'The Emigration of Talent' debate[40]). The second current, described by Witoszek as 'sceptic–apocalyptic', provides an 'instance of the intelligentsia's equivocal stance'. This poetic tradition, inaugurated by Krasiński with his *Un-divine Comedy* (1833), 'displays the fear of cosmic disorder and confusion, of the disappearance of absolutes and, implicitly, of the loss of culture under the rule of the mob'.[41] Certainly the sceptical voices of the Polish romantic tradition resonate in a number of Conrad's texts, and critics have shown us how, as a displaced individual, Conrad himself reflected the romantics' uneasy response to the distinction between personal and public duty in the presentation of his male protagonists. Like the protagonist of Conrad's *Lord Jim*, Słowacki's *Kordian* (1834) is paralysed by doubt when confronted with a fundamental moral test. As Kordian is about to release his people from Russian oppression by taking the life of the Tsar, he fails, at the final moment, to act.[42] Kordian's discourse with the Doctor, in which the latter questions the validity of Kordian's sacrifice, resembles Jim's discussions with Marlow

[40] It is possible that Conrad began to compose *Lord Jim* in response to Eliza Orzeskowa's article 'The Emigration of Talent', published in *Kraj* in Warsaw, 23 April 1899, in which she accused Conrad of betrayal of his homeland by writing in English. Conrad nevertheless achieved considerable popularity in Poland. Paradoxically, Orzeskowa's presentation of women in her fiction, read in translation, is remarkably reminiscent of Conrad's style. See e.g. the image of Frieda's wife in *An Obscure Apostle*, trans. C. S. de Soissons (London: Greening, 1899), 21, 'questioning' her husband 'with her eyes only'—reminding us of Emilia's silent responses to Charles Gould in *Nostromo*.

[41] See Nina Witoszek, *The Theatre of Recollection: A Cultural Study of the Modern Dramatic Tradition in Ireland and Poland* (Stockholm: University of Stockholm, 1988), 102. See n. 40 above for Eliza Orzeszkowa's accusation of Conrad's betrayal in the 'Emigration of Talent' debate, 1899. See also Conrad, 'Amy Foster', *Typhoon and Other Stories* (1903), for an imaginative reconstruction of the dilemmas of isolation experienced by a man stranded on foreign soil without knowledge of the language or customs.

[42] See Adam Gillon, *The Eternal Solitary: A Study of Joseph Conrad* (New York: Bookman Associates, 1960), 92.

about his experience of a dislocation of consciousness at the fatal moment, as well as his inability to take responsibility for his crucial action: 'I had jumped . . . It seems' (111).

Conrad therefore borrowed from the Polish writers a structure that bore within it the seeds of its own critique of the romantic ideal. But doubts about the efficacy of heroism are not only expressed by the male protagonists of this literature. They also emerge in the dynamics of male/female relations. Critics of Conrad have overlooked the fundamental position occupied by the women of Polish romantic drama, whose roles often function as a reminder of the inadequacy of the male hero or the futility of his pursuit of an idealist quest. The women of Conrad's preferred poems, Mickiwiecz's *Konrad Wallenrod* and *Grażyna*, offer two such paradigms of the critique of the hero in Polish romanticism.

Grażyna (1823) represents the exemplary sacrifice and bravery of a female knight who acts effectively in the face of her husband's betrayal of national loyalties. She refuses to acknowledge her husband's alliance with the national enemy, the Teutonic knights, and leads an army into battle against them. She sacrifices her life and dies fighting for the homeland. After the battle, her husband confronts his shame and leaps onto the funeral pyre beside her. The most obvious parallel in Conrad is represented by Lena in *Victory* (1915), who dies heroically for her lover Heyst, her selfless action constituting the moral triumph of the novel, and whose sacrifice is swiftly followed by Heyst's belated self-recognition and suicide, as he sets fire to their bungalow.[43] Another echo of the Grażyna type appears in Conrad's earlier work, as Aïssa in *An Outcast of the Islands* (1896) fights with equal status alongside her father in battle.[44]

---

[43] See Busza, 'Conrad's Polish Literary Background', 216. Busza also suggests the close affiliation of *Victory* with Stefan Żeromski's *Dzieje Irzechu* (*The History of a Sin*, 1908). Żeromski was a writer of the French sensationalist school, influenced by Zola. The end of *History of a Sin* bears a close resemblance in content and style to the end of the penultimate chapter of *Victory*. See also Batchelor, *Life*, 236. Another Grażyna type exists in *Postlannicy* (*The Envoys* (1876)), by the minor dramatist and poet, Stefan Buszczyński (1821–92), Apollo's contemporary and friend (who became Conrad's first guardian). See Busza, 'Conrad's Polish Literary Background', 153: 'the story of a woman who sacrifices her own happiness for the good of the country'.

[44] See Ch. 3. Conrad would have been reminded of the Grażyna type by Marguerite Poradowska's *Popes et popadias* (1892), which he read while working

Conrad testifies to his preference for the model of female selflessness which is combined with an unquestionable integrity and
a disposition for action. He wrote to Marguerite Poradowska
on 6 or 13 December 1894 that 'I think only women have true
courage', and that in Polish literature, 'women will have more
character than the men, which with us is unquestionably the
case'.[45] In his Author's Note (1917) to *Nostromo* (1905), he
employs the language of chivalry to describe how a childhood
sweetheart became the model for Antonia Avellanos. To him,
his schoolfriend had always represented the Polish patriotic
ideal of womanhood, 'the standard bearer of faith to which we
were all born' (p. xlvi). Indeed, Adam Gillon argues convincingly
that Conrad's Polish upbringing accounts for this female type
to be found in the fiction:

> It seems to me . . . that Conrad's attitude toward women and love comes
> partly from what he himself accepted as the romantic chivalrous tra-
> dition of the Polish gentry in the Ukraine, and from the tradition of
> Polish romantic poetry.[46]

But Polish romanticism also questioned, as well as idealised, the
position of women in a chivalric tradition. These writers offered
a critical commentary on the closure of romance. In their work,
maids in towers were not exclusively rescued, but often con-
demned to a life of anguish and stasis. As I outlined in Chapter
1, Mickiewicz provides a striking example of the sacrifice of
female identity to the male heroic quest in his epic poem *Konrad
Wallenrod*, a nationalist drama in which the hero infiltrates enemy
lines in order to betray them. The curious presentation of a
tortured, solitary hermitess, once a princess, but now locked in
her tower, occupies an uneasy role in a narrative describing the
formation of nationalist identity.[47] Princess Aldona became the
wife of Konrad Wallenrod before he set out on his adventure of

---

on *Outcast* (see letter 20 May 1895, *CL* i, 221). Poradowska makes several refer-
ences in this novel to the extraordinary heroism of the legendary Polish Queen
Wanda. See Norman Davies, *God's Playground: A History of Poland*, i: *The
Origins to 1795* (New York: Columbia University Press, 1982), 61.

[45] *CL* i, 191.   [46] Gillon, *Eternal Solitary*, 89.
[47] Mickiewicz presents the trope of the isolated, abandoned woman elsewhere.
See his lyric poem, *The Romantic* (1822), trans. W. H. Auden, in Czesław Miłosz,
The History of Polish Literature (1969; Berkeley: University of California Press, 1983),
208, where the lonely female figure is characterised by her 'Medusa's stare'.

national recovery against the Teutonic enemies of Lithuania. She reappears in the narrative as a schematic figure, an archetypal embodiment of loss, a Gothic wraith, abandoned by the active male to her passive grief and self-imposed isolation in a lonely tower—'an unknown woman found in a living grave'.[48]

Her pose registers the hero's movement between genres. Her shift in role from one of domesticity ('Prince's daughter sits by her loom'[49]), to one of marginalised solitude (hermitess in the tower) also signals the moment of Konrad Wallenrod's transformation from the locus of domestic comedy to the broader sweeps of social duty and national epic. Victim of a narrative of male assertion, Mickiewicz's hermitess claims that she has been reduced, by grief, to a ghostly representation of her former self, and declines Konrad Wallenrod's invitation to leave her tower: 'Back to the world wouldst thou be bringing—whom? | A phantom!'[50] Her story is one of unrelieved anguish, her presentation that of an identity unfulfilled, since her personal sacrifice is unable to match that of her husband's crusading heroism. Zygmunt Krasiński, the third of the 'great' Polish romantics creates, in his *Un-divine Comedy*, an example of a woman's descent into grief and madness after being betrayed and abandoned by the husband to whom she is devoted.[51] In this bitter critique of romanticism Krasiński finally presents the dutiful spouse of Count Henry in a position of permanent enclosure in the garden of an asylum.

Such figures emerge in Conrad's fiction as ghostly repetitions rather than as direct influences, suggestively recalling, rather than directly borrowing from a tradition that often ironises as well as idealises the notion of self-sacrifice in women. Several examples spring to mind—Lena's presentation at the beginning of *Victory*, as a 'phantom-like apparition' (83), a 'white and spectral' figure (86), eluding the advances of Ziangiacomo, or the ghostly presence of Arlette in *The Rover* (1923), haunted by

---

[48] Adam Mickiewicz, *Konrad Wallenrod*, trans. George Rapall Noyes and others (Berkeley: University of California Press, 1925), 17. The presentation of stasis and despair originates in a long oral tradition. The Polish romantics frequently assimilated medieval tropes in their poetics (cf. Mickiewicz's *Forefathers' Eve*).

[49] Mickiewicz, *Konrad Wallenrod*, 43.

[50] Mickiewicz, *Konrad Wallenrod*, 69.

[51] Zygmunt Krasiński, *The Un-divine Comedy* (1833), in Harold B. Segel (ed. and trans.), *Polish Romantic Drama* (Ithaca, NY: Cornell University Press, 1977).

memories of the French revolution; the psychologically isolated Flora, metaphorically imprisoned on *The Ferndale* in *Chance*; the domestic claustrophobia of Winnie Verloc, Mrs Hervey in 'The Return' in her urban bourgeois 'grave'; or the sullen Alice, prisoner of a sinister 'hortus conclusus' in 'A Smile of Fortune' (*'Twixt Land and Sea* (1912)).

In his plays, *One Day More* and *Laughing Anne*, Conrad explores the issue of female entrapment in the web of domestic relations and the histories of male identity.[52] In *One Day More* Bessie is locked in a master/slave relationship with her possessive, blind father and in *Laughing Anne*, Conrad gives us a portrait of an isolated woman who tells us she 'stuck to my men through thick and thin',[53] but who is nevertheless sacrificed to the plot—she dies at the end of the play, while the son she raised alone survives, ensuring the male 'inheritance' of the narrative. In the final scene, her friend Davidson exclaims, 'Poor Anne! You are on my conscience, but your boy shall have his chance.'[54] The dramatisation of *The Secret Agent* (first performed on 2 November 1922), emphasises Winnie's 'enclosure' by framing the action at the outset with the domestic scene and closing with her pre-suicide soliloquy.

Mickiewicz's hermitess, whose personal narrative is unfulfilled, also provides the model for a familiar device in Conrad in which the female characters signal an uneasy gap in the text, the shady presence of a woman's story, hinted at, but not fully expressed. In 'The Tale' (1917), for example, the female auditor, who initially expresses the desire to hear the story, constantly intervenes in the male narrator's account of a wartime experience:

She interrupted, stirring a little.
   'Oh, yes. Sincerity—frankness—passion—three words of your gospel. Don't I know them!'

---

[52] *One Day More* was written in 1904, adapted from the short story 'To-morrow', performed in June 1905 in London, and published, with *Laughing Anne*, and with an introduction by John Galsworthy (London: John Castle, 1924). *Laughing Anne* was an adaptation of Conrad's short story, 'Because of the Dollars' (*Within the Tides*, 1914 and as 'Laughing Anne' in *Metropolitan Magazine*, 1914), reminiscent of the title of Apollo Korzeniowski's comedy *Because of the Money* (1859). See also *Three Plays by Joseph Conrad* (London: Methuen, 1934).
[53] *Laughing Anne*, 13.   [54] Ibid. 29.

'Think! Isn't it ours—believed in common?' he asked, anxiously, yet without expecting an answer, and went on at once . . .[55]

The male narrator's expression of discomfort at her response suggests the tantalising presence of an alternative story—*her* story. But it is one that is never uttered, as the male narrator briskly 'papers over the cracks' of the text constituted by her reply, and hurries on with his own narrative.[56]

To some extent Conrad's female figures represent the widely recognisable elements of enclosure, stasis and madness associated with the feminine of many nineteenth-century Gothic narratives. But the Polish examples provide a convincing model for his highly schematic mode of presentation. The fate of the hermitess of *Konrad Wallenrod*, or of the abandoned wife in Krasiński's *The Un-divine Comedy*, suggest the elusively defined, yet charismatic presence of Conrad's often silent but imposing heroines.[57]

Conrad's ironic perspective alludes closely to the Polish tradition, where works of high romanticism are often tempered by a coexistent parody of the form. The Polish romantics experimented widely with genre. Mickiewicz's *Forefathers' Eve* interweaves folklore and medieval motifs with a lack of linear chronology; Krasiński's *Un-divine Comedy* locates its critique of romanticism within a framework of domestic and political drama. Both exemplify the self-reflexive nature of the texts and the parody of strictly romantic forms.[58]

---

[55] 'The Tale', *Tales of Hearsay and Last Essays* (London: Dent, 1955), 64.

[56] See Cedric Watts, *The Deceptive Text: An Introduction to Covert Plots* (Brighton: Harvester Press, 1984), 53: 'one corollary of Conrad's interest in covert narratives is his interest in *latent*, if unrealisable narratives: the stories of what might have been.'

[57] Consider also Hermann's niece in 'Falk', *Typhoon and Other Stories* (1902).

[58] See Busza, 'Conrad's Polish Literary Background', 208. Busza draws attention to the influence of the Polish 'gawęda' or literary yarn—a traditional narrative technique—on Conrad's fiction (especially in *Lord Jim*, *Under Western Eyes*, and *Chance*): 'a loose, informal narrative, told by a speaker in the manner of someone reminiscing. It is often involved and full of digressions. Little attention is paid to chronology. At first, seemingly important details and fragmentary episodes come to the fore, then gradually a coherent picture emerges. By the time the speaker has finished everything has fallen into place.' The technique originated with the oral tradition, but first appeared in Polish literature during the romantic period, in the poetry of Mickiewicz, Pol, and Syrokomla, and in the prose of Rzewuski, Chodźko, and Kaczowski.

Conrad's preference for the work of Juliusz Słowacki can be attributed to his interest in the potentially subversive nature of the romantic quest. Słowacki's less well-known drama *Fantazy* (written between 1830–40) offers an extravagant parody of romantic self-sacrifice. It was first published posthumously in 1866, under the title *Niepoprawni* (*The Incorrigible*). Since the narrator of 'Prince Roman', Conrad's only overtly 'Polish' story, refers to 'the great exasperation of our enemies who have bestowed upon us the epithet of Incorrigible' (29), we can assume Conrad's familiarity with the play which he may have known as a boy from its original edition.[59]

Słowacki's play offers a convincing model for both Conrad's caricatured revolutionaries, Madame de S—— and Peter Ivanovitch in *Under Western Eyes* (1911). In *Fantazy*, Countess Idalia is 'something on the order of a Madame de Staël, a letter-writing steam engine'.[60] And Count Fantazy's portrait of the heroine Diana refers to her experience of exile, 'whitened by the bind of Siberia', and who, 'with those black eyes of hers sees graves and crosses there, hears chains rattling, and clasps her hands to her bosom like a statue of obedience and pain'.[61] Fantazy's description resembles the familiar imagery of Peter Ivanovitch's first speech at the Haldins' as he recalls his escape from prison, 'the loose end of the chain' fastened to his leg 'to deaden the clanking' and his praise for the exemplary Russian womanhood that saved him with 'the sacredness of self-sacrifice and womanly love' (121).

In this context, the portrait of Conrad's mother in *A Personal Record*, as well as the texts of Ewa's letters, suggest a sacrifice to her husband's revolutionary idealism that reads like the fruitless self-denial of the women of Polish romantic drama.[62] But while the presentation of female self-sacrifice may often be ambivalent, the mother figures of Polish romanticism usually represent integrity, and are rarely tainted by a sceptical treatment. Mickiewicz's Mrs Rollinson offers such a model, one that

---

[59] *Tales of Hearsay* (1925). 'Prince Roman' was initially published in October 1911 in the *Oxford and Cambridge Review*.

[60] Juliusz Słowacki, *Fantazy*, in Segel, *Polish Romantic Drama*, 264.

[61] Ibid. 258.

[62] Segel, *Polish Romantic Drama*, 182. Count Henry's wife, in Krasiński's *The Undivine Comedy*, proclaims to her husband: 'I will sacrifice myself on your anger.'

is taken up by Conrad in his presentation of motherhood.[63] The action of the blind mother, who in scene viii of Mickiewicz's *Forefather's Eve III* (1832)[64] pleads for the life of her son, a Polish nationalist imprisoned by the Russians, resembles the heroic self-sacrifice of the few mothers of Conrad's fiction. The *gravitas* of Mrs Rollinson's scene in Mickiewicz's drama contrasts jarringly with another moment in the play when Moscow intellectuals discuss the unsuitability of using 'bloody scenes of violence and stress' as a 'true subject' for Polish poetry. Although such events represent the Polish political reality, of which Mrs Rollinson's son is a victim, the 'Men of Letters', superficially posing in a Moscow salon, would prefer the pastoral mode as a generic form for nationalist poetry:

> One should sing village courtships, peasant bridals,
> Flocks, hillsides, shady trees. We Slavs love idylls.[65]

The flippant exchanges of the 'literati' offer a bitterly ironic juxtaposition with Mrs Rollinson's despairing exhortation to the Russian official on behalf of her son.

III

Mickiewicz's use of the tragic figure of Mrs Rollinson as a moral gauge of events suggests a method adopted by Conrad in his presentation of female self-sacrifice in *Under Western Eyes*. Mrs Haldin's marginal but statuesque presence on the periphery of the action in Geneva constitutes just such a standard or medium of interpretation, reminiscent of the unwavering moral status of Mickiewicz's Mrs Rollinson. A closer reading of this novel reveals the analogies between the presentation of the mother-figure of the Polish tradition and Conrad's personal tribute to his mother's memory in the fiction.

---

[63] I am referring principally to Conrad's presentation of European women. Mrs Blunt in *The Arrow of Gold* presents an exception, but even she works tirelessly to further her son's prospects. Likewise, Joanna Willems is hardly idealised in *An Outcast of the Islands*, and also represents the devoted mother type.

[64] Mickiewicz, *Forefathers' Eve III* in Segel, 162.

[65] Scene vii, *Forefathers' Eve III* in Segel, 138.

In December 1907 Conrad began working on 'Razumov', a short story that developed into the novel *Under Western Eyes* (1911). At the same time, he was contemplating an autobiographical work. In August 1908, Conrad discussed with Ford the idea for a series of autobiographical sketches for Ford's *English Review*, later published in one volume, initially as 'Some Reminiscences' and then as *A Personal Record* (1912).[66] As Conrad addressed his memories of the homeland in the autobiographical work, he was also composing his most painfully wrought fictional presentation of Russia, a narrative focusing on the psychology and consequences of Razumov's betrayal of his friend Haldin. The story of his protagonist's treacherous behaviour, and his subsequent activities as a double agent, set in the context of revolutionary resistance to Russian autocracy, constitutes one of Conrad's bleakest confrontations with the issues of private and public loyalties. But this novel also reflects the author's personal conflict surrounding the memories of his parents' subversive politics in Poland. The revolutionary enthusiasm displayed by Haldin and his sister Natalia is reminiscent of his father's idealistic sacrifice, while Conrad's cynical presentation of Peter Ivanovitch and Madame de S—— indicates his own emphatic mistrust of revolutionary values. The attenuated role of Mrs Haldin, who hovers anxiously on the periphery of the action in Geneva, awaiting news of her son, perhaps represents Conrad's most poignant tribute to his own mother, whose letters to Apollo expressed so intensely her agony of uncertainty during their separation in the days of his political activity in Warsaw.

Conrad's presentation of Mrs Haldin initially resembles the description of his mother in *A Personal Record* as the figure dressed in the perennial black of mourning, a 'loving, wide-browed, silent, protecting presence' (23). The English teacher, narrator of *Under Western Eyes*, describes Mrs Haldin as if she were Conrad's own mother, now older: 'a tall woman in a black silk dress', whose 'wide brow, regular features . . . testified to her past beauty', and who 'received me very kindly' and spoke 'in a gentle voice' (101). Like Conrad's mother, Mrs Haldin also displays a capacity for the traditional, maternal self-sacrifice: 'I have an idea that Mrs Haldin, at her son's wish, would have set

---

[66] See Knowles, *Chronology*, 72.

fire to her house . . . without any sign of surprise or apprehension' (100). But unlike her daughter's conviction that 'concord is not so very far off' (104), she maintains no romantic ideals about Russia. 'That is what my children think' she tells the English teacher, with steady scepticism (104). From her first entrance into the narrative in Part Second, she embodies one of the few detached political perspectives of the novel.

Conrad closes Part First with Councillor Mikulin's searching question to Razumov, 'Where to?' and opens Part Second with a sweeping shift of location from the Russian political stage to the domestic enclosure of the Haldins' apartment in Geneva. By following the scene in Mikulin's office at the centre of Russian autocratic politics with the private locus of a family displaced from the homeland, Conrad shows the way in which events set in motion at a political level inevitably reverberate throughout the domestic sphere. Evoking a faint echo of Mickiewicz's *Forefather's Eve III*, where Mrs Rollinson's private suffering is seen in the light of an offhand and unfeeling debate of public events, Conrad deftly handles the bitter irony of Razumov's situation by juxtaposing public and private spaces within the novel, drawing attention to the far-reaching implications of Razumov's act of betrayal. He carefully choreographs the gestures and movements of the Haldin women within the confined domestic space to suggest both their moral integrity and their political helplessness. While Natalia's presence alternates between the political and the domestic realms, her scenes at home are chiefly characterised by a passive quality as she glides between rooms: 'Miss Haldin in a plain black dress came lightly out of her mother's room with a fixed uncertain smile on her lips' (111). She strikes attitudes, watching, waiting, listening with quiet dignity, as she learns of the terrible consequences of her brother's engagement with the politics of revolutionary idealism. Her response to Razumov's confession is one of emotional petrification—'I feel my heart becoming like ice' (356). Her attainment of knowledge is accompanied by a symbolic 'unveiling'. The moment is registered as a ghostly tableau, Razumov transfixed with Natalia's veil at his feet, 'framed in the opening, in the searching glare of the white ante-room . . . standing before the empty chair, as if rooted for ever to the spot of his atrocious confession' (355).

While avoiding the crude sensationalism of melodrama, Conrad nevertheless drew on the theatrical effects of a genre associated with domestic drama in order to establish the significance of Razumov's anagnorisis. The confession occurs, notably, in the 'ante-room'—the space between home and the outside world. Razumov finally confronts his act of political betrayal when he brings the truth into the domestic space. The theatrical device also emphasises the role of the English narrator (and by implication the reader of *The English Review* or *The North American Review*[67]), as Western observer looking on with a limited understanding of the relationship of politics and domesticity in the structures of Russian life:

The thought that the real drama of autocracy is not played on the great stage of politics came to me as, fated to be a spectator, I had this other glimpse behind the scenes, something more profound than the words and gestures of the public play.   (339)

While Natalia may represent the catalyst of Razumov's self-recognition, Mrs Haldin herself plays a fundamental role in encouraging him to confess. Although she never articulates her suspicions, Razumov senses her disbelief in his story after their meeting, and, when confronted by Natalia, realises there is no escape from an admission of guilt. His dissimulation fails to convince Mrs Haldin, and he leaves her contemplating the ghost of her son: 'lost in the ill-defined mass of the high-backed chair, her white, inclined profile suggested the contemplation of something in her lap, as though a beloved head were resting there' (339).

Without the guide of a reliable narrator in the novel, the figure of Mrs Haldin indicates the moral direction of the narrative. When the English teacher encounters Peter Ivanovitch (the caricatured revolutionary mystic) at the Haldins' for the first time, the narrator significantly observes that 'Mrs Haldin's armchair by the window stood empty' (118). This is the only reference to her during the scene, as if the abandoned chair signalled both the moral redundancy of Ivanovitch's bogus feminism, as well as the generic movement from realist domestic drama to parody.

The subtle modifications of Mrs Haldin's posture in the armchair register her steady psychological decline throughout the

---

[67] *Under Western Eyes* was serialised in these journals from 1910 to 1911.

course of the novel. At first her position suggests a patient stoicism as she awaits news of her son Victor. The English teacher
remarks that 'she had not made the slightest allusion to her son
for the last week or more', yet 'she sat, as usual, in the armchair
by the window, looking out silently on that hopeless stretch of
the Boulevard des Philosophes'.[68] But as evidence of Haldin's
fate filters through to the Geneva apartment from 'Western' eyes,
reported in the 'three weeks' old number of the *Standard*' (113),
Mrs Haldin's pose soon deteriorates, her 'extinct gaze' making
'another woman of her' (114). When Razumov arrives in the
city the English teacher inadvertently summarises the Russian's
moral dilemma, with unintentional and unknowing accuracy,
as one in which he must 'deal with the morbid state of the
mother' (192). At this point Conrad uses the narrator's lack of
knowledge to exploit the painful irony of Razumov's position.
Razumov's response to her—'Must I go then and lie to that old
woman!' (190)—suggests, even to the limited understanding of
the English teacher, a profound disturbance: 'it was not anger;
it was something else, something more poignant, and not so
simple' (190–1). Razumov's acknowledgement of Mrs Haldin's
compelling presence marks a significant step in his path towards
self-recognition.

Meanwhile, a further shift in Mrs Haldin's pose now indicates
the extent to which her silent, shadowy existence, transfixed in
her peripheral but emblematic posture not only acts as a catalyst of Razumov's confession, but as a repository of his guilt. As

[68] One of many ironic references to Jean-Jacques Rousseau, whose birthplace was
in Geneva. His major work of political philosophy, *Du contrat social* (1762) argues
that sovereign power in the state should reside in the will of the people. As Najder
observes in his Introduction to *A Personal Record* (Oxford: Oxford University Press,
1988), p. xviii, Conrad 'specifically scorned the "confessional" form of reminiscences
and taunted its most eminent practitioner, Jean-Jacques Rousseau in "A Familiar
Preface" to this work'. Indeed, the affirmation afforded by Rousseau's compassionate
philosophy is at odds with Conrad's sense of self-restraint, his 'distrust of unbridled
emotionalism' in *A Personal Record* (Najder, p. xviii) in revealing details of his personal life. And the tragic irony of Razumov's case shows that confession bought
redemption at a high price. See also Claude Lévi-Strauss, *Structural Anthropology*,
ii, trans. Monique Layton (Harmondsworth: Penguin, 1978), 36, for a discussion
of Rousseau's *Discourse on the Origin of Inequality* (1754). Lévi-Strauss comments
that 'the ethnographer must learn to know himself', to discover 'a self who reveals
himself as *another*'. If we substitute Razumov, the spy, the observer, for 'ethnographer', then we can see how, in the context of Geneva, he fails to 'know himself'
until his final confession to Natalia.

if intuitively aware of Razumov's arrival in Geneva, 'her immobility in the great armchair in front of the window' took on 'an air of expectancy' (200–1). But her posture soon assumes a more frenzied aspect—'the poignant quality of mad expectation' (319) —as her physical appearance echoes her psychological disintegration, once the news of her son's death grips her with the notion of his betrayal. She responds physically to Razumov's anxieties, her pose resembling the agonised stasis of Mickiewicz's Gothic hermitess, and, like Krasiński's mother-figure, Count Henry's wife in the *Un-divine Comedy*, Mrs Haldin represents the female figure of Polish romanticism, whose descent into madness follows betrayal.

After Razumov's confession we catch a final glimpse of Mrs Haldin, 'her whole figure had the stillness of a sombre painting' (355). Once more the pose signifies the generic shift. The English teacher again records how Natalia 'pointed mournfully at the tragic immobility of her mother, who seemed to watch a beloved head lying in her lap' (355). The initially confident image of the formal portrait, reflecting Mrs Haldin's domestic harmony, has been transformed into the iconography of the *Pietà*. Razumov's 'redemption' after his public confession is confirmed by a repetition of this very image—as Tekla, the lady companion to Mme de S—— takes Razumov's head on her lap in the tram after he suffers his near-fatal accident (371).

Throughout *Under Western Eyes* the image of the self-sacrifice of three women, of Mrs Haldin, Natalia, and Tekla, is set against the single act of Razumov's betrayal of Haldin. Conrad repeatedly shows us that domestic well-being is disturbed by the male protagonists' engagement in the political spheres of the novel. In *Under Western Eyes* Conrad developed further the strategies of his other political novels, *Nostromo* and *The Secret Agent*, where Mrs Gould and Winnie Verloc, distanced from the public lives of their husbands, are marginalised by their limited domestic existences. Emilia Gould, locked in the domestic spaces of her 'medieval castle' is far from impervious to the effects of her husband's obsession with the San Tomé mine. Winnie Verloc's brutal and despairing solution to her betrayal in *The Secret Agent* pointedly debunks the notion of 'home' as a locus of security and affection. In all three political novels Conrad's use of irony invokes the register of the Polish romantics in their exploitation of the generic shift between realist domestic drama and political narrative. The revolutionary 'family' of *Under Western Eyes* is perhaps most reminiscent of the domestic parodies of Krasiński's *Un-divine Comedy* or Słowacki's *Fantazy*. In Conrad's novel the term *chez nous*, in revolutionary jargon, refers to 'Russia in general, and the Russian political police in particular' (163). Conrad further undermines the notion of harmonious domesticity with his presentation of the exiled Madame de S—— (who, the narrator, tells us, was 'very far from resembling the gifted author of *Corinne*' (142)[69]). She appears, a Gothic parody, 'like a galvanised corpse out of some Hoffman's Tale' (215), setting up house in the run-down Chateau Borel, holding court amongst 'the refuse the banker's widow had left behind her' (216).

The position of both Haldin women and the lady companion Tekla exposes the vulnerability of the domestic sphere and the futility of sacrifice to its service. Tekla, as an outcast like Razumov, makes an appropriate partner for him in the context of a debased 'comic' closure. Yet the sacrifices of all these women retain a moral dignity that is largely absent elsewhere in the novel. Mrs Haldin's stoic expression of grief unsettles Razumov to the point of confession: 'He could not shake off the poignant impression of that silent, quiet, white-haired woman' (340). Tekla first appears as a caricatured figure of futile devotion in the service of the brutal Peter Ivanovitch. Her early experiences of domesticity with the 'journeyman lithographer' had also been 'like a nightmare' (152). Nevertheless her story of sacrifice to this 'simple martyr' of revolutionary activity retains a notable sincerity. Natalia, who loses both her family and her faith in Razumov nevertheless sustains a positive outlook in her final sacrifice to Russia. The English teacher remarks that her decision to give herself to the sick and needy had matured her: 'It was the perfection of collected independence' (373). All three women are in some way sacrificed to Razumov's *story*, since it is after his confession that Mrs Haldin dies, Natalia gives herself to the poor of Russia, and Tekla saves him.

---

[69] Germaine Necker de Staël (1766–1817), *Corinne, où l'Italie* (1807). Madame de Staël, who was forced to leave Paris during the 1789 revolution, and exiled by Napoleon, took up residence near Geneva.

We have seen that Conrad began work on *Under Western Eyes* while writing his personal reminiscences. As if compelled to relive and confront all the old memories of Poland, the accusations of guilt associated with leaving his native land, writing in a foreign language, and by implication, abandoning the nationalist struggle against Russian hegemony, Conrad devised, in *Under Western Eyes*, his most harrowing narrative of loyalty and betrayal, amongst whose protagonists was Poland's traditional enemy itself. The personal cost of exhuming these memories was considerable.[70] It therefore seems reasonable to identify Conrad with his protagonist Razumov, who achieved his painful anagnorisis at a price. But what of the women of the novel, who accept self-denial and sacrifice themselves to Razumov's narrative without a fight? Must we agree with Terence Cave's view, that Natalia is not 'an individual' at all, but 'a symbol of transcendent value' in which she functions as an uncomplicated two-dimensional figure?[71]

Keith Carabine's extensive work on the texts of 'Razumov' and *Under Western Eyes* has shown that Natalia Haldin's role had initially captured Conrad's interest to a much greater extent.[72] Miss Haldin's final characterisation, however, expresses less of the depth and nuance of the earlier story, and Conrad himself drew attention to the unfulfilled potential of his heroine. He admitted in a letter to Olive Garnett of 11 October 1911 that he could have done more with the female role: 'if I had allowed myself to make more of her she would have killed the artistic purpose of the book . . . Still I need not have made Miss Haldin a mere peg as I am sorry to admit she is.'[73] Yet in spite of Conrad's anxieties, the vital presence of the self-sacrificing women in *Under Western Eyes* offers a firm standard in a world of moral

---

[70] See Najder, Introduction, *Conrad's Polish Background*, 12. Najder makes an important observation about Conrad's reasons for leaving Poland. In 1872 Tadeusz Bobrowski had failed to secure Austrian citizenship for Conrad. Najder cites this moment as the turning point in Conrad's life: 'it meant that he could not stay indefinitely in ethnic Poland without risking possibly as many as 25 years of military service in the Russian army, to which he was liable as the son of a convict.'

[71] Terence Cave, *Recognitions* (Oxford: Clarendon Press, 1988), 482.

[72] Keith Carabine, 'From *Razumov* to *Under Western Eyes*: The Dwindling of Natalia Haldin's "Possibilities"', *The Ugo Mursia Memorial Lectures* (Milano: Mursia International, 1988), 147–71.

[73] Edward Garnett (ed.), *Letters from Joseph Conrad* (New York, 1928), 234.

uncertainty (like the role of the mother in Polish romantic drama). Jocelyn Baines talks of Natalia Haldin as 'Conrad's most effective portrait of a woman', perhaps because, as he sees her, she fits the model of selflessness already mentioned above: 'a noble, intensely idealistic girl' who acts as a catalyst for Razumov's self-discovery.[74] However, like their Polish counter-parts, these women fade from the narrative, marginalised, destined to a lifetime of self-sacrifice. Only Sophia Antonovna survives intact. Of all the women in the novel, with her frank and earnest demeanour, 'the true spirit of destructive revolution', perhaps it is she who provides the greatest challenge for Razumov. He experiences great difficulty negotiating with her in his pose as double agent because she was 'stripped of rhetoric, mysticism, and theories'. She was, in fact, 'the personal adversary he had to meet' (261). Yet her last words on the subject of the bogus feminist, 'Peter Ivanovitch is an inspired man', leaves unsettled the question of her independence and integrity at the end of the novel (382).[75] How seriously should we take her championing of Ivanovitch? Does she too ultimately join the ranks of the self-sacrificing women of the novel?

Conrad's evocation of female self-sacrifice, and even his denial of Natalia's part, shows Conrad's tendency, as he developed his female roles, to draw on, and yet engage more critically with the signification of the Polish tradition. Originally, as Carabine has outlined, the love affair between Natalia and Razumov was far more explicit. Only after the marriage of the two would Razumov confess. The problem here for Conrad may have been that in this version the marriage plot threatened to overtake the political one, and, in a sense embroil the reader too thoroughly in a realist domestic drama. Conrad's highly sceptical presentation of the male emphasis on female sacrifice questions and undermines this very tradition of womanly duty. But part of the subversive effect arises from the fact that, ironically, he shapes Natalia's role according to the codes of a Polish tradition where men privilege 'love for the cause above love for the

---

[74] Baines, *A Critical Biography*, 362.

[75] See Carabine, 'From *Razumov* to *Under Western Eyes*', 3–29. Carabine provides detailed textual evidence to show how Conrad sacrificed Natalia's role in order to preserve Peter Ivanovitch's credibility as an influence on the women of this novel.

person'.[76] Ultimately Razumov's love for Natalia is sacrificed, not to the cause of liberation, but, paradoxically, to the survival of Russian autocracy.

As the Polish material has shown, the full significance of Conrad's identification with the women of his early life and reading has so far been neglected. Conrad explores the dilemmas of male protagonists, but the female roles, when they arise from a distinctively Polish tradition, constitute an important expression of his critique of romanticism. By tracing this influence on his presentation of women in the fiction we perceive a sense of continuity in his career denied by the traditional bifurcation of the canon into early and late works. It has been customary to see Conrad's breakdown, following the completion of *Under Western Eyes* in 1910, as the end of his achievement, but from another point of view his recovery freed him to produce a work in which a female protagonist dominates the narrative. Like Natalia Haldin, Flora de Barral makes her sacrifices. But it is she, and not the male protagonist who constitutes the narratorial preoccupation of *Chance*. Having confronted the ghosts of his Polish life and the loss of his mother, Conrad produced the first novel in which a woman finally achieves the status of the mysterious and 'unknowable' Conradian hero.

[76] Witoszek, *The Theatre of Recollection*, 178 n. 22.

3
Conrad and Marguerite Poradowska

The difficulty in describing the significance of Conrad's creation of a female protagonist in *Chance* stems from our inability to imagine a predominantly female readership of his work. But his serious engagement with women's issues and audience was not as adventitious as it may seem. He had addressed the question of female identity in the colonial encounters of the first two Malay novels, offered sympathetic portraits of female frustration and domestic entrapment in the marriage plots of 'The Return', *Nostromo*, and *The Secret Agent*, and given a biting critique of Peter Ivanovitch's blatant insincerity in his attitude to feminism in *Under Western Eyes*. Yet because Conrad has been situated by critics in an almost exclusively masculine literary world, we think of him as empathising with a male reader. The author's enduring friendships and prolific correspondence with a number of men of letters have added weight to the argument that he not only wrote about men but predominantly *for* them. However, Conrad was far from isolated from women writers or readers of his work. He admired and encouraged the literary achievements of a number of female friends. To name but a few examples, he commented extensively on the work of Gabriela Cunninghame Graham,[1] Ada Galsworthy, Katherine Sanderson,[2]

---

[1] Gabriela Cunninghame Graham was an active member of the Spanish women's movement, who had published a life of *Santa Teresa* (2 vols., 1894), and a collection of essays, 'Family Portraits', reprinted in *The Christ of Toro* (1908). See letters to R. B. Cunninghame Graham, 31 Jan. 1898 and 4 Feb. 1898, *CL* 2, 29–30, 35; and letter to Gabriela Cunninghame Graham, 24 Feb. 1899, *CL* 2, 171.

[2] Soon after reading Ada Galsworthy's book on Rousseau in 1907, Conrad began work on 'Razumov', the short story that eventually incorporated, in *Under Western Eyes*, a response to Rousseau's philosophy. In 1910 he sent Katherine Sanderson a detailed critique of her series of South African sketches, written for publication in *Scribner's* magazine. See letter of 16 or 23 October? 1910, *CL* 4, 374–5.

and Constance Garnett,[3] and respected their responses to his fiction.[4]

One female figure in particular occupies an outstanding position in Conrad's development as a writer, offering a background for his encounter with the woman reader of the later fiction. His relationship with Marguerite Poradowska, herself a writer of French fiction with whom he corresponded most frequently during the period of his transition from sailor to novelist, offers a neglected but vital influence on his career, not only in the early stages, but one that was sustained as his audience more frequently encompassed, with the publication of *Chance*, the women readers of romance.

Conrad's letters to Poradowska, the widow of his distant Polish cousin, reveal a depth and intimacy that dispels any doubts about Conrad's empathy with women. But while Poradowska's moral support of Conrad is well documented, her creative input has gone unrecognised. In drawing attention to the French influences on Conrad's work, critics have engaged in a canonisation of sources, emphasising the importance of his borrowings from famous male writers such as Gustave Flaubert, Anatole France, and Guy de Maupassant. They have overlooked the possibility that a less highly rated female author of French romance fiction (whom Conrad is known to have read) might also have offered him creative inspiration. Yves Hervouet, for example, in his otherwise exhaustive catalogue of Conrad's allusions to French literature, occasionally cites the correspondence with Poradowska, but mentions none of her fiction, referring to her

---

[3] When Constance Garnett, the well-known translator of Dostoevsky, wrote to Conrad to congratulate him on the publication of *The Nigger of the 'Narcissus'*, he had pasted her letter into his personal copy of the novel. See letter to Edward Garnett, 7 January 1898, *CL* 2, 6: Conrad declared that her response constituted 'the most prized words of praise and specially interesting as disclosing the woman's point of view'. The remark not only expressed the high esteem in which he held Mrs Garnett's opinion, but also the importance to him of reaching a female audience.

[4] In 1895, when Conrad tried to publish *Almayer's Folly* in the internationally respected literary journal, *Revue des Deux Mondes*, he sent the manuscript not to the editor Ferdinand Brunetière, but to a woman reader, herself a prolific feminist writer, Thérèse Bentzon (pseudonym of Marie Thérèse [de Solms] Blanc (1840–1907), who wrote *The Condition of Woman in the United States* (1895)). Conrad believed his novel would receive a more enlightened reading from her. See *CL* 1, 204. See also Letter to Katherine Sanderson, 6 April 1896, *CL* 1, 271. On this occasion, Conrad had been delighted with the favourable response to *Outcast* of Katherine Sanderson's sister Monica.

as a close friend rather than a literary figure in Conrad's life.[5] Likewise, in *A Preface to Conrad*, Cedric Watts includes a section entitled 'Short Biographies', specifically referring to the literary influences of Flaubert, France, and Maupassant. The entry under Marguerite Poradowska identifies her simply as a 'prize-winning writer of tales and novels' who 'doubtless encouraged him to persevere with *Almayer's Folly*'.[6]

Throughout his career, Conrad drew on a variety of sources, responding to the methods of both popular and 'highbrow' fiction. And while he was scornful about certain contemporary women writers, he constantly praised Poradowska's romances, even after the period of their most intimate correspondence.[7] Her work dealt, however superficially, with the struggles of religious and political factions in rural communities of partitioned Poland, subjects of personal concern to the displaced Conrad. Her novels stimulated his interest in the plots and situations of romance, beginning with *Almayer's Folly*, and provide evidence of a considerable creative impact that extends also to Conrad's later fiction, when he turned more frequently to the genre of romance.

I

Marguerite Poradowska (née Gachet, 1848–1937) was already a well-established author when Conrad first met her. Her romances, based on Polish themes, drew on her experiences in Galicia, in the Austrian part of Poland, where she had lived during the early months of her marriage to Alexander Poradowski.

[5] See Yves Hervouet, *The French Face of Joseph Conrad* (Cambridge: Cambridge University Press, 1990), 10–11, 220–1, 237–8. Writing of *Chance*, Hervouet remarks: '[Anatole] France contributed to a few of the observations about women sprinkled throughout the book' (118). He cites a few phrases from *Le Jardin d'Épicure*. See also J. H. Stape, 'An Allusion to an Eastern Tale in the "Author's Note" to *Chance*', *L'Époque Conradienne* (1988), 69–75, on Conrad's borrowing from a tale presented by France in his essay 'M. Thiers, historien' collected in the first volume of *La Vie littéraire* (1888) and retold in *Les Opinions de M. Jerome Coignard* (1893).

[6] Cedric Watts, *A Preface to Conrad* (1982; London: Longman, 1993), 200–6.

[7] J. A. Gee and P. J. Sturm (eds. and trans.), *Joseph Conrad: Letters to Marguerite Poradowska: 1890–1920* (1940; repr. Port Washington, NY: Kennikat Press, 1973), 117.

She published fiction in the internationally respected journal, *Revue des Deux Mondes* in Paris, as well as French translations of Polish writers (including Henry Sienkiewicz) in both Paris and Brussels. She was the only living writer known to Conrad as he worked on his first draft of *Almayer's Folly* (begun in 1889). Shortly after their first meeting in Brussels, Conrad had taken this manuscript and a copy of Poradowska's novel *Yaga* (1887) with him on a visit to the Ukraine.[8]

Poradowska occupies a place in Conrad's biography as the author's most intimate correspondent between 1890 and 1895. She was French by birth, daughter of an eminent medievalist associated with the Royal Belgian Archives, but her husband (like Conrad's father, Apollo Korzeniowski) was a Polish patriot who had participated in the 1863 insurrection. Poradowski eventually settled in Brussels with Marguerite, where he helped to found a benefit society for Polish exiles.[9] Conrad first met Marguerite in 1890, when he broke a journey to Poland by visiting Brussels to pay his respects to his dying relative.

The meeting occurred at a moment when Conrad was struggling with a sense of isolation and lack of direction. It was almost a year since he had returned to London from his command of the *Otago* (of which he was master from January 1888 to March 1889), and even longer since he had visited his guardian, Uncle Tadeusz Bobrowski, in Poland in 1883. He was still undecided about settling in England, and at the age of 33 his professional position was precarious. He felt uncertain about his future as a seaman in Western Europe, and, given his parentage, a permanent return to Russian-dominated Poland offered even fewer prospects, where, as the son of political prisoners he would have been obliged to serve in the Russian army.[10] Under the circumstances, Poradowska the writer provided fundamental encouragement for his first attempts at a new vocation.

After Poradowski's death Marguerite and Conrad corresponded frequently in French, meeting occasionally in Brussels or Paris, where in 1891 Poradowska had taken an apartment

---

[8] See Letter to Poradowska, 14 Feb. 1890, *CL* 1, 39. *Yaga*, a novel of Ruthenian life, was published in serial form in the *Revue des Deux Mondes* 82 (Paris, 1 and 15 August 1887) and in book form by Ollendorff, Paris, 1888.

[9] See Frederick R. Karl, *Joseph Conrad: The Three Lives* (New York: Farrar, Straus, and Giroux, 1979), 278.   [10] See Ch. 2 n. 70.

at 84, rue de Passy. They shared personal and professional confidences until 1895, after which no letters are known to exist until 1900, when their tone loses its emotional intensity. By this time Conrad had married Jessie George (1896) and settled in England, and Edward Garnett had become his chief mentor in literary matters. Nonetheless, the affection between the two endured, as Conrad's comments on her novel *Hors du foyer*, written to her in 1913, clearly show: 'in those genuine and well-written pages I am very near you in thought and feeling.'[11] While critics have made much of a possible romance between Conrad and Poradowska, they do not always acknowledge the importance for Conrad of the intellectual aspect of their relationship, and tend to overlook the fact that his first *literary* friendship was with a woman.

His letters to Poradowska demonstrate an extraordinary empathy with his correspondent, whose spirited independence he so obviously admired and with whom he shared confidences of a profound and often philosophical nature. Conrad's initial intimacy with Poradowska developed rapidly through the correspondence conducted during his trip to Africa in 1890. She had helped Conrad to secure the post in the Congo that would inspire *Heart of Darkness*,[12] and in April of that year he acknowledged her assistance as a gesture that 'touches me more than I can express'.[13] In his letters to her from Africa he surmised that an imaginary 'other' self, a 'secret sharer' remained behind with Poradowska. In mid-May, for example, he wrote: 'Happily there is another me who prowls through Europe, who is with you at this moment.'[14] His former apathy about his destiny had been replaced by an interest in her: 'this makes me forget the petty miseries of my own path.'[15]

His sense of a strong female presence accompanying him to the Congo creates a vivid contrast with Marlow's presentation of the European women of *Heart of Darkness*, who are categorically 'out of it'. Unlike the Intended, who hovers on the novella's periphery, and from whom Marlow withholds knowledge of Kurtz's experiences in Africa, Poradowska received, in

[11] 12 April 1913, *CL* 5, 213.
[12] See Karl, *Three Lives*, 282 for Poradowska's intervention, on Conrad's behalf, with Albert Thys in Brussels.   [13] *CL* 1, 48.
[14] *CL* 1, 51.   [15] *CL* 1, 55.

Europe, a detailed account of Conrad's journey. In late September he appealed to her in confidence 'to keep secret from *everybody* the state of my health.'[16] Far from representing the passive, ineffectual white women of *Heart of Darkness*, Poradowska was acknowledged by Conrad as a successful woman writer who lived at the centre of European culture. In the same letter from Kinshasa, he referred to her prize-winning novel, *Demoiselle Micia*: 'I learn with joy of your success at the Academy, which, of course, I never doubted.'[17] Watts's claim that Poradowska's chief influence on Conrad was that 'she was evidently a model for the Intended'[18] seems inadequate in the context of Conrad's response to her in his letters from Africa.

The earliest letters show an instant rapport, yet are characterised by a greater formality than the modern reader might expect.[19] His formal voice leaves us with the sense of a private and intensely intimate ritual being enacted within the texts of these letters, a strategy which concealed a dialogue of equal integrity conducted at the profoundest level. Perhaps the formality of the letters created a medium for handling the developing intimacy with an older woman. As the emotional relationship extended to one of professional interest, Conrad's voice remained governed by a sense of decorum on many occasions. Having read the manuscript of her novel *Marylka*,[20] he immediately sent the first page of *Almayer's Folly*, accompanied by a gentlemanly comment: 'This I owe you, since I have seen yours. I for one like to observe the decencies.'[21] Yet whatever Conrad's intention, the formal gestures failed to mask the sense of reciprocity that had been quickly established at the outset of the relationship. Marguerite's immediate acceptance of Conrad's friendship after the death of her husband had provided a lifeline for the displaced Conrad. And when Tadeusz Bobrowski died (in 1894) she represented for him the only living link (albeit by marriage) to his family outside Poland. With first-hand experience, she could accept both his Polishness and his status as émigré, while he also

---

[16] 26 Sept. 1890, *CL* 1, 62.   [17] *CL* 1, 62.
[18] Watts, *Preface to Conrad*, 204.
[19] See Owen Knowles, 'Conrad's Correspondence: A Literary Dimension', *Conradiana* 23 (Spring 1991), 19.
[20] *Marylka* was published in the *Revue des Deux Mondes* 11 (15 Aug. 1895) and 12 (1 and 15 March 1895).   [21] 29 March or 5 April 1894, *CL* 1, 151.

understood her sense of isolation and could share with her their grief for the departed.

Conrad wrote to Poradowska from Warsaw on 11 February 1890, shortly after her husband Alexander's death (on 7 February), addressing her in French as 'My dear and good Aunt': 'I was with you in thought and spirit yesterday, sharing, though far from you, your sorrow, as indeed I have not stopped doing since I left you.'[22] Translation cannot adequately render the formalities of Conrad's written French: 'J'étais avec Vous de pensée et de coeur hier partageant, qoique [sic] loin de Vous, Votre douleur comme du reste je n'ai cessé de le faire depuis que je Vous ai quitté.'[23] The letters contain frequent grammatical and spelling errors, like 'qoique', but often convey an expressive overflow of feeling which belies the almost ritualistic formality of their mode of address. Throughout the period of their most prolific correspondence (1890–5), Conrad continued to write to Poradowska as 'Tante', a gesture not only of respect, but one that positioned him in a specifically unthreatening relation to her: that of a younger, less experienced family member. In many instances he also carried over from the Polish the practice of capitalizing 'You' and 'Your', a convention which, seen on the page in manuscript, strikingly elevates the status of the addressee. Nevertheless, a strongly emotional tone also characterises the letters. Conrad excused his idiosyncratic but expressive use of French in the postscript to a letter of 14 February 1890: 'I write to you in French because I think of you in French; and these sentiments, so badly expressed, come from the heart, which knows neither the grammar nor the spelling of a studied sympathy.'[24]

Conrad had, of course, already begun his first novel in English before meeting Poradowska (presumably he had hoped eventually to capture the wider English and American markets). But the development of a relationship with a French novelist at this time may also have had some impact on his decision to continue his creative work in English. In spite of the mistakes in grammar and spelling, he developed a style of writing to Poradowska that suggests at times an extraordinary ease with the French language, especially when writing to her in confessional mode. Conrad stated in the Author's Note to *A Personal*

[22] CL 1, 37.   [23] CL 1, 36.   [24] CL 1, 39.

Record that it was 'natural' for him to write in English (p. v). But in his letters to Poradowska he repeatedly initiates in French some of the most strenuous philosophical issues later discussed in English in the fiction.

Conrad's emotional involvement with Poradowska during his change of career was complex. The tone of the letters is intimate, but often tinged with awe for the accomplished older woman (she was ten years his senior), showing the admiration of the novice for the successful professional. Conrad may have felt the need to distance himself from the already accomplished French author to avoid comparison with her. At the same time, he might also have associated his writing of French with the *private* language of his letters to Poradowska. We cannot eliminate the possibility that she may have indirectly assisted in his decision to continue writing in English.[25]

Poradowska was the first person to whom Conrad suggested a shared authorship. In late July 1894, he tentatively approached his 'chère Maitre': 'we might perhaps be able to have *Almayer* appear not as a translation but as a collaboration.'[26] Later, in August of the same year, before hearing that Fisher Unwin had accepted his first manuscript,[27] Conrad again pursued the idea, this time asking her to translate *Almayer's Folly*, but offering her full acknowledgement as author and proposing to reduce his own identity on the title page to the letter 'K'.[28] The letter confirms Conrad's lack of confidence in his position before he secured Unwin as publisher, but may also indicate his indebtedness to Poradowska for her creative inspiration as he persevered with his first novel.

Ultimately Poradowska did not collaborate with Conrad or translate *Almayer's Folly*, although she did later translate 'An

---

[25] See James Clifford, *The Predicament of Culture: Twentieth-Century Ethnography, Literature and Art* (Cambridge, Mass.: Harvard University Press, 1988), ch. 3, 'On Ethnographic Self-Fashioning: Conrad and Malinowski', 92–3. Clifford's discussion provides an anthropological perspective on the effect on Conrad's fiction of his use of three languages—English, French, Polish—during the period of his close relationship with Poradowska.   [26] 30? July 1894, *CL* 1, 165.

[27] See letters of 4 Oct. 1894 to T. Fisher Unwin and to Poradowska, *CL* 1, 176–8.

[28] 18? Aug. 1894, *CL* 1, 170. Conrad wrote that 'K' represented the Malay word *kamoudi*, meaning 'rudder,' but it might also suggest his family name, Korzeniowski. See also Ch. 4 on Conrad's doodles with the letter 'K' in the manuscripts of *Under Western Eyes* and *Chance*.

Outpost of Progress' and 'The Lagoon'. Conrad acknowledged receipt of her translation of 'Outpost' on 16 May 1900,[29] an important date because it suggests the continuity in the relationship during the years of the missing letters and detracts from the theory of a fundamental rift between them at this time.[30] Henri Davray of the *Mercure de France* subsequently took over the translation of all Conrad's work. It made good business and artistic sense to obtain a uniform translation from Davray, but Conrad's tactful handling of the situation confirms his desire to remain on good terms with Poradowska.[31] In early April 1902 he suggested that Davray use Poradowska's manuscript as a basis for his translation of 'Outpost', and she complied willingly with his request. He quite frankly suggested some improvements to both her and Davray's work:

Davray has allowed me to make some changes in his translation of 'Karain'. Will you permit me to do the same with 'An Outpost of Progress' and 'The Lagoon'? The latter especially needs to be shortened, tightened a little, don't you think?[32]

This episode demonstrates the endurance of a candid professional relationship, as well as a sustained affection between the two as Conrad gradually moved away from Poradowska's sphere of influence.

But during the years of their greatest intimacy, the emotional confidences exchanged in the correspondence clearly informed Conrad's creative development. The letters to Poradowska offer an intriguing opportunity to observe some of his earliest 'rehearsals' of later fictional themes. Beneath the surface formalities, at the most profound level of exchange, Conrad encouraged her to explore an inward vision, the growth of knowledge through the spiritual adventure that occupied the lives of his male protagonists:

---

[29] *CL* 2, 270.

[30] See Bernard C. Meyer, *Joseph Conrad: An Analytic Biography* (Princeton: Princeton University Press, 1967), 107.   [31] *CL* 2, 401.

[32] 5 January 1907, *CL* 3, 401. Conrad refers to Poradowska's translations again in a letter to Davray of 8 Jan. 1907 (*CL* 3, 402); and in a letter to T. Fisher Unwin on 26 April 1911: 'I did some time ago authorise Mme Poradowska my relation by marriage to translate the *Outpost* which appeared serially in a French publication the name of which has escaped me altogether' (*CL* 3, 434–5). Karl and Davies (435 n. 1) observe that this translation, which had been considered for, but not published in, the *Mercure de France*, is not known to have appeared elsewhere.

Your letter is so human in that sadness of all beginnings. I understand you perfectly. It is the hesitation at the threshold, the distaste for
new things, the uncertainty of the darkness where one fearfully inches
along.[33]

Again, in a letter of early November 1893, we recognise the
isolation of consciousness perceived by the individual who is
projected into the darkness of insecure psychological states: 'I
have seen nothing, see nothing and shall always see nothing.'[34]
These remarks are reminiscent of the painful encounters with
the abyss expressed in the fiction by Marlow in his journey
to the 'heart of darkness', by Jim in his fateful leap from *The
Patna*, or by Razumov in his confession to Natalia Haldin
in *Under Western Eyes*.[35] We are most familiar with Conrad's
'rehearsals' of his fiction from much-quoted letters to Garnett
and Cunninghame Graham;[36] but he also wrote to Poradowska
of moments in which 'the unguided soul strays into an abyss'.[37]
In early November 1893 he expressed his own sense of isolation: 'I could swear that there is nothing but the void outside
the walls of the room where I write these lines.'[38] Three years
earlier, in mid-May 1890, Conrad had summed up a view of
life that recurs in the experiences of Almayer and Willems, the

---

[33] 22 Oct. 1891, *CL* I, 100.   [34] 5 Nov. 1893, *CL* I, 131.

[35] See Vincent Pecora, '*Heart of Darkness* and the Phenomenology of Voice', *Journal
of Literary History* 52 (1985), 993. Pecora identifies the parallels between Conrad
and Schopenhauer in their representations of 'the abyss', citing Schopenhauer, *The
World as Will and Representation*, rev. edn., trans. E. F. J. Payne (New York, 1969),
i 2788 n. Pecora suggests that Conrad uses Marlow's voice as a device through
which to discuss the subject of language, showing its tentative and unstable quality as a register of human consciousness. I will argue that Marlow's voice per-
forms a similar function in *Chance*, where his unreliable narrative exposes the
epistemological difficulties of understanding the central female character. See
also Edward Said, *Joseph Conrad and The Fiction of Autobiography* (Cambridge,
Mass.: Harvard University Press, 1966), 102. Said suggests that Conrad was familiar with Schopenhauer through the work of Ferdinand Brunetière (1849–1906), 'La
Philosophie de Schopenhauer et les consequences du pessimisme', in *Essais sur la
litterature contemporaine* (1892). This was not necessarily Conrad's first encounter
with Schopenhauer, but it is of interest here since Poradowska sent Conrad copies
of the *Revue des Deux Mondes*, of which Brunetière was editor, and in which he
published his work.   [36] See Ch. 1.

[37] 23 March 1890, *CL* I, 43. See also Conrad's reference to Mrs Almayer in
Almayer's Folly (Cambridge Edition): 'she felt . . . the narrow mantle of civilized
morality in which good meaning people had wrapped her young soul . . . fall away
and leave her shivering and helpless as if on the edge of some deep and unknown
abyss' (33).   [38] *CL* I, 131.

protagonists created during the years of his most intimate correspondence with Poradowska: 'A little illusion, many dreams,
a rare flash of happiness followed by disillusionment, a little anger
and much suffering, and then the end.'[39]

These letters point to a paradox in Conrad's work. As he fixed
the energy engendered by this kind of emotional conflict in his
male protagonists, he initially found an attentive response to
his own sense of moral and psychological despair in a woman.
Yet it was not until the creation of *Chance* (1913) that Conrad
explored the psychology of isolation in a central female protagonist for the first time. The way in which Conrad and Poradowska
had interacted as correspondents provides an important insight into Conrad's fictional presentations of female identity. In
Chance the same expression of psychological isolation found in
Conrad's letters to Poradowska resides in the portrait of Flora
de Barral. Caught within, but nevertheless alienated from the
world of seamen narrators—'the girl was like a creature struggling under a net' (140)—her plight offers a parallel with the
dimensions of despair evident in these letters.

Yet the letters are by no means exclusively introspective or
philosophical in character. They display cross-currents of emotional honesty, gentlemanly decorum, and playful didacticism
tempered occasionally with an astonishing and radical departure from traditional nineteenth-century attitudes to women in
which Conrad entered into a dialogue of impassioned and rigorous frankness. The tone oscillates between idealisation and
empathy; the voice sometimes decorous and affectionate, sometimes patronising. Like Marlow and his interlocutor in *Chance*,
who both at some stage of the novel idealise the heroine—'a young
girl, you know, is something like a temple' (311)—Conrad put
his 'aunt' on a pedestal. Alluding to Dante, he claimed that—
'Without realizing it, you doubt that the Divine Spark is within
you.'[40] On other occasions he identified with her totally in her
sense of isolation following the death of her husband: 'I understand you perfectly' (*CL* 1, 99). Alternatively, he sometimes
addressed Poradowska with a rational male voice, chiding the
chaotic female who needs protection: 'Aunt of mine, you are
very, very slightly "impractical" . . . let yourself be guided (for

[39] *CL* 1, 51.   [40] 22 Oct. 1891, *CL* 1, 100.

once in your life) by the light of pure reason.'[41] We can hear in this Marlow's way of deploring the apparent irrationality of Flora's despair, while finding her suicide pose 'attractive' (46).

The rhetorical jousting of Marlow and his interlocutor in *Chance* may suggest that in this novel Conrad commented on the shifts in tone which he himself had used to address a woman he admired and respected.[42] He undermines the male narrators' attempts to fix the identity of Flora de Barral, presenting a variety of perspectives which they impose upon her. Conrad himself had idealised, cajoled, and sympathised with Poradowska, while the narrators of *Chance* adopt positions ranging from irritation to empathy, in which the heroine is variously categorised as a 'minx' (53), the 'damsel' of the title page for Part 1, or a 'victim' of the governess's cruelty (119). In the letters, Conrad's decorous mode of address sustained a sense of playfulness which concealed the otherwise painful exchange of confessions. A similar effect occurs in *Chance*, in the presentation of Marlow's growing attachment to Flora, brought about because, in discussing her suicide attempts, they had shared 'the most intimate and final of subjects, the subject of death' (177). Conrad himself had dropped the patronising tone to Poradowska when he exchanged with her the experiences of loss and displacement as individuals facing 'the void'. The shift in register signals instead the equality of their dialogue, where they exchange both private and professional anxieties. Yet the interplay of voices in *Chance* shows that Conrad himself cannot be associated so closely with Marlow. His method in the novel was to undermine the narrators' traditional views of Flora, to create a structure in which all potential definitions are unstable, constantly subverted by opposing perspectives.[43]

Just as Conrad's voice struggled to settle on a consistent register through which to correspond with Poradowska, so the

---

[41] 28 May? 1891, *CL* 1, 80.

[42] Conrad first thought of this narrative at a time close to the 'Poradowskan' period: in 1898–9 he was thinking of a story about 'a captain's wife' (*CL* 2, 62, 169). See Ch. 4.

[43] See Jane Miller, Introduction, *Chance* (London: Hogarth Press, 1984), p. ii: 'Marlow, tussling with his waif and his feminist, returns almost obsessively to the question, are they loyal, reasonable, vindictive? Is it men who cause their problems? Does he like them, understand them?'

narratorial structures of *Chance* suggest a comparable uneasiness in dealing with its unfathomable heroine. Yet, rather than expressing confusion, Conrad's transformation of the varied tones of the letters into the text of *Chance* shows an awareness of the contradictory nature of contemporary suppositions on the subject of women. It is as if Poradowska had early on provided the inexperienced sailor-turned-writer with a medium through which to experiment with his writing voice on the subject of women. Whether self-consciously or not, he may have parodied the tones expressed in his earlier letters to his most intimate woman friend.

The letters raise the question of how we read the abundant presentations of female self-sacrifice in the fiction. Given Conrad's usual restraint on this subject (his reticence about his mother's sacrifices, for example), did Conrad intend us to look with a more ironic eye upon the 'sublime' sacrifice of Lena in *Victory* or the women of *Under Western Eyes*, who seem to act as repositories of the guilt expressed by Razumov? In *Chance*, one of the fundamental causes of Flora's entrapment and victimisation arises from her experience of emotional redundancy in her dealings with a jealous father, to whom she can never sacrifice enough. But she has also been scarred by the actions of a cruel governess, a woman who represents a perfect example of the problems of sacrificing too much when, as he had warned Poradowska in early March 1892, such action 'whets the appetite for evil'. In this letter Conrad had, in his petulant objection to Poradowska's excessively dutiful behaviour towards an elderly aunt, reprimanded her for her self-effacing actions, suggesting that her position bordered on the 'dangerous' rather than the worthy: 'abnegation carried to an extreme . . . becomes not just a fault but a crime . . . that dormant human tendency towards hypocrisy in the . . . benevolent.'[44] Here Conrad's voice shifts from that of the decorous admirer—'I tell you all this because I love you so very much, admire you so immensely'—towards a more radical form of address in which he contradicted the most conventional Victorian perceptions of duty in a woman: 'I cannot imagine on what ethical grounds you base your conduct' (*CL* 1, 107).

[44] 5 March, 1892, *CL* 1, 107.

Read in the light of Conrad's letter, Marlow's account of the governess's story deserves close attention. Marlow embarks on one of his characteristically moral discourses, explaining Flora's response to her governess's accusations when she confronts her with the de Barral disaster:

She stood, a pale and passive vessel into which the other went on pouring all the dislike for all her pupils, the accumulated resentment, the infinite hatred of all these unrelieved years of—I won't say hypocrisy. The practice of hypocrisy is a relief in itself . . . the passionate bitter years, of restraint . . . had been like living half strangled . . . (119)

Marlow expresses a grudging sympathy for the governess. His analysis of her cruelty as 'relief' for the 'passionate, bitter years of restraint' in the service of others suggests a verbal echo of Conrad's discussion with Poradowska, when he feared for Poradowska's moral integrity if her 'abnegation' were 'carried to an extreme'. While Marlow presents Flora as the 'pale and passive' victim of the governess's wrath he also concedes the passivity of the governess during her life of sacrifice to her charges (119). Subsequently, Conrad provides the governess's story with a psychological dimension reaching beyond the conventional structures of the stale romance. Marlow initially categorises the governess as the 'wicked-stepmother' type of fairy tales: 'hatching a most sinister plot under her air of distant, fashionable exclusiveness' (90).[45] But on this occasion he expresses considerable insight into the economic circumstances that kept women like her entrapped in dependency relationships.[46] Marlow's limited compassion for the governess masks the presence of an alternative version of the story of female self-sacrifice, a subtext in which the governess herself assumes the passive role as 'strange victim of the de Barral failure' (106). His ironic view of her disturbs the categories of popular romance where she occupies the

---

[45] See E. E. Duncan-Jones, 'Some Sources of *Chance*', *Review of English Studies* 20 (Nov. 1969), 468–71, for a comparison with the governess of Henry James's 'Turn of the Screw' (first published in serial form in 1898).

[46] See Kathryn Hughes, *The Victorian Governess* (London: Hambledon Press, 1993); Mary Poovey, *Uneven Developments: The Ideological Work of Gender in Mid-Victorian England* (Chicago: University of Chicago Press, 1988).

unambiguous status of villainess.[47] Some of the complexities of Conrad's position on this subject can be traced to his Polish romantic heritage, in which female self-sacrifice is both idealised and parodied.[48] The letter to Poradowska and the presentation of the governess in *Chance* show that the issue was far from reconciled in his mind or in his fiction. With the governess's story Conrad gave us one of his most convincing, as well as troubling, female characterisations. While our sympathy remains with Flora during this episode, Conrad used the medium of Marlow's oscillating voice to demonstrate the range of possible interpretations, breaking through generic restrictions that classify women according to received definitions. It is easy to over-identify Conrad with his narrator, and Marlow's quirky changes of opinion in *Chance* have been attributed to his own ideological confusions.[49] The intertextual resonance of the passages on self-sacrifice demonstrates just how complex the issue was for Conrad.

In *Chance* Conrad experimented daringly with epistemological issues relating to the representation of women in fiction. The novel's rhetorical structure exposes the central female role as an unknowable figure isolated from the world inhabited by the male narrators. However, something of the history of Conrad's problematic relationship to his women characters emerges much earlier in the correspondence with Poradowska. Contrary to the received image of Conrad, his empathy with Poradowska's isolation, with her creative impulse, his rejection of the self-sacrificing elements of her personality, all suggest a sensitivity to the position of women in his society, as well as an interest in their psychology. The shifting tones of the letters, in which Conrad often reverts awkwardly to a somewhat ingratiating voice, betray the habitual conservatism of his responses, and perhaps something of his inexperience with women, sustained during the

---

[47] Conrad presents the deeds of his female murderesses, Aïssa in *An Outcast of the Islands*, Mme Levaille in 'The Idiots' or Winnie Verloc in *The Secret Agent*, from a similarly ambivalent perspective, using an omniscient, rather than a dramatised narrator.   [48] See Ch. 2.

[49] See Jeremy Hawthorn, *Joseph Conrad: Narrative Technique and Ideological Commitment* (London: Edward Arnold, 1990), ch. 4: '*Chance*: Conrad's Antifeminine Feminist Novel'.

years at sea. Yet the frequent relaxation of the decorous tone, the sharing of philosophical insights and professional anxieties, indicates Conrad's desire to explore the psychological challenge of at least one particular woman. The creation of *Chance* showed that Conrad began to transform his confusions and developing sympathies into a narrative of complex and nuanced observations of woman's contemporary status.

II

Critics have been reluctant to associate Poradowska's fiction with Conrad's work, since her somewhat florid prose now seems dated and over-written. The first editors of Poradowska's letters, for example, were baffled by Conrad's enthusiasm for her romances, implying that her writing was second-rate, and that Conrad had in some way been exploited by her femininity.[50] Yet, as Conrad worked on his first novel, his relationship with her had flourished with a frequent exchange of ideas and discussions of her novels, moving towards a serious professional correspondence.

He paid minute attention to Poradowska's fiction, reading and rereading *Yaga* not twice, but at least three times, and later recommending the novel to literary friends (probably Garnett[51] and certainly Ford[52]). On his voyage to Australia in the *Torrens* he urged her to send him her most recently published work: 'Joujou'[53] or *Popes et popadias*.[54] He seemed most favourably impressed by Poradowska's descriptive abilities, claiming in early April 1892 that 'you possess the author's insight, which sees characteristics that escape the eye of those whose business is not that of observing their fellows'.[55] In February 1893, he

[50] Gee and Sturm, *Letters to Marguerite Poradowska: 1890–1920*, p. xvi.

[51] Letter to Poradowska, 14 or 21 November, *CL* 1, 188: 'The other Saturday I spent the evening with one of my friends . . . we chatted about *Yaga*. He knows the book better than I. We recalled scenes which gripped us; we argued about them, and we admired many a passage with a touching unanimity.'

[52] Letter to Poradowska, 10 May 1900, *CL* 2, 267.

[53] 19 October 1892, *CL* 1, 120, and 119 n. 3. 'Joujou' appeared in the *Figaro illustré* for 29 July 1893.

[54] *CL* 1, 120. *Popes et popadias* appeared in the *Revue des Deux Mondes* 114 (15 Nov. and 1 Dec. 1892). It was published in book form by Hachette, Paris, 1893.

[55] 6 April 1892, *CL* 1, 110.

wrote that *Popes et popadias* was 'full of charming touches—of discriminating observations', praising her particularly for the 'atmosphere' she had created for her characters and the 'landscapes you have painted for them'.[56] He complimented her by suggesting that in the 'striking simplicity of your descriptions, you remind me a little of Flaubert'.[57]

On the rare occasions on which Conrad used Polish themes in his fiction, we hear echoes of the style in which Poradowska describes the expansiveness and the extreme contrast in the physical landscapes of rural Galicia, Podolia, or the Ukraine, which form the backdrop to most of her narratives. Discussing her novel *Marylka*, Conrad wrote in February 1895: 'there is space, the blowing of the wind in your description of the Ukrainian countryside. It's astonishing. You have never been there?'[58] Her romantic style conveys a sweeping panorama of the winter plains at night:

Novembre! Il gèle à vingt-cinq degrés . . . Sur la steppe infinie, blanche comme un linceul [winding-sheet], s'étend un ciel d'un bleu métallique criblé d'étoiles cristallines . . . le vent siffle, le vent se déchaîne, ce vent terrifiant qui vient de Sibérie.[59]

November! At twenty-five degrees everything freezes . . . over the infinite plain, white as a shroud, a metallic blue sky pierced with crystalline stars stretches out . . . the wind whistles, the wind breaks loose, that terrifying Siberian wind.

Conrad echoes this juxtaposition of images of mortality and cosmic infinity in his setting for the French army camp in 'The Warrior's Soul':

the boisterous north wind had dropped as quickly as it had sprung up, and the great winter stillness lay on the land from the Baltic to the Black Sea. One could almost feel its cold, lifeless immensity reaching up to the stars.[60] (17)

In fact we might speculate that Poradowska was a model for Tomasov's French lover in this story. A cultured woman of 'sheer beauty' (8) and 'imagination' (10), she is 'not a woman in her

[56] *CL* I, 125.   [57] *CL* I, III.   [58] 23? February 1895, *CL* I, 202.
[59] Poradowska, *Marylka*, *Revue des deux Mondes* 12 (1 March 1895), 160.
[60] 'The Warrior's Soul', in *Tales of Hearsay and Last Essays* (1925). First published in *Land and Water*, 1917.

first youth. A widow, maybe' (8), who 'was a secret delight and a secret trouble' (9) to the younger man. In this late tale Conrad may have recalled the precariousness of his own feelings of devotion as a younger man towards his beautiful 'aunt'.

Conrad was by no means unreservedly enthusiastic about Poradowska's work, and we can detect a hint of occasional frustration at the limitations of her fiction. In February 1895 he expressed severe disappointment at the published version of *Marylka*—'My dear and Good Aunt, you have mangled this poor book'[61]—although he was careful to blame Ferdinand Brunetière, the editor, rather than Poradowska herself, for being an 'imbecile' in cutting the original manuscript. But on the whole he expressed genuine admiration for her novels, and his own work benefited from his acquaintance with her narrative methods. Poradowska's ability to manipulate pace and create anticipation is evident from her structuring of conventional plot devices and situations. As Conrad struggled with the manuscript of *Almayer's Folly*, his letters suggest that he was alert to her skills, often taking the smallest hint from her methodology and recasting it to great advantage in his early Malay fiction.

One notable example concerns Conrad's extension of the father–daughter role in *Almayer's Folly*. He had read and discussed with Poradowska the early versions of *Marylka* when he began to revise *Almayer's Folly* in April 1894.[62] In early March he referred to a proposed visit to her, and Frederick R. Karl and Laurence Davies surmise that he probably took the first ten chapters of *Almayer's Folly* with him to Brussels later that month.[63] On that visit they also discussed *Marylka*.[64] In late April Conrad wrote to Poradowska that he was 'rewriting the first four chapters' of *Almayer*, and on 2 May he again mentioned 'revising my first three chapters'.[65] The editors of the Cambridge Edition of *Almayer's Folly* have noted that these particular revisions refer to an intervening stage between manuscript and typescript, recorded in a text which is now lost. However, they have been able to deduce from the extant evidence that in this intermediate document 'the most important revisions' of the novel were achieved, and that one of Conrad's most fundamental

[61] 23? February 1895, *CL* I, 202.   [62] *CL* I, 154–5.   [63] *CL* I, 150.
[64] *CL* I, 151.   [65] *CL* I, 156.

changes occurred in the extension of the relationship between Almayer and Nina: 'The major addition, two pages of dialogue between them near the end of Chapter 1, refocuses the misunderstandings of each other.'[66] This dialogue takes place in the domestic situation, at Almayer's evening meal, during which Almayer shares with his daughter his dreams of escaping with her to live in Amsterdam, while the narrator implies Nina's love for Dain Maroola and her quite contrary intentions.

According to John Dozier Gordan, neither of these themes was suggested in the manuscript of *Almayer*, but they both appear in the typescript completed well after Conrad's visit to Poradowska.[67] His letters to her, showing evidence of their professional relationship at this time, suggests that their discussion of *Almayer* and of *Marylka* prompted Conrad to develop the conflict between Almayer and Nina after seeking Poradowska's advice. In February 1895, after reading the final version of *Marylka* in the *Revue* Conrad wrote, 'I am not mistaken in thinking the scene between father and daughter has been shortened?'[68] He had obviously been impressed with the possibilities of the father–daughter relationship of Poradowska's earlier version of the novel, which, along with his problems with *Almayer*, they had presumably discussed during his visit in March 1894. What remains of the scene between father and daughter in *Marylka* (an altercation between them takes place at the dinner table), suggests that Conrad may well have realised the dramatic potential of presenting the conflict of interests in this relationship during a ritual associated with domestic harmony. Poradowska's scene consists in the daughter's petulant verbal display of resistance to patriarchal authority. Conrad's methods are far more subtle: Almayer voices his hopes and intentions, while Nina's restlessness is revealed in Almayer's responses to her, conveyed by the narrator's oblique hints.

Poradowska may have inspired Conrad to extend not simply the father–daughter relationship, but the exterior and interior presentation of Nina's character during these first three chapters, which he revised after his visit. Poradowska's heroines always

---

[66] *Almayer's Folly*, ed. D. L. Higdon and F. Eddleman with an Introduction by Ian Watt (Cambridge: Cambridge University Press, 1994), 167.

[67] John Dozier Gordan, *Joseph Conrad: The Making of a Novelist* (Cambridge, Mass.: Harvard University Press, 1940), 125-7.   [68] *CL* 1, 202.

enter theatrically—'à ce moment la porte s'ouvrit, et, dans le cadre lumineux apparurent les figures éffarées'[69]—and Nina enters the novel (in the final version) 'through the curtained doorway', accompanied by the dramatic lighting effects and contrasts in colour and texture of a northern oil painting: Nina 'stood there all in white . . . her low but broad forehead crowned with a shining mass of long black hair that fell in heavy tresses over her shoulders, and made her pale olive complexion look paler still by the contrast of its coal black hue'.[70] But Conrad develops much further the statuesque quality of Poradowska's female portraits. Using an omniscient narrator who negotiates between the still, iconographic poses of the silent Nina, he also achieves in these first three chapters a subtle indication of Nina's self-possession, and the reticence developed through the experience of a divided cultural identity. Pulled between conflicting influences—of native mother and Europhile father—the narrator suggests the inner tensions of her existence, claiming that 'Nina's life for all her outward composure—for all the seeming detachment from the things and people surrounding her, was far from quiet'.[71] It is through his presentation of women that Conrad initiates the underlying critique of imperialism in the opening chapters of this novel. His treatment of the bedraggled, scheming Mrs Almayer, unlike that of his European mothers, is far from idealised. Yet his portrait of her 'abduction' by the white man Lingard, who forces her to appropriate an alien culture, is empathetic in its presentation of female entrapment: 'had she known of the high walls, the quiet gardens and the silent nuns of the Samarang Convent, where her destiny was leading her she would have sought death in her dread and hate of such a restraint.'[72] Ultimately Nina chooses to follow her mother's tradition rather than that of a 'feeble and traditionless father'. Conrad's narrator is explicit in his critique of the white man: 'To [Nina's] resolute nature . . . the savage and uncompromising sincerity of purpose shown by her Malay kinsman seemed at last preferable to the sleek hypocrisy, to the polite disguises, to the virtuous pretences of such white people as she had the misfortune to come in contact with' (35).[73]

---

[69] Poradowska, *Demoiselle Micia, Revue des Deux Mondes* 90 (1 Dec. 1888), 523.
[70] *Almayer's Folly*, Cambridge edn., 15.
[71] *Almayer's Folly*, Cambridge edn., 30–1.   [72] Ibid. 19.   [73] Ibid. 35.

If Poradowska had advised and contributed towards Conrad's first major thematic revisions to *Almayer*, then his offer to acknowledge her as principal author of a French translation of the work makes more sense.[74] Nonetheless we can see the gulf between Poradowska's two-dimensional romance and the level of sophistication that Conrad had already attained with his first novel. In fact, the father–daughter scene demonstrates the way in which Conrad, from the very outset of his writing career, developed a creative opportunism, learning to convert the smallest suggestions into his individualised narrative strategies.

Only once did Conrad attempt something closer to Poradowska's actual style and tone, although this was in a novel he never completed. Conrad began *The Sisters* late in 1895, during a period of his life in which we know little of his personal affairs. He was unsure what direction his fiction would take after the Malay novels. However, Ford sheds some light on the professional dilemma Conrad experienced at this time. In his introduction to the remaining fragment, published posthumously in 1928, Ford emphasised that the theme of this story failed to fit the market to which Conrad was addressing his early work:

Conrad still faced un-shaped destinies. Henley, who had just published *The Nigger of the Narcissus* in *The New Review* impressed upon Conrad that his only chance of making a living lay in writing about the sea . . . Readers might be found for books about the sea; it was unthinkable that they would support Slav introspections passing in Paris. So, as I have said, the manuscript and the very thought of 'The Sisters' was as it were put away in a locked drawer.[75]

At the same time Poradowska's role of literary mentor to Conrad was being replaced by others. Following the publication of *Almayer's Folly*, no more was said about collaboration with her. But in *The Sisters* Conrad explored a domestic subject in something like the manner of her own romances; and while Conrad abandoned the novel at the time, it nevertheless

---

[74] See above, CL 1, 165, 170.
[75] Ford Madox Ford, Introduction, *The Sisters* (New York: Crosby Gaige, 1928), 4–5. See also, Todd G. Willy, 'The Conquest of the Commodore: Conrad's Rigging of the "Nigger" for the Henley Regatta', *Conradiana* 17:3 (1985), 163–82, for a discussion of Conrad and Henley; and P. D. McDonald *British Literary Culture and Publishing Practice 1880–1914* (Cambridge: Cambridge University Press, 1997), ch. 1 n. 20.

constituted an important experiment. He would later return to
domestic plots in *The Secret Agent* and in sections of *Nostromo*
and *Under Western Eyes*, in *Chance*, parts of *Victory*, *The
Arrow of Gold*, and *Suspense*. The later fiction can help us to
evaluate more closely the place of this fragment in the context
of Conrad's whole career.

The Sisters was set in Europe and written in an over-romantic
and mannered style which, as Zdzisław Najder has remarked,
translates surprisingly well into Polish.[76] The early descriptive
passages are also closely reminiscent of Poradowska, and we
have to remember that she frequently translated from Polish to
French, and that her romances aimed to suggest a Polish style.
It is possible that at the time of the break in correspondence with
Poradowska in 1895 Conrad had been contemplating a novel
that would in some way reinforce his association with her as
a writer, if only to reach the market she had found for her
romances in the *Revue*.[77]

The lengthy description of Stephen's homeland in *The Sisters*
has some remarkable correspondences with Poradowska's landscapes. Conrad borrowed from her the expansiveness of her
sketch of the plains, as well as the heaviness of her sometimes
over-written prose: 'Stephen, unwinking, looked on—smiling at
Immensity.' From his mother's arms he saw the trees stirring
'in the gentle and powerful breath of the indolent steppe'. Over
a hill 'the wide plains would open out again . . . the uniform level
of ripe wheat stretched out into unbounded distances, immensely
great, filled by the hum of invisible life of the infinitely little.'[78]
In *Marylka*, Poradowska had provided a model for this luxuri-
ant, sensuous description (suggestive of the Symbolists), comparing the vast scale of the landscape to the 'infinitely little'
inhabiting it: 'Au loin, la moire mouvante des blés verts ondule,
bercée par le vent, cette âme mystérieuse de la steppe, qui mêle,
en l'endormant, sa plainte amoureuse aux mille sursurremens des
insects.'[79] (Far away, the undulating sheen of green corn ripples,

---

[76] Zdisław Najder, *Joseph Conrad: A Chronicle* (Cambridge: Cambridge
University Press, 1983), 48–9; See also Karl, *Three Lives*, 170; John Batchelor, *The
Life of Joseph Conrad: A Critical Biography* (Oxford: Blackwell, 1994), 258.

[77] See 12 March 1895, CL I, 204.

[78] Joseph Conrad, *The Sisters* (New York: Crosby Gaige, 1928), 28.

[79] *Marylka*, *Revue des Deux Mondes* 12 (15 March 1895), 453–4.

lulled to sleep by the wind, that mysterious spirit of the plain that mingles its tender lamentation with the insects' thousand whisperings.) The light imagery characteristic of Poradowska —'le soleil descendait, dorant l'émeraude transparente des feuilles'[80]—translates in *The Sisters* into a somewhat starker Conradian perspective: 'far off . . . another village showed above the monotony of yellow corn, the green path of its few trees, and lay lone, minute and brilliant, like an emerald negligently dropped on the sands of a limitless and deserted shore.'[81]

There is another, even closer association with Poradowska. In his introduction, Ford does not comment on the obviously autobiographical element of *The Sisters* associated with 'Slav introspections passing in Paris'. Stephen, the restless Ukrainian artist of Conrad's unfinished novel, travelling through Europe to Paris, could easily be identified with Conrad himself. Conrad situates Stephen not only in Paris but specifically in Passy, the district where Poradowska was living in 1895, at the time of the break in their correspondence. The omniscient narrator of Conrad's story tells us that Stephen 'had found on the outskirts of Passy an almost ideal retreat' (46).[82] The narrative then shifts to the concerns of the Ortega family and the sisters Rita and Thérèse, presumably precursors of characters in *The Arrow of Gold* (1919). Perhaps for this reason, most critics have felt that the antecedents of 'The Sisters' are to be found chiefly in Mediterranean experiences that occurred much earlier in Conrad's life.

About a year before embarking on *The Sisters*, Conrad began discussing the progress of Poradowska's *Pour Noémi*. Although this novel did not appear in the *Revue* until 1899, he wrote to her as early as October 1894, responding favourably to her outline for its story. In December, he remarked: 'The development of the plot seems to me absolutely faultless. I foresee a series of dramatic situations.'[83] In *The Sisters*, Conrad exploited the dramatic situation of Poradowska's opening of *Pour Noémi*, which also tells of an artist who left his Ukranian homeland and works for sometime in Paris, where he fails to conform to the

---

[80] Marguerite Poradowska, *Pour Noémi* in *Revue des Deux Mondes* 154 (15 Aug. 1899), 723. Published in book form by Plon-Nourrit, Paris, 1900.
[81] Conrad, *The Sisters*, 28.   [82] Ibid. 46.   [83] *CL* I, 191.

style of the academic salons, preferring to follow his individual creative instincts. The conflict between father and son occurs in both novels, the father resisting the son's choice of profession. André's father in *Pour Noémi* complains of his son's reputation in Paris as 'L'Impressioniste, l'Estétique moderne',[84] mocking him for his choice of subject and style: 'à quoi sert la peinture, je vous prie, si ce n'est à exalter ou à réveiller dans nos coeurs ce qu'il y a de plus noble'.[85] Like André, Conrad's artist Stephen 'would look to no one as teacher. He stood aloof from the world' (22), while his father 'could not understand the ambition of the youth . . . Paint! . . . What's the good of it?' (31).

In Conrad's novel Stephen refuses his brother's offer to return home after their father's death, while in Poradowska's the artist André returns to the Ukraine. But this is not the end of the correspondence between the two works. Najder has disputed Ford's claim that Conrad intended to write about incest in *The Sisters*. According to Ford: 'The pensive Slav painter was to have married the older sister and then to have had an incestuous child by the other.'[86] Conrad abandoned the story before the painter meets either of the Ortega sisters; but Ford's testimony recalls the principal plot of *Pour Noémi*, which tells of André's love for two sisters, Noémi and Malva, and of his inability to face life without either of them. Poradowska's nineteenth-century decorum never allowed her to write literally of the consummation of love affairs in her fiction, but the sensuous and voyeuristic descriptions of André's painting of their portraits serves as a sufficiently transparent metaphor for the painter's physical possession of the sisters.

The evidence also suggests that *The Sisters* represented, in part, Conrad's gesture of thanks to Poradowska for their professional exchanges. Initially she had drawn inspiration from Conrad.[87] She reproduced her understanding of his national inheritance in *Pour Noémi*, in the artist's struggles of conscience, his frustration with his homeland, his worries about leaving it, his turning, as a professional writer, towards the methods of

---

[84] Poradowska, *Pour Noémi, Revue des Deux Mondes* 154 (15 Aug. 1899), 727.
[85] Ibid. 729.   [86] Ford Madox Ford, Introduction, *The Sisters*, 5.
[87] See also Poradowska, *Mariage romanesque, Revue des Deux Mondes* (15 Nov. 1902), 77, for another possible allusion to Conrad's biography in her description of a protagonist of this story: 'C'est qu'il était fils d'un insurgé polonais de 1863.'

'impressionism' and a 'modern aesthetic'. As André contemplates a return to his nomadic life away from Poland he reflects on his sense that 'l'homme n'a pas le droit de déserter sa patrie', but that 'si je reste içi, mon talent s'atrophiera'.[88] Perhaps Conrad wished to reciprocate by developing a Poradowskan plot for *The Sisters*, acknowledging that much of his own early inspiration to persevere with his writing had come from suburban Paris.

III

The direction of Conrad's work, as Ford rightly remarked, took him away from the subject of *The Sisters* for many years. When he returned to the genre of popular romance with the serialisation of *Chance* in 1912, he once again found occasion to draw on his relationship with Poradowska. Her version of romance had already awakened in Conrad a striking response to the inadequacies of conventional representations of women in fiction. The revisions of *Almayer's Folly* show how he may have learned from Poradowska's example while developing his own methods in his presentation of Nina Almayer. But the way in which Conrad and Poradowska had interacted as correspondents also provides an important insight into Conrad's presentations of female identity, especially in his later works. We have seen how his letters to Poradowska are distinguished by a range of tones, oscillating from idealisation and empathy to a decorous, affectionate, but sometimes patronising voice, combined with an occasionally unguarded openness.

At the same time, Conrad was equally indebted to Poradowska's fiction when it came to the representation of his romance-heroine in *Chance*. With the marketing of this novel for a female readership of romance in 1912, Conrad faced the question of how to address women readers without resorting to the methods of popular writers whom he despised, such as Grant Allen or Marie Corelli.[89] While critics may now regard Poradowska's novels with equal scorn, the evidence of the letters shows that Conrad had always been generous and attentive

---

[88] *Pour Noémi, Revue des Deux Mondes* 155 (1 Sept. 1899), 76.
[89] See letter to Aniela Zagórska, Christmas 1898, *CL* 2, 137.

to her work, and was not above borrowing from her conventional stories of the quest for a husband that lay beneath the surface narratives of rural Polish politics. Since *Chance* initially appeared in *The New York Herald* in the fiction-slot represented by such items as 'Her Little Young Ladyship', an unsophisticated adventure of the heart,[90] Conrad's intimate knowledge of Poradowska's novels may well have furnished him with some readily available and highly suitable raw materials for his own later romance.

Critics have recognised Conrad's allusions to Dickens and James in *Chance*, and Yves Hervouet has identified the borrowings from Anatole France, but in the context of Conrad's critique of romance conventions, the initial impact of Poradowska's fiction on the writer during his formative years has been overlooked. Bearing in mind that in 1890, while in the Congo, Conrad had congratulated Poradowska on her prize-winning early novel, *Demoiselle Micia*,[91] a close reading of this novel reveals how, much later in his career, Conrad appropriated aspects of its narrative to provide the basis of his sceptical presentation of domestic structures in *Chance*.

Although Poradowska's *Demoiselle Micia*, a novel of romance and intrigue set in a mining community in rural Ruthenian-Poland could hardly have been located further from the setting of *Chance* (in the English countryside, in London, and aboard ship), there are some striking parallels between certain plot elements of the two works. Like *Chance*, *Demoiselle Micia* is about a young girl whose father is a financier and whose mother dies

[90] Myra Kelly, 'Her Little Young Ladyship', in *The New York Herald* Sunday Magazine, 18 June 1911, 3.

[91] Marguerite Poradowska, *Demoiselle Micia: moeurs galliciennes*, in the *Revue des Deux Mondes* 90 (1 and 15 Dec. 1888) and 91 (1 Jan. 1889). The novel was published in book form by Hachette, Paris, in 1889. *Demoiselle Micia* was one of six works receiving French Academy prizes of 500 francs in 1890. An announcement appeared in *Le Temps* for 31 May 1890. Since Poradowska sent Conrad copies of all her work, it is more than likely that he read this novel. Amongst others, works by Poradowska include: 'Vers Lemberg', in *Figaro* (Supplément littéraire, 27 April 1895); 'La Madone de Busowiska', from the Polish of Władisław Łosiński, *Revue* (1 September 1891), see *CL* 1, 94; *Le Mariage du fils Grandsire* (Paris: Hachette, 1894), see *CL* 1, 145–7; 'Simple Récit', from the Polish of Sophie Kowerska, *Revue des Deux Mondes* (1 Aug. 1889); *Hors du foyer* in the *Correspondant* (25 Feb., 10 and 25 March, 10 April, 1912) and in book form, (Paris, 1913).

young.[92] In both novels the child is left in the care of an un-sympathetic governess. In *Micia*, the governess dominates the early part, and in both novels the reader is encouraged (by an omniscient narrator in *Micia*, by a dramatised one—Marlow—in *Chance*) to empathise with the plight of the innocent hero-ine, particularly in her sense of entrapment in the hands of the governess. In *Micia*, however, a secondary protagonist, Helen, is also the daughter of a wealthy man who wasted the family fortune, and subsequently she marries for money. Thus the com-bined fates of Micia and Helen are mirrored, to some extent, in Flora de Barral, and those of both fathers in de Barral himself. Moreover, the ending of Poradowska's novel somewhat under-mines the harmony of an otherwise neatly symmetrical, rather conventional romance plot. In *Micia* the survival of the hero is left uncertain, and at the end a bohemian character, Tarasia, declares: 'La vie des créatures est entre les mains de Dieu',[93] pre-senting a lack of closure that may have appealed to Conrad.

While corresponding elements of both novels may be famil-iar enough to readers of nineteenth-century fiction—the banker with a young daughter left motherless in the care of a harsh governess, or the woman beset by economic difficulties, marry-ing out of necessity on account of paternal neglect—one specific incident in *Chance* suggests an even more direct borrowing from *Micia*. An almost identical scene occurs in both narratives —in the description of the banker's grief after the death of the heroine's mother. In *Micia* the narrator tells us that immedi-ately after the funeral the father was inseparable from the child: 'il l'entoura d'une sollicitude presque maternelle'.[94] However, the banker soon emerges from his mourning: 'Il éprouva comme un irrésistible besoin de revoir ses anciennes connaissances, retourna à son club, fréquenta salons.'[95] Likewise, in *Chance*, Marlow tells us how de Barral 'was extremely cut up' (at the funeral), 'and holding the child tightly by the hand wept bitterly at the side of the grave' (73). He 'clung to the child like a drowning man'

---

[92] The romantic hero of Poradowska's novel is actually called Conrad, although this probably refers to Konrad Wallenrod, the hero of Adam Mickiewicz's poem.

[93] Poradowska, *Micia*, *Revue des Deux Mondes* 91 (1 Jan. 1889), 141.

[94] Poradowska, *Micia*, *Revue des Deux Mondes* 90 (Dec. 1888), 528.

[95] Ibid.

(73); yet, like Micia's father, 'He managed, though, to catch the half-past five fast train . . . bolted back to his suite of rooms in the hotel' (73). Again, like Micia's father, de Barral rapidly returns to business, abandoning Flora to an indifferent governess.

This, however, is as far as the correspondence goes between the two fathers. The banker in *Micia* remains a fairly innocuous figure throughout. In *Chance*, Conrad takes the possessive element of the pose at the graveside and uses it as a portent of de Barral's recurrent behaviour, both destructive and selfish, when he is released from jail. De Barral fails to understand Flora's sacrifice in marrying to provide for him, thinking of her marriage only in terms of his loss: ' "My Flora! You went and . . . I can't bear to think of it' "(369). Conrad's sharper characterisation of the egotistical de Barral again typifies his refinement of narrative elements to be found in Poradowska's novels.

Conrad's narratorial complexities and his manipulation of conventional romance forms in *Chance* did not prevent him from borrowing directly from Poradowska's outward description of the tragic heroine. A repetitive reference to Flora's suicide pose, for example, suggests another intriguing appropriation of her work. Conrad's image bears a striking resemblance to Poradowska's treatment of suicide in another novel, *Popes et popadias*, to which he refers on several occasions in his letters.[96] Poradowska's version of this trope is of particular interest in relation to Conrad because it is one that she undoubtedly drew from the Polish romantic tradition and its presentation of female self-sacrifice (she frequently quoted Mickiewicz and Słowacki in her work). As we have seen, this version of the suicidal romance heroine is far from passive, suggesting instead a specifically heroic image in which the heroine dies for her country or some particular cause (cf. Mickiewicz's *Grażyna*). Poradowska reproduces the type in *Popes et popadias*, where the female protagonist, Binia, is fascinated with the history of a legendary Polish monarch, Wanda. Binia reads that Wanda 's'est jetée dans la Vistule'[97] rather than

---

[96] Letters to Poradowska, 3 Feb. 1893, *CL* 1, 124; 17 May 1893, *CL* 1, 127; 20 May 1895, *CL* 1, 220 n. 1.

[97] Poradowska, *Popes et popadias*, *Revue des Deux Mondes* 114 (15 Nov. 1892), 261. *Popes et popadias* appeared in the *Revue* for 15 Nov. and 1 Dec. 1892, and was published in book form as *Les Filles du popes* by Hachette, Paris in 1893. See Ch. 2 n. 44.

lose her virginity to a German knight who has invaded the homeland. Like Grażyna, Wanda represents the trope of the female knight: 'elle s'élance elle-même au combat . . . elle lève la visière de son casque'.[98] When Binia is later disappointed in love, she contemplates following Wanda's example. She hesitates for a moment on the edge of the river, 'son ombre fit . . . une tache indécise'. Like Flora de Barral hovering on the cliff-top, Binia is presented as a wraith-like figure, 'pâle et impénétrable', trapped by her situation: 'ce qu'elle voulait, c'était fuir, échapper au sort qui la menaçait, trouver un refuge. Mais où, comment? elle le savait à peine'.[99] While Conrad draws on a similar linguistic register to describe Flora's desire to escape from the 'wretchedness' of 'an unjust and prejudiced world', to find a refuge in suicide—he makes clear that her dilemma stems as much from despair at the need to protect her father as despair for herself: 'What to do with him? Where to go? How to keep body and soul together?' (246).

Poradowska's heroine represents a somewhat sentimentalised version of a Polish literary trope, while Conrad's adaptation of the pose is highly ironic, since he employs a male voyeur (Marlow) who finds the pose of the suicide victim 'attractive'. Yet it is more than likely that Conrad took note of the Polish resonances in Poradowska's story, and particularly its evocation of active sacrifice in the face of isolation and despair. He had certainly emphasised the importance of female heroism in a Polish story in his letters to Poradowska.[100] The possibility that Conrad was echoing *Popes et popadias* in *Chance* helps us to understand his use of chivalry in the novel, where he deliberately ironises the conventional gender roles of romance. Flora's pale, strained figure bears a resemblance to the marginalised wraiths of the Polish romantics, but her role as her father's champion when he emerges from prison is closer to the Polish representation of the activity of the female knight than to that of the 'pale and passive vessel' elsewhere described by Marlow. As if Conrad had reconstructed the Polish romantic trope through his reading of Poradowska, he transforms the self-sacrifice of the Polish romantic heroine into the female 'heroism' of the

[98] *Revue des Deux Mondes* 114 (15 Nov. 1892), 260.
[99] *Revue des Deux Mondes* 114 (1 Dec. 1892), 510, 511.   [100] CL 1, 191.

contemporary English woman forced to save a now dependent father from destitution. Indeed, Conrad would again allude to the Polish tradition in his representation of Lena's heroic death in *Victory* (which also resembles the self-sacrifice of Mickiewicz's heroine, Grażyna) and in the sacrifice of Adèle de Montevesso, the heroine of *Suspense*, who agrees to a loveless marriage in order to achieve economic security for her parents, exiles of the French Revolution.[101]

Conrad's intimate and influential relationship with Marguerite Poradowska shows that he was far from insensitive to the interiority and emotional isolation in a woman. Despite his break in intimacy with her in 1895, she offers an unexpected source for a deeper understanding of Conrad's early experimentation and his change of direction towards the bleaker, more philosophical work of the middle years. Her specific impact on Conrad then resurfaced in his later career. As he confronted issues of gender and genre in the late fiction he once again alluded to the intricate interplay of voices in the letters to Poradowska, as well as to the methods and conventions of her romances to create his individualised responses to the romance genre, and to address the problematic issue of representing the female consciousness. Drawing on his own difficulties in addressing a close woman friend whom he both admired and respected, her influence enabled him to question received assumptions about what it is to be a woman. Without Poradowska's early support *and* her novels Conrad may have been reluctant to engage with the issue of gender in *Chance*. By reading this novel in the light of their complex relationship, we see that Conrad addressed a fundamental contemporary dilemma with far greater sophistication than has often been acknowledged.

---

[101] Conrad identifies his model for Lena in the Author's Note (1920) to *Victory* (p. xli), as a woman he had seen playing in a café orchestra in the south of France. But for a possible literary model for Lena, see Poradowska, *Mariage romanesque*, *Revue des Deux Mondes* (15 Dec. 1902), 896. The heroine, Mauve, plays the violin in a travelling orchestra. Lena appears in *Victory*, like 'le spectre de Mauve', as a 'white and spectral figure' (86). See Ch. 8 for echoes of Poradowska in Conrad's presentation of the heroine in *Suspense*.

4
Chance: 'a fine adventure'

Chance represented a turning point in Conrad's career. Initially serialised in the United States in *The New York Herald* in 1912, the novel brought him the popularity and economic rewards that had earlier eluded him. Its success was due partly to the modern marketing strategies employed by the newspaper, whose advance publicity included a bold advertising campaign and a full-page illustrated interview with Conrad. Subsequently the book version was promoted imaginatively by the up-and-coming publisher Alfred Knopf (at that time working for Doubleday). Yet the major breakthrough in sales occurred because, for the first time, a Conrad novel was aimed at a female readership.[1]

Conrad was not unprepared for the challenge of writing for and about women. He frequently drew on the presentation of women in Polish literature in his work, and his friendship with Marguerite Poradowska had offered him material and resources for writing a romance as well as engaging with the woman reader. He had created important female roles in the early Malay fiction, and in subsequent work, in his presentation of Emilia Gould, Winnie Verloc, and Natalia Haldin he explored female identity compromised by the moral failures and iniquitous actions of a male-dominated society. The issue of feminism and the position of women in a world of predominantly male politics constitutes an important subplot of *Under Western Eyes*. So although *Chance* signalled a departure for Conrad in one

[1] *Chance* was serialised from January to June 1912 in *The New York Herald*, appeared in book form in England in 1913 (London: Methuen), and in the United States in 1914 (New York: Doubleday). Conrad was paid (by prior agreement with J. B. Pinker) £4 per thousand words plus £100 on delivery of the first instalment (*CL* 4, 359). By 2 June 1913 the novel had earned him £1,400 (Jean-Aubry, *Life and Letters*, ii. 146). By February 1914, about 12,000 copies of the book had been sold in Britain, a figure which increased with the American publication in March 1914 (Frederick R. Karl, *Joseph Conrad: The Three Lives* (New York: Farrar, Straus, and Giroux, 1979), 746–7). For a full discussion of the genesis of this novel see Ch. 5.

respect, in other ways it suggested a continuity with issues aris-
ing in earlier work. Yet these novels derive their main plots from
sources other than women's lives. The story of *Chance*, however, is *about* the female protagonist in the way that Henry
James's women are 'shown as "mattering"'.[2] Flora de Barral's
life may be manipulated by the plots of her governess, her husband Captain Anthony, and her father, but what happens to *her*
constitutes the principal dramatic interest.

The orientation of the narrative around a woman's history constitutes an important development in Conrad's work, but critics
have traditionally dismissed the shift in emphasis towards the
female protagonist as an inferior attempt at a Jamesian narrative.[3] However, by always placing the novel in Henry James's
shadow, they have effectively prevented it from standing on
its own terms. While Conrad undoubtedly admired James and
responded in this novel to his narrative methods, we shall see
that in *Chance* he also distinguishes himself from a Jamesian perspective on women. By evaluating *Chance* in its own right, this
chapter ultimately resituates Conrad's relationship to James,
the novel offering instead an individual, but equally searching
account of a heroine.

The theme of *Chance* was timely. The militant phase of the Suffragist Movement had begun with 'Black Friday' on 18 November 1910, five months before Conrad took up *Chance* again
after a long break. As instalments of *Chance* initially appeared
in *The New York Herald*, the activities of the Woman's Movement were already established as headline news in the United
States, and the Reform Bill debate and the Suffragist struggles
with Asquith were under way in Britain.[4] But it was not merely
the political position of women that occupied contemporary

[2] Henry James, 'Preface' (1907) to *Portrait of a Lady* (1881; Oxford: Oxford
University Press, 1981), 17.

[3] See e.g. Fredric Jameson, *The Political Unconscious: Narrative as a Socially
Symbolic Act* (London: Methuen, 1981), 222.

[4] See Ray Strachey, *The Cause* (1928; London: Virago 1978), 321–36; Sylvia
Pankhurst, *The Suffragette Movement* (1931; London: Virago, 1977); Lady
Constance Lytton and Jane Warton, *Prisons and Prisoners: Some Personal
Experiences of a Suffragette* (London: Heinemann, 1914); Millicent Garrett
Fawcett, *The Women's Victory—and After: Personal Reminiscences, 1911–18*
(London: Sidgwick and Jackson, 1920); Ida Husted Harper (ed.), *The History of
Woman Suffrage Vol. VI, 1900–1920* (New York: National American Woman
Suffrage Association, 1922).

argument. Their economic, social, and indeed, ontological status was a prominent theme for discussion in a wide variety of publications, ranging from scientific and theological pamphlets to the New Woman novels that had first appeared in the 1880s.[5] Conrad's portrait of a young girl struggling to establish an autonomous identity therefore provided a topical and challenging response to the contemporary debate about 'being' a woman.[6]

Nevertheless, Conrad's attitude to the popular marketplace was somewhat ambivalent, his dilemma amounting to an acute sense of guarding his reputation as an artist of 'literary merit', producing 'good quality', rather than undiscerning 'sensational' prose. He shared with Ford a certain contempt for the popular novelist (which they expressed together by creating the character of the writer Callan in The Inheritors (1901), probably an attack on Hall Caine). Nor did Conrad praise Grant Allen's The Woman Who Did (1895), with its controversial pro-feminist heroine. He claimed that this work was 'not art in any sense', and that it was written by 'a man of inferior intelligence'.[7] Yet his preferences tended to be stylistic rather that ideological,[8] and they did not finally prevent him from exploiting the market for

[5] In his presentation of Mrs Fyne, the feminist, who is writing a 'Pankhurstian' tract on women's education in Chance, Conrad may have parodied the position of Sarah Grand (pseudonym of Frances Elizabeth McFall), a member of the Woman Writer's Suffrage League, a 'New Woman' novelist whose The Heavenly Twins (1893) dealt with sexual double standards and woman's desire for emancipation. Conrad claimed that 'serious criticism treats The Heavenly Twins by Mme Sarah Grand with the scorn it deserves' (CL 1, 185). Another possible model for Mrs Fyne was the suffragist and educationalist Emily Davies, who became mistress of Girton College, Cambridge 1873–5. See also Harper, History of Woman Suffrage, vi. 440, for an American 'Mrs Fyne': 'Mrs Gertrude Nelson Andrews conducted for two years classes on public speaking and knowledge of suffrage principles in the New York headquarters'.

[6] In the context of contemporary fiction, these themes were also emerging among male authors such as H. G. Wells. See Ann Veronica (London: Heinemann, 1909), 10, who 'wanted to live . . . she did not clearly know for what—to do, to be, to experience'.   [7] See letter to Aniela Zagórska, Christmas 1898, CL 2, 137.

[8] Conrad expressed similar reservations for Edward Garnett's play The Breaking Point (London: Duckworth, 1907), which he read in a pre-publication copy (letter to Garnett, 17 Nov. 1906, CL 3, 378). The play, which had been at the centre of a censorship controversy, deals with the crisis of a woman who conceives outside wedlock and is torn between duty to her father and love for the father of the child. Conrad was sympathetic to the situation in which Garnett had placed the woman, but he was unconvinced by his treatment of the woman's response. He may have had a similar response to Allen's handling of the female figure.

romance fiction while commenting on its stale plots and gestures. Neither did they influence his support for the political rights of women. In spite of his apparently anti-feminist ironies in *Chance*, he joined such writers and social reformers as Laurence Housman in signing a Writer's Memorial Petition, sent to Asquith in May 1910 to endorse the claims of a women's suffrage bill.[9] Given the context in which Conrad was writing, he created a sensitive account of female isolation in *Chance*, the protagonist caught within a web of male perspectives on women.

His representation of the heroine is both radical and astute. Far from capitulating to the formulaic romance, the final version of *Chance* offers a challenging portrait of psychological isolation in a woman, subverting generic expectations and questioning assumptions about gender. While many critics emphasise its success in the marketplace, implying that Conrad denied his aesthetic principles in writing a 'woman's novel',[10] they fail to see, in the emergence of Flora de Barral, the continuity in the ongoing preoccupations of his work, or the development of a sensitive attitude to the characterisation of women.[11] In *Chance*, the repetition of well-worn gestures and poses reinforces the reader's perception of a gap between being and representation, drawing attention to the disparity between what a woman is, or might choose to be, and the roles that have been prescribed for her.

I

The novel's technical complexity poses problems for interpretation, its success all the more remarkable because of its exceptional involution. We are dealing with a tale that has often been recounted through multiple narrative voices, a feature that is

[9] See Ray Stevens, review of *The Collected Letters*, ed. Karl and Davies, in *English Literature in Transition 1880–1920* 35 (1992), 240. See Conrad's letter to Housman [14?] May 1910, *Letters* 4, 327: 'with the greatest sympathy for the object I cannot share the optimism of the memorial . . . nothing would please me more than to find myself utterly wrong in the light of the facts.'

[10] Cedric Watts, *Joseph Conrad: A Literary Life* (Basingstoke and London: Macmillan, 1989), 114–19.

[11] Marlow's changing perspective on the white figure of *Lord Jim* (1900) suggests a parallel with his voyeuristic relationship to Flora. But Jim's conflict results from the protagonist's inability to live up to his own definition of 'hero'.

signified in some editions by no less than three sets of quotation marks at one moment. It requires considerable effort on the part of the reader to decipher the chronological order of events, keep track of the subplots, and identify the significance of the individual fragments of the tale. In view of the potential for misreading of the central figure we have to engage in a very careful reconstruction of the story. It requires detailed, close analysis of the narrative framework and the presentation of the female protagonist in order to reveal the experimental nature of Conrad's discussion of genre and female identity in this novel.[12]

The bare details of the plot indicate a debt to the structures of melodrama. Flora de Barral is the daughter of a parvenu financier, jailed for fraud.[13] She loses her mother at an early age and suffers severe psychological mistreatment at the hands of a conniving governess. Abandoned to her own resources when her father goes to prison, she first attempts suicide, and later marries a sea captain, motivated by poverty and the need to provide for her father on his release. Her jealous father tries to poison Flora's husband, Captain Anthony, but, when discovered by the young seaman Charlie Powell, de Barral kills himself. After a brief period of happiness for Flora, her husband drowns at sea.

---

[12] Discussions of narrative method and gender in *Chance* include Jeremy Hawthorn, *Joseph Conrad: Narrative Technique and Ideological Commitment* (London: Edward Arnold, 1990), ch. 4, '*Chance*: Conrad's Anti-feminine Feminist Novel'; Jakob Lothe, *Conrad's Narrative Method* (Oxford: Clarendon Press, 1989); Laurence Davies, 'Conrad, *Chance* and Women Readers', Andrew Michael Roberts, 'Secret Agents and Secret Objects: Action, Passivity, and Gender in *Chance*, Robert Hampson, '*Chance* and the Secret Life: Conrad, Thackeray, Stevenson', all in Andrew Michael Roberts (ed.), *Conrad and Gender* (Amsterdam: Rodopi, 1993); Paul B. Armstrong, 'Misogyny and the Ethics of Reading: The Problem of Conrad's *Chance*', in Keith Carabine, Owen Knowles, Wiesław Krajka (eds.), *Contexts for Conrad* (Boulder, Colo.: East European Monographs, 1993); Robin Truth Goodman, 'Conrad's Closet', *Conradiana* 30:2 (1998), 83–124.

[13] See Watts, *A Literary Life*, 118, for contemporary models for de Barral: 'Jabez Balfour, founder of the Liberator Permanent Benefit society, who had been jailed in 1895, or Whitaker Wright, of the London and Globe Empire, who had committed suicide after being sentenced to prison for fraud in 1904.' See also, Samuel Smiles, *Thrift* (London: John Murray, 1897). One of de Barral's financial ventures,'the "Thrift and Independence" Association' (69), alludes (ironically given the outcome), to the titles of popular late nineteenth-century self-help manuals. See also, John Galsworthy, *Joy: A Play on the Letter "I" in Three Acts* (1909; New York: Scribner's, 1916), 89. Conrad's references to de Barral's speculations with 'quarries in Labrador' (81) are reminiscent of Galsworthy's emphasis on high risk investment in the 'Tocopala Gold Mine' plot of *Joy*, a play that exposes public gullibility during the rise of twentieth-century capitalism.

Some years later, Flora and Powell meet again and the novel closes with a prospective marriage. However melodramatic the plot, Conrad employs his customary narratorial sophistication in handling the dissemination of the story to create a complex characterisation of an elusive female figure. He frames the account with discussions between Marlow, a retired seaman, and his interlocutor who meet Powell at a Thameside inn. They listen to Powell's story of his initiation into seamanship, his encounter with Flora and Captain Anthony during his first commission. Although Marlow reconstructs the occasions on which he met Flora himself, providing her with a few brief moments of something closer to self-dramatisation, Flora's story is mostly reproduced by Marlow from second-hand accounts.

Conrad constructs an intricate framework for the novel, drawing on the methods of a number of sub-genres: the romance, with a bipartite division of the text into sections entitled 'The Damsel' and the 'Knight', references to maidens in distress, heroic rescues, and a harmonic closure; the detective novel, with its uncovering of fraud in the financial world and the discovery of an attempted poisoning (the narrator Marlow thinks of himself as 'an investigator—a man of deductions' [326]); the sensation novel and melodrama, complete with family jealousies, a wicked governess, intrigues, domestic enclosure, and the sense of female entrapment on board ship. Flora's story emerges obliquely from an interweaving series of set pieces consisting of a 'rites of passage' narrative of a young sailor, a Victorian family saga, the biography of a fraudulent financier, and anecdotes of seamen delivering a cargo of explosives to the colonies on Anthony's ship, *The Ferndale*. Marlow's overarching narrative, spoken to an often bewildered interlocutor, links the chronologically disparate events and stories. Straining to make sense of Flora's story, Marlow attempts to pull together the fragments of the plot, with all its diversions and temporal dislocations. Yet his assertions are constantly undermined by others' testimony, the interlocutor's interruptions, and his own, often outrageous assertions on the subject of women. As plots overlap and figures and narrators move between set pieces, generic boundaries dissolve. Flora's brutal governess, for example, belongs to the category of the Victorian sensation novel where her 'wicked' actions ensure her role as scapegoat. We learn that she is 'hatching a sinister plot' (90) and she is duly expelled from the narrative. But when Flora herself enters the marketplace for women's work as a governess, lady's companion, or kindergarten assistant, the generic framework shifts in order to elicit our sympathies for the damsel in distress and 'the miserable dependence of girls'(172) of a modern romance.

However topical the narrative of *Chance* may have been, we have discovered from the example of Poradowska's *Demoiselle Micia* that Conrad exploited the generic possibilities of nineteenth-century romance fiction, a move that gives his novel its melodramatic tone. Yet Conrad's oblique presentation of Flora hardly conforms to Poradowska's somewhat flat, formulaic romance heroine, described by her omniscient narrator as 'la personnification idéal'.[14] Flora de Barral is seen from a number of different perspectives, drawing attention instead to the inaccessibility of the woman and her indeterminate identity. Marlow is struck by the elusiveness of her expression (215); Captain Anthony sees her only as 'a "possible" woman' (217). Her actuality, her presence, is always in question, she seems always 'about to become' (or about to die) rather than 'being'. Except for a few brief moments of self-dramatisation, knowledge of Flora is always mediated, filtered a number of times through a hermeneutic web. In spite of its echoes of nineteenth-century romance, Flora's evasion of a schematic role at the centre of the text suggests the novel's modernism, where Flora is alienated from the other characters in the tale, endlessly debating the question 'who is she?' and imposing on her the traditional characteristics of the romance heroine.

While Conrad deliberately tailored the narrative for a popular market, he nevertheless created a compelling portrait of a woman trapped by rigid cultural expectations. Paradoxically, these expectations to some extent arose and received reinforcement from the representational codes of the popular novel. So Conrad both exploited and commented on the market in which he now placed his fiction, showing how the representation of the heroine is also conditioned by the market's propagation of enduring generic conventions.

[14] Marguerite Poradowska, *Demoiselle Micia, Revue des Deux Mondes* 90 (Dec. 1888), 805–6.

Given the complexity of its generic texture, we need first to explore the ways in which Conrad invites a questioning of the novel's genre. He undermines our assumptions both about romance, and what constitutes a romance heroine. Marlow constantly refers to his uneasiness about the story's generic status, offering a defining category of 'tragi-comedy' in which his style of narration veers 'between jest and earnest' (23). Nevertheless, a strong narrative drive propels the tale, stimulated by the inaccessibility of the figure of Flora de Barral, promoting our desire to learn the outcome of her 'romance'. Marlow suggests that we are 'the creatures of light literature'—and the desire for a 'lived happy ever after termination' is strong (288). Yet, contrary to the reader's anticipation of a comic closure, Conrad displaces the romance plot by offering instead, at the centre of the novel, an unconsummated marriage that threatens to destabilise social conventions, assumptions about gender roles, and the structure of romance itself.

On the surface Flora's role appears to follow the conventions demanded by a sentimental Victorian romance—she occupies the position of female dependent, first as the innocent, motherless child of an up-and-coming financier, then as the dutiful wife of a sea captain. But Conrad's complex plotting enmeshes her in a web of relationships that offer instead a critique of the patriarchal values and structures that limit female identity within a contemporary social framework. Traditional gender roles are undermined as the father-figure, de Barral, fails to provide a life of economic security for his daughter. Instead, he is seduced by the world of capitalist venture and exploits a credulous public into speculating on unsafe investments, a plot that itself ironises the ill-advised speculations about Flora pervading the narrative. De Barral's actions set in motion a series of disasters that disturb our assumptions about familial roles. De Barral goes to prison for fraud, while Flora's ambitious governess plots a marriage between her charge and her young nephew (possibly her lover). The governess, herself a substitute mother-figure who occupies no clearly defined social position,[15] terrorises the 'daughter' when *her* hopes of financial gain are thwarted by the collapse of the de Barral fortune. Flora, traumatised by the governess,

---

[15] See Ch. 3 n. 45 for discussions of the social position of governesses.

isolated and abandoned by the father, finds that at her weakest moment roles have been reversed—her father now depends on her for survival when he is released from jail. But just as Flora appears to re-enter the conventional patterns of dependency— by marrying Captain Anthony—Conrad subverts the romance plot further by suggesting a form of 'rescue' that merely prolongs the tragedy of Flora's position. Believing that Flora does not love him, but is marrying him solely to save her father, Anthony matches Flora's chivalrous behaviour with his own supreme sacrifice—offering a legal marriage without consummation.

We can now analyse Flora and Anthony's marriage plot in its full context. The genre of the novel is destabilised, at a formal level, by the non-consummation of the marriage. But genre is always closely associated with gender in this novel. Flora's psychological drama unfolds in a medium where her 'coming into being' depends on her liberation from a network of schematic gender roles—those of the 'domineering' fathers, de Barral and Anthony (to the extent that he inherits something of his father's temperament: 'He certainly resembled his father, who . . . wore out two women . . . because they did not come up to his supra-refined standard' [328]); and the 'unsupportive' mother-figures of the governess and, latterly, Mrs Fyne. Conrad questions the sanctity of received Victorian notions of family as the parental figures fail to operate as good parents but nevertheless try to shape Flora's role according to traditional assumptions about what it is to be a woman—the damsel in distress, the worthy wife, the unscrupulous fortune hunter.

Conrad organises the plot in such a way that the displaced romance forms part of an overall critique of patriarchy throughout the novel. Roderick Anthony is himself reacting against the harsh behaviour of an authoritarian father. Like Flora, he is something of an isolated figure, abandoning the family home when his father takes the role of 'domestic tyrant'. Conrad matches de Barral's irresponsibility with the brutality of Roderick's father, Carleon Anthony, a parody of the poet Coventry Patmore, best known for his literary idealisation of woman in his poem 'The Angel in the House' (1854–63).[16] Thus Conrad presents

[16] See also Sarah Grand (possibly a model for Mrs Fyne), *The Heavenly Twins* (New York: Cassell, 1893), 7. The father of the heroine Evadne is described as 'liable to become a petty domestic tyrant at any moment'.

a sceptical view of the patriarchal voices that delineate female roles, both in social practice and in literature. While Patmore claimed that 'the true happiness and dignity of women are to be sought, not in her exultation to the level of man, but in her inferiority and in the voluntary honour which every manly nature instinctively pays to the weaker vessel',[17] Conrad ironises the paternalistic tone when he describes Flora's 'weaker' position, as she is forced, in her role as governess before her marriage, to endure the unwanted advances of an employer who thought 'he would be safe with a pretty orphan' (181).

Roderick Anthony, on the other hand, behaves in a quite contrary fashion, withholding physical affection when he marries Flora. But Conrad shows that, paradoxically, his response is equally brutal, given her situation. Flora has suffered 'all the possible phases of anguish' (121) during the governess's verbal onslaught. Her psychological disintegration follows this episode as she is abandoned by her father, patronised by uncaring relatives, and forced to work for a living, utterly unprepared for life. The experience of profound loss and an all-encompassing sense of insecurity drives her to attempt suicide. In addition, she must now support both herself and her father, whose possessiveness is equal to his dependency on her. It is within this context that she meets Captain Roderick Anthony and accepts his offer of marriage. However, far from gaining a sense of security, Flora is devastated by Anthony's physical rejection of her.

Conrad's complex presentation of this issue has caused one critic to presume that the renunciation was all on Flora's part.[18] But we need to unpack the narrative detail carefully to avoid misunderstandings of the dynamic between Flora and Anthony. The textual evidence shows that the decision to avoid physical intimacy lay squarely with Captain Anthony: 'he had never given her time, that he had never asked her!' (330) and later she confirms that: 'Neither am I keeping anything back from you' (343). Anthony attempts to disguise a repressed, but 'savage passion' (226) with his scrupulously chivalrous behaviour. But he misjudges Flora's state of mind, assuming that her restraint signifies her lack of physical interest in him. Flora, psychologically

---

[17] Coventry Patmore, 'The Weaker Vessel', *Principle in Art: Religio Poetae and Other Essays* (1889; London: Duckworth, 1913), 347.
[18] Goodman, 'Conrad's Closet', 92.

damaged and unstable, at this point finds she cannot realistic-
ally contemplate any relationship (except the familiar one with
her father, with its expectations of duty) or to trust herself: 'in
truth, she did not know' (330) quite how she felt about Anthony.
Conrad presents Anthony's position as a delicate balance between a primitive desire to seize sexual fulfilment and a sense
of honour and compassion for Flora's unfortunate plight. Flora,
on the other hand, unsurprisingly has no resources for dealing
with the emotionally charged situation, while an urgent economic premise drives her to hasty acceptance of marriage in name
only. Subsequently, through the course of shifting narrative perspectives we discern that her attraction to Anthony had in fact
been developing since their initial meeting. Flora reveals in her
final interview with Marlow that at first she *had* believed that
she was 'selling' herself, but, once rejected physically, she realised
that she had been far from indifferent to Anthony's advances.
She says that his so-called 'honourable' behaviour was what
stimulated her 'awakening'. She claims to have discovered 'my
love for my poor Roderick through agonies of rage and humili-
ation' (443). At the moment of renunciation, however, caught
between the possessiveness of father and prospective husband,
and suffering from a lack of belief in herself, she remains speech-
less and unable to protest. Instead, Anthony's physical rejection
of her merely projects her back into the patterns of insecurity
governing her life: 'it was as that abominable governess had
said. She was insignificant, contemptible. Nobody could love her'
(335). Later in the novel, following her father's death, Anthony
agrees to let her go. This represents her ultimate crisis: 'she had
arrived at the very limit of her endurance' (427), and at last she
finds her voice: 'But I don't want to be let off' (430).

We need to draw back for a moment to grasp the full significance of this plot in its wider political context. For, while
undermining patriarchal strategies in the novel, Conrad also questions contemporary feminist forms of resistance. He draws on a
number of contemporary discussions of sexuality here (we are
perhaps most familiar with those expressed by sexologists such
as Havelock Ellis and Stella Browne). In his presentation of
the unconsummated marriage, however, he alludes to opposing
feminist perspectives on chastity. Like the feminist writer Mona
Caird, who saw marriage in terms of prostitution, 'the purchase

of womanhood',[19] Flora had initially perceived her union with Captain Anthony as a financial arrangement. Many of the contemporary leading feminists such as Christabel Pankhurst and Cicely Hamilton envisaged chastity and the single life as the most effective path to female liberation, one that was preferable to licensed 'prostitution' within marriage.[20] But Flora's relations with Roderick Anthony, following her suicide attempts, and her growing attraction to a man who rejects her physically, more accurately reflect a problem identified by the radical Legitimation League, a group that had investigated the adverse physical effects of chastity on women. Dora Kerr informed a League meeting that 'women suffer as much from enforced celibacy as men',[21] while Eleanor Marx and Edward Aveling had claimed in 1886 that ungratified sexual instincts in a young woman could lead to madness and even suicide.[22] Alternatively, other feminists advocated chastity within the marriage union. In fact, in the immediate context of the publication of *Chance*, Roderick Anthony takes the initiative of this particular feminist advice, his action giving him the appearance of being 'lifted up into a higher and serene region by its purpose of renunciation' (334). But, paradoxically, he fails to perceive the fragility of his partner's psychological state and enforces his will in a conventionally patriarchal fashion: 'he had dragged the poor defenseless thing by the hair of her head, as it were, on board ship' (396). Contemporary radicals, such as E. M. Watson and Kathlyn Oliver, writing in 1912 in Dora Marsden's journal, *The Freewoman*, had advocated chastity for women and men within the *married* state, to avoid becoming 'slaves of our lower appetites'.[23] Presenting the isolation of a woman caught between conflicting ideologies, Conrad ironises both patriarchal and feminist positions in the novel.

Flora's individual potential is limited further by her relationship to Mrs Fyne (Roderick Anthony's sister and an ardent feminist). Zoe Fyne and her husband carry out the first 'rescue' of 'the damsel' in the novel, saving Flora from total abandonment after her confrontation with the governess. Mrs Fyne is initially

[19] Mona Caird, 'Ideal Marriage', *Westminster Review* 130 (Nov. 1888), 635.

[20] See Lucy Bland, *Banishing the Beast: English Feminism and Sexual Morality 1885–1914* (Harmondsworth: Penguin, 1995), 282.

[21] Dora Kerr, *The Adult* (Oct. 1897), 40, quoted in Bland, 172.

[22] See Eleanor Marx Aveling and Edward Aveling, *The Woman Question* (London: Swan Sonnenschein, 1886).

[23] Kathlyn Oliver, *The Freewoman* (15 Feb. 1912), 252.

sympathetic. She too had suffered as a young girl at the hands of the father, the 'domestic tyrant', Carleon Anthony. She even offers an empathetic view of Flora's suicide attempt (one that Marlow cannot fathom), claiming, according to Marlow, that a woman 'had the right to go out of existence without considering any one's feelings' (59), 'to escape in her own way from a man-mismanaged world' (183). Her views again resemble those of Mona Caird, who in her articles in the *Westminster Review* in 1888 had addressed 'the obvious right of the woman to *possess herself* body and soul, to give or withhold herself . . . exactly as she wills'.[24] Caird is talking specifically about the woman's right to withhold sexual favours within marriage, but in Conrad's novel Mrs Fyne extends the notion to include all aspects of autonomy over her body. However, when Flora does take her life into her own hands by eloping with Mrs Fyne's brother, Mrs Fyne responds with a conventional attitude of disapproval, identifying Flora as 'a heartless adventurer' (444).

An ambivalent representation of gender and sexuality in the novel contributes to its generic indeterminacy. But it is the uncertainty of Flora's role that draws together the various threads of the plot and focuses the narrators' attention, so that a desire for knowledge about *her* history drives the tale. One of the ways in which Conrad structures this epistemological uncertainty is to exploit the device of a 'missing letter', a document that represents an uneasy textual hiatus in the novel and symbolises the narrators' quest.[25] Mrs Fyne rejects Flora after receiving a letter from her in which she informs her former friend of her intention to marry Captain Anthony. Marlow strains to interpret Mrs Fyne's response to Flora, unable to imagine the letter's contents, which no one will inform him of directly. Without full knowledge of what Flora actually said to Mrs Fyne, Marlow's authority over the narrative threatens to break down, his assumptions falter over the missing information, whose absence leaves an epistemological gap in his reconstruction of the story. When Flora does eventually reveal its contents to Marlow, he discovers that she had told Mrs Fyne, 'I did not love her brother

---

[24] Mona Caird, 'Marriage', *Westminster Review*, 130 (Aug. 1888), 198.
[25] It is interesting to note that in the serial version of the novel Marlow refers to 'Edgar Poe's writing' (see Ch. 5 n. 50). In the final version he alludes, not to the missing letter, but to the elopement of Captain Anthony, as 'the affair of the purloined brother' (148).

but that I had no scruples whatever in marrying him' (443). At this point Conrad confirms the crisis of interpretation that faces all participants in Flora's history. All take her letter to some extent literally. Mr and Mrs Fyne are insulted; Roderick (who, like Marlow, hears of the letter from John Fyne) believes that Flora cannot love him; and Marlow, who flounders between interpretations to some extent shapes her role as conventional heroine from this letter, basing his assumptions about her elopement from what he presumes she wrote in it. However, Flora herself confesses that the letter did not represent her situation accurately, but instead reflected the precariousness of her psychological state at the time: 'it was simply crude', she remarks, and merely 'the echo' (443) of the very ideology suggested to her by Mrs Fyne, written in anger and despair at her seemingly untenable role when she is forced to support her father although she is already destitute.

The letter is important because Flora's revelation of its contents at the end of the novel forces us to reconsider Marlow's authority. For one thing, it reminds us that Marlow's presentation of feminism in the novel is purely subjective. He quite clearly disapproves of Mrs Fyne's 'moral fire-and-sword doctrine' (187), believing that 'a passive attitude' is a woman's 'best refuge' (378). But because he does not know what Flora said to upset Mrs Fyne, much of Marlow's interpretation of Flora relies solely on his *personal* view of women rather than on her testimony, and he therefore presumes that in marrying Roderick, Flora has rejected Mrs Fyne's feminism in order to accept the 'passive' but 'proper' role for women. He fails to perceive the subtlety of Flora's case, caught between positions, unable to conform to any of the more reductive alternatives offered to her, including his own. Hovering between 'divided duty' to father and husband, where her excessive loyalty to an egocentric father conflicts with her desire to find individual expression of her own life, Flora cannot imagine a tolerable solution to her situation. Mrs Fyne's thesis does not work for her either, not because she believes, like Marlow, that her 'best refuge' is a 'passive attitude', but because ultimately no theoretical position adequately accounts for her actual experience. And as Mrs Fyne shows in her reaction to Flora's letter, neither does *she* accept the outcome of her own theories. Finally, it is only after the removal of the patriarchal authority, the literal death of the father, that Flora comes into 'being'.

We are now in a position to assess Conrad's experimentation with the structures of romance. He shows how the contemporary struggle to improve women's social and political position, and to express radical views of their ontological status often generated misunderstandings and sometimes elicited counter-productive perspectives. He draws attention to some of the conflicting, and also potentially reductive aspects of contemporary views of gender. But he also uses the issue of the non-consummation of the marriage to experiment fully with the relationship between gender and genre. Flora fulfils her role as romance heroine, or 'damsel in distress' as long as she maintains her passivity and accepts her rescue at the hands of the chivalrous 'knight'. But the circumstances of her 'rescue' force her into an equivocal position balanced between roles and hovering between generic boundaries. As the Polish material has shown, her role in protecting her father puts her in an active rather than a passive position, but Anthony's 'heroic' refusal to consummate the marriage forces her into a passivity that nevertheless annihilates the possibilities of a conventional romance closure.

Thus Conrad subverts the conventionally 'active' role of the male 'knight'. Again there is an echo of Polish romanticism's questioning of the hero's 'failure to act'. However, Conrad shows how Anthony's fastidiousness only negates Flora's sense of autonomy further: 'she existed, unapproachable, behind the blank wall of his renunciation' (396). Despite his 'heroic' refusal to take sexual possession, Anthony nonetheless keeps her on board his ship, where she is metaphorically possessed, even imprisoned. Marlow describes this moment with great pathos:

> then when she understood that he was giving her her liberty she went stiff all over, her hand resting on the edge of the table, her face set like a carving of white marble. It was all over.   (335)

It is true that Marlow empathises with Flora's sense of entrapment.[26] Yet he chooses a sculptural image through which to

[26] Gail Fraser, 'Mediating Between the Sexes: Conrad's *Chance*', *Review of English Studies* 43 (Feb. 1992), 86: Fraser has remarked of this passage that at this point 'the narrator suddenly takes us inside the feminine consciousness'. But we should note that Marlow imagines her thoughts through the medium of a second-hand account.

mediate her thoughts. The frozen pose reminds us that Flora is always viewed from outside and that her inner states of consciousness are almost exclusively filtered through another's voice.

   Now we can take a closer look at the narrative method itself. Flora's resistance to any narrow generic classification represents a structuring principle throughout the narrative, and needs to be understood in the context of Marlow's attempts to establish a framework for defining the heroine. This framework, based on discussions between Marlow and an interlocutor, reflects the chivalric motif of the novel, where the narrators fight over their shifting perceptions of what it is to be a woman. Marlow considers himself well qualified to make pronouncements about women: 'there is enough of the woman in my nature to free my judgement of woman from glamorous reticency' (53). Yet he is equally capable of delivering a blatantly misogynistic view of women: 'For myself it's towards women that I feel vindictive mostly' (150). On other occasions he accuses the dramatised listener of adopting an overtly chivalrous attitude: 'Nothing can beat a true woman for a clear vision of reality; I would say cynical vision if I were not afraid of wounding your feelings' (281). While his interlocutor fights back, he fails to draw attention to Marlow's reductive classification of women in the same speech: 'a woman's part is passive, say what you like' (281). Elsewhere in the novel Marlow himself adopts the role of chivalrous knight, idealising Flora as damsel in distress (46). But Conrad undermines the lofty tone with the combative style of his narrators' exchanges. Marlow's interlocutor admits that 'we were always tilting at each other' (102), yet the resulting dialogue produces a comic subversion of the medieval romance and the conventionalised images of women that have developed out of that form, particularly those associated with Victorian reconstructions of medievalism. Conrad's handling of the voices that classify women in *Chance* contributes a ludic quality to the novel while simultaneously isolating Flora as a tragic, misunderstood heroine.

   Besides these two narrators, other voices and second-hand accounts contribute to the prevailing social register in the novel (represented by Powell, the Fynes, Franklin, and Flora herself). Traditional views of women appear to be upheld, only to be disturbed by contradictory assertions, or tempered with a more empathetic identification with a female figure. Powell, for example, holds 'preconceived ideas as to captains' wives' (288), where alternative possibilities are limited to either 'stout or thin', 'jolly or crabbed', but 'always mature' (289), and his shock at discovering Flora's youth and frailty causes 'a sort of moral upset' (289). Franklin, the first mate of Captain Anthony's ship, *The Ferndale*, presents the most reductive and misogynistic view of Flora, implying that the presence of a woman on board ship engaged him 'in an active contest with some power of evil' (305), only to be challenged by Powell's increasingly chivalrous attitude to the captain's wife. Marlow's account of Flora constitutes the principal theme of his narration and although ultimately he comes close to understanding her predicament, he nevertheless exposes the reader to the inadequacy of his endlessly commonplace representations. But then, none of the women of this novel are exempt from Marlow's scrutiny. He rebukes Mrs Fyne, the feminist, for her 'individualist woman doctrine', calling her 'a ruthless theorist' (126), at the same time satirising her role as a 'guileless' but 'worthy wife' (62). Marlow strains most of all for a definition of Flora:

Flora de Barral was not exceptionally intelligent but she was thoroughly feminine. She would be passive (and that does not mean inanimate) in the circumstances, where the mere fact of being a woman was enough to give her an occult supreme significance. And she would be enduring, which is the essence of woman's visible, tangible power. (310)

Subjected to Marlow's classifications, the women in his story retain a figurative, emblematic quality. But by limiting Marlow's voice so that it never achieves final authority, Conrad registers the dilemma of women who are unable to form identities untrammelled by plots, poses, gestures that have not already been invented for them, and that are not already entrenched at a cultural level. Marlow's antagonistic and unreliable voice forces the reader to question his more dogmatic assumptions. Since Marlow is also challenged by his interlocutor, Conrad creates a narrative frame in which he can distance himself (as author) from the classifications of the male storytellers of the novel, and destabilise the reader's confidence in the authority of their voices.

Conrad also registers Marlow's unreliability through the narrator's changing perspectives on the heroine as he struggles to understand her motives for suicide. Marlow's presentation of his first encounter with Flora contains a number of contemporary resonances, most notably the image of the Dickensian 'pure young girl'.[27] His obsessive return to the pose suggests his own difficulties in identifying the genre of Flora's story.[28] As Marlow becomes more familiar with the details of Flora's life, he recollects her seemingly rash act with increasing empathy, remembering with greater insight his first encounter with the white figure of a frail young girl perched on the edge of a quarry ready to leap (an episode he initially presents with a lighthearted touch, invoking a comic reference to the yapping dog that actually saved her life).[29] He gradually modifies his acerbic tone in describing her suicide attempts. Following her dismissal from the home of crude and unsympathetic cousins, Flora then tries to run from the Fynes, who have taken her in, 'with the haste, I suppose, of despair and to keep I don't know what tryst,' says Marlow (177). The tone has shifted from the ironic mode (with its initially dismissive assessment of Flora) towards a more substantial empathy with the tragic dimensions of her case. However, it is only after Flora confesses her desire to end her life to Marlow in person, outside a hotel in London, that he offers her his full sympathy. Even then he refuses to relinquish his chivalric fantasy that he rescued her. During her interview with Marlow, she utterly rejects his 'chivalrous' part in preventing her suicide:

[27] See Jeremy Hawthorn, *Joseph Conrad: Narrative Technique and Ideological Commitment*, ch. 4 on *Chance* and Dickens; and also John Batchelor, *The Life of Joseph Conrad: A Critical Biography* (Oxford: Blackwell, 1994), *Life*, 211–12, on Marlow's recollection of Mrs Fyne's view of Flora and her father as 'Figures from Dickens—pregnant with pathos' (162). Batchelor identifies the reference to Florence Dombey and her father in *Dombey and Son* (1848).

[28] I have already discussed the allusions to Poradowska's presentation of suicide as Flora hovers on the cliffside, but the pose suggests a number of other references— a parody of nineteenth-century commentaries of fallen women, such as George Frederic Watts's 1848 painting, *Found Drowned*. The image represents a prostitute who, in the act of committing suicide, is saved by a benevolent gentleman. Conrad plays on the idea of Flora's potential suicide, ironic in this case, since Flora's father, the authority figure, is responsible for her 'fall', not into prostitution, but into poverty and exploitation in the market for women's work. There may also be an allusion to Henry James's Milly Theale, hovering on a precipice in *The Wings of the Dove* (1902).

[29] See also paintings by James Whistler or John Singer Sargent in this context. For example, Sargent's strained, stiff portrait of Miss Elsie Palmer, all in white against a dark panelled background, used for the front cover of the Penguin (1974) edition of *Chance*; Conrad himself drew attention to a portrait by John Lavery (1856–1941) entitled *The Girl in White* (shown at the Goupil Gallery, London, June 1891). See letter to R. B. Cunninghame Graham, 14 April 1898, *CL* 2, 56 and 56 n. 3.

'I see you will have it that I saved your life. Nothing of the kind. I was concerned for that vile little beast of a dog' (213). Thus the subjectivity of Marlow's narration contributes to the impact of her few moments of self-dramatisation. Conrad gives his heroine the power to undermine Marlow's authority as narrator, or as 'knight', and to subvert generic expectations by converting his view of her tragic pose into a moment of pure absurdity.

The novel moves uneasily between genres: on the one hand, it is a romance, where the isolated heroine experiences sexual awakening. But far from being a conventional romance, the harmonic closure is less dependent on the marriage plot than on the positive outcome of Flora's endurance as an individual, her recovery from the loss of faith in herself and her perception of a fragmented identity. On the other hand, it is a story of initiation in another sense, taking its lead from Powell's tale of his first professional appointment as second mate of *The Ferndale*. Flora's entry into the professional world, inexperienced as she is, and where, according to Fyne, 'she had no value, either positive or speculative' (114), pairs her appropriately with Powell, who says he had also been 'looked over' by a prospective employer 'as if I had been exposed for sale' (19). Conrad links these two as novices entering a capitalist world, where sailors depend on commerce with the colonies to keep them in employment, and women without means, hovering between identification with father or husband, can only maintain economic independence by adopting a precarious role, ill-defined in terms of social status (such as governess or companion). Thus the heroine's brief appearance in Powell's story, where he refers to the unusual presence of the captain's wife on board ship, is converted into a romance about the young woman's realisation of the harsh realities of female dependency in a masculine world. The stories of two 'innocents', Flora and Powell, whose 'youth had created a sort of bond between them' (315), offers one structuring device for the novel in their journeys of experience.

At the same time, *Chance* is a *bildungsroman* where Flora and Captain Anthony's education—learning how to be and how to love—depends on their passage through psychological crisis and confrontation. Conrad experiments radically with genre, subverting expectations by constantly shifting the perspective from which we view events, questioning the construction of conventional plots and assumptions about stories, limiting the view of his narrators, drawing attention to the subjectivity of their assertions, the various agendas they bring to the shaping of their reports. He creates a vast structure of surveillance, where Marlow, always on the lookout for a story, picks up hints and fragments of Flora's history, piecing them together from his imaginative reconstruction of his informers' observations. Conrad demands a discerning reader who can never assume the authority of the narrators because they themselves are caught in an epistemological dilemma, struggling to know the woman whose status as heroine they obsessively discuss.

The epistemological issue—how to know the woman—lies at the heart of the narrative's structure. But the method of constructing the story exposes the unreliability of the narrators' observations. Conrad creates a network of voyeurs, who, tantalised by the object of their view, nevertheless fail to represent her accurately. Marlow, however, believes firmly in his own authority as interpreter of all he sees and hears. His comments about the other narrators' failures of vision reflect his own self-confidence as the central narratorial authority. He remarks on the inaccuracy of John Fyne's reports (49, 352); he claims that Zoe Fyne cannot interpret Flora's glance (170); Powell, he believes, is unable 'to interpret aright the signs', and that 'the inwardness of what was passing before his eyes was hidden from him' (426); whereas Marlow assures us that he 'visualized the story' for himself (177). Yet his perceptions are rarely as accurate as he makes out. On one occasion he fails to understand Mrs Fyne's jealousy of Flora's elopement with her brother: 'What could it matter to her one way or another . . .?' (193) he asks. Like many recent critics, Marlow himself puzzles over the possibilities of Mrs Fyne's fondness for her 'girlfriends' (whose ranks Flora joined when Mrs Fyne 'rescued' her). But earlier in the narrative Mrs Fyne had explained at length to Marlow that 'I felt very much abandoned' (185) when her brother had gone to sea, leaving her to face 'the domestic tyrant' alone. Marlow never considers the possibility that it may be Roderick Anthony, and not Flora of whom she feels most possessive.

Marlow is also slow to pick up on the importance of de Barral's obsession for his daughter and the extent to which Flora's identity has been defined by her attachment to the patriarchal figure. He prides himself on his ability to extract confidences from

Flora during his protracted conversation with her outside a London hotel. Yet in spite of her confession of the circumstances of her elopement with Captain Anthony, it is not until his subsequent conversation with Fyne that he realises that de Barral may have played a fundamental role in influencing Flora's actions in marrying Anthony. Fyne has to spell out the facts for Marlow: 'that girl looks upon her father exclusively as a victim' (242). Marlow admits that he had completely forgotten about de Barral at this point, expressing total incredulity: 'So she thinks of the father?' (245). The suggestion of an incest plot (Mrs Fyne and her brother, Flora and her father) escapes Marlow's attention in both cases, as he struggles to imagine a conventional romance closure for Flora's story.

Marlow is unable to rest on a consistent reading of Flora's character. At one moment she is 'too simple to understand my intention' (236), but two pages later she becomes an 'intelligent girl' (238). He never really relinquishes his perspective of Flora as damsel, neither does he deny his own chivalric pose in any fundamental sense. Conrad uses Marlow's voice to show how Flora's consciousness is finally isolated from the textual space, while her story has been 'rescued' by a narrator whose subjective interest in her life colours his perception of the case. His physical description of Flora outside the hotel, dressed in her 'close-fitting' garment (205), speaking from 'under the brim of her hat' with her head down, in a manner that 'gave me a thrill' (215) suggests an eroticism that betrays his own attraction to his 'heroine'. Marlow's retelling of his encounter with Flora emerges as yet another displaced romantic closure—where he himself attempts, and fails, to occupy the part of 'knight'.

Conrad increases the narrators' anxiety surrounding Flora by juxtaposing interior and exterior methods of presentation—building a relationship between what is seen from the outside, and what is consciously imagined. Much of our knowledge of the governesses's story, for example, relies on Marlow's ability to recreate her inner life—he presumes to understand her motivation for inflicting psychological cruelty on her pupil. Marlow shows how knowledge of de Barral's financial fraud had been withheld from the innocent Flora. Conrad's method hinges on Marlow's expression of the governess's interiority by placing her in an intimate relationship with her surroundings, while Flora remains passively excluded from an understanding of the de Barral plot. Marlow expresses the governess's active panic in terms of the disruption of objects around her as she herself prepares to move out: 'wardrobes opened, drawers half pulled out and empty, trunks locked and strapped, furniture in idle disarray' (101).[30] At this point in the narrative, Flora remains the 'pale and passive vessel' (119).

Marlow's relation of the concluding episodes of her adventures on her husband's ship also shows how she is excluded from the main events of the story. Again the style of narration is important for the way in which it determines our final reading of Flora. Powell now takes centre stage for the scenes outlining the discovery of de Barral's attempt on Anthony's life on board *The Ferndale*. We penetrate Powell's consciousness as Marlow relates, at second hand, the moment when Powell enters Anthony's cabin, having watched through the skylight above as de Barral puts poison in the captain's glass. Powell is transfixed, stopping in his tracks: 'What checked him at the crucial moment was the familiar, harmless aspect of common things, the steady light, the open book on the table, the solitude, the peace, the home-like effect of the place' (419). We gain access to Powell's consciousness in a passage of dramatic intensity, the stillness of familiar objects contrasting with his mental turmoil. Yet in the next scene, the knowledge of his discovery is withheld from Flora. Flora's exclusion from Powell's perceptive account of her father's crime is expressed once more through her pose of innocent passivity: 'At that moment the appearance of Flora could not but bring tension to breaking point. She came out in all innocence but not without vague dread' (423). She appears like one of Poradowska's romantic heroines: 'her hair was down. She looked like a child, a pale-faced child with big blue eyes and a red mouth, a little open, showing a glimmer of white teeth. The light fell strongly on her as she came up to the end of the table' (423).[31] Even her

---

[30] Conrad's writing at this point can be described appropriately as phenomenological on the basis of this passage, especially when compared with Gaston Bachelard, *The Poetics of Space*, trans. Maria Jolas (1958; Boston: Beacon Press, 1964), 78: 'Wardrobes with their shelves, desks with their drawers, and chests with their false bottoms are veritable organs of the secret psychological life.'

[31] See Marguerite Poradowska, *Pour Noémi*, *Revue des Deux Mondes* 154 (15 Aug. 1899), 723: 'éclairée par les rayons obliques du soleil, une jeune fille, mince, très blanche . . . aux yeux doux et allongés . . . le regardait avec une expression . . . confuse.'

father's suicide is later concealed from her, a fact that Marlow never reveals to her in their final interview.

Flora is excluded from the world of narration, yet dominated by men who wish to possess her self *and* her story. Marlow suggests Flora's fulfilment of identity in the last pages of the novel, when he assures us that 'she was now her true self' (363). But Marlow's final view of Flora reinforces the emblematic representation imposed on her throughout the novel: 'The lamp had a rosy shade; and its glow wreathed her in perpetual blushes, made her appear wonderfully young as she sat before me in a deep, high-backed armchair' (443). As she resumes the familiar pose of Poradowska's two-dimensional heroines, Marlow expresses his satisfaction. It is, he says, 'all very proper' (443). Marlow's failure to release Flora from the traditional literary and iconographic poses with which she is closely associated throughout the novel points to a deliberate strategy on Conrad's part to deflect the box-office closure.[32] Flora gets a prospective 'happy ending', but she is forever locked in the manipulative web of the narrator.

For the most part, Marlow presents the heroine from the outside, providing a tension in the novel between what he sees and what the reader might imagine her to be. However, within his own narrative confines, which ultimately fail to liberate the heroine from narrow generic expectations, he achieves at times a limited understanding of Flora's inner life. When reconstructing the incident with the governess Marlow achieves dramatic effect by presenting Flora almost exclusively from the outside. Again, when he reproduces Flora's tale of her rejection by Anthony, he initially objectifies her pose by describing her as a

---

[32] Conrad had encountered problems with the ending of the novel. The editors of the *New York Herald* had found his original ending for the serialised version unacceptable. See letter to J. B. Pinker, 20 Nov. 1911, *Letters* 4, 507: 'It positively pains me not being able to do with the end what I should like to do. However I don't think it will be bad.' We do not know what Conrad had originally planned, but in the manuscript, (in the Berg Collection of the New York Public Library) which was finished on 25 March 1912 (see Ch. 5), the novel ends as Powell finishes his story of Captain Anthony's death, and he gives only a hint of his visits to Flora (in the Dent edition, the last line of the manuscript coincides with Powell's exclamation, ' "Pah! Foolishness. You ought to know better," he said' [441]. For the serial version Conrad added Marlow's scene with Flora, in which he strengthened the idea of a prospective marriage between Flora and Powell (*Herald* Sunday Magazine, 30 June 1912, 6). He retained this scene for the book-version.

'carving of white marble'. But later Marlow's narrative enters into the young woman's consciousness, reconstructing her interior 'adventure' as she swiftly absents herself from her confrontation with Anthony: 'Flora, relieved, got clear away to her room upstairs, and shutting her door quietly, dropped into a chair' (228), where she reflects extensively on her current predicament. Her action is highly suggestive of a method outlined by Henry James in the Preface to *The Portrait of a Lady*, where the writer imagines Isabel Archer sitting up by the dying fire, 'motionlessly *seeing*'. James's intention is to 'make the mere still lucidity of her act as "interesting" as the surprise of a caravan or the identification of a pirate'.[33] Flora's contemplation, like Isabel's 'extraordinary meditative vigil' also represents for *Conrad's* heroine 'the occasion that was to become for her such a landmark'.[34] Flora looks back on a secure past with her father, but now defines herself as isolated, rejected, caught in a moment of intolerable stasis that leads to further thoughts of suicide.

The episode allows the reader a moment of close identification with the novel's heroine, showing that the psychological 'adventure' was indeed, as she claims, hers, and offering the reader, in a heroine who 'matters', a sense of her interiority in the Jamesian manner. However, Marlow does not sustain a 'narrative' of Flora's consciousness, and, uncertain of the linear construction of the story, unable to fathom Flora's actions, ultimately unwilling to relinquish his part in her 'rescue', he slips back into a role that makes this novel less reminiscent of James's *Portrait* than of his *Daisy Miller*, whose female protagonist is misunderstood by an unreliable male narrator, or *The American*, where Madame de Cintré represents a distanced and somewhat unfathomable figure whose deeper consciousness James's narrator finally fails to penetrate.[35] Conrad's method ultimately emphasises

[33] James, Preface (1907), *The Portrait of a Lady* (1881; Oxford: Oxford University Press, 1981), 17.   [34] Ibid.

[35] On the other hand, we also have Conrad's testimony of his admiration for Turgenev, whose representation of Lisa, or *A Nest of Gentlefolk* he preferred to the heroines of most 19th-cent. English writers (*Last Essays*, 133). James had also drawn on this novel for his presentation of Madame de Cintré in *The American*. Like Turgenev with Lisa, he experimented with the crisis of consciousness that takes place within a heroine who is nevertheless chiefly 'seen' through the eyes of others. Conrad repeats the experiment in yet another form with Flora de Barral. See Daniel Lerner, 'The Influence of Turgenev on Henry James,' *The Slavonic and East European Review* 20 (Dec. 1941), 43–4.

the telling of the tale, where a strained and elusive figure struggles into being in spite of the misrepresentations of the narrators.

II

Conrad's relationship to James was clearly significant but also uneasy. The awkwardness stems in large measure from James's review of *Chance* in the *Times Literary Supplement* in 1914, later enlarged and revised in the same year under the title of 'The New Novel'. It is worth looking more closely at what James had to say not only for the light it casts on their interaction and mutual assessment, but because the review has exerted considerable influence over subsequent critics who have interpreted it as wholly unfavourable, seeing Conrad's novel as a failed attempt to emulate James. This conclusion has had direct implications, in turn, for the placement of the work within the Conrad canon.

To conclude this chapter, I shall briefly explore James's connection to *Chance*, but I suggest that rather than emulating James, Conrad was engaging in a technical debate with 'The Master' in this novel.[36] During the course of *Chance* Conrad both acknowledges his debt to Jamesian narrative theory, and distinguishes himself from it by introducing his individual approach to the issue of 'knowing' the heroine. Irrespective of its associations with James, Conrad's experimentation in *Chance* ultimately emerges, in its own right, as a significant contribution to contemporary explorations of female identity, and discussions about the relationship between gender and genre in the romance form.

Conrad's esteem for James is well documented in the letters.[37] And while the tone of the review is on one level acerbic, James actually concedes his admiration for the novel, albeit rather

[36] See Ian Watt, 'Conrad, James, and *Chance*', in Maynard Mack and Ian Gregor (eds.), *Imagined Worlds: Essays on Some English Novels and Novelists in Honour of John Butt* (London: Methuen, 1968), 301–22; E. E. Duncan-Jones, 'Some Sources of *Chance*', *Review of English Studies* 20 (Nov. 1969), 468–71; Batchelor, *Life*, 211, and 203–4 on 'The Younger Generation'. On 2 Jan. 1904, *Harper's Weekly*, New York, published the Preface to *The Nigger of the 'Narcissus'* under the title, 'The Art of Fiction' (690).

[37] See letter to Galsworthy, 12 March? 1899, *CL* 2, 174; to Garnett, 12 Nov. 1900, *CL* 2, 303; to James, Oct.? 1906, *CL* 3, 361–2; 20 Sept. 1907, *CL* 3, 477; 12 Dec. 1908, *CL* 4, 161–2; Oct.? 1911, *CL* 4, 497.

obliquely. James's critique focuses on the question of method.[38] For James, Conrad's 'extraordinary exhibition of method' in *Chance* places him 'absolutely alone as a votary of the way to do a thing that shall make it undergo most doing'.[39] This sounds like an underhand remark, but he then compares Conrad's novel favourably with the methods of contemporary realist writers (he alludes in the same review to Arnold Bennett and H. G. Wells), who, he feels, 'saturate' their texts with physical detail and description to the detriment of the 'interest' of the novel ('interest' for James implies the 'real' subject matter of the novel—not events and descriptions in themselves, but that which stimulates the intellectual pleasure of the reader through the presentation of the complexity of situations, points-of-view, consciousness). According to James, the contemporary novels that often gained (for him, unmerited) public acclaim were those that had required the 'least' methodological effort on the part of their authors. Under these terms, Conrad comes off well in James's estimation: 'the author of "Chance" gathers up on this showing all sorts of comparative distinction.'[40]

So far, in spite of a somewhat wry handling of the terms of praise, James appears to sympathise with Conrad. But in due course he takes issue with Conrad's narrative method in *Chance*, implying that the intricate strategy was somewhat gratuitously imposed. He cites the work of his close friend, the writer Edith Wharton, as 'an eminent instance of the sort of tonic value most opposed to that baffled relation between subject-matter and its emergence which we find constituted by the circumvalations of *Chance*'.[41] He reinforces his preference for developing interiority as a means of directing the narrative. While Flora's story is imparted obliquely through the subjective voices of a number of dramatised narrators, James may have preferred to receive it principally through her centre of consciousness or through the medium of a single, less intrusive narratorial consciousness. James's chief concern lies in Conrad's handling of multiple

---

[38] Letter to Warrington Dawson, 1 June 1913, *CL* 5, 298. In discussing with Warrington Dawson the 'general question' of the art of fiction, Conrad observed that 'the sheer methods' were 'the only part of our art in which advance or at any rate novelty (of effects) is possible'.
[39] Henry James, 'The New Novel' (1914), in *Henry James: Essays, American and English Writers* (New York: The Library of America, 1984), 147.
[40] Ibid.   [41] Ibid. 155.

narrators whose voices are in danger of obscuring 'those . . . in whom the objectivity resides', a pitfall normally avoided, he says, by keeping the narrative voice 'comparatively impersonal' or 'inscrutable'.[42] He finds Conrad's method too clumsy, one demanding that 'the sense and the interest of the subject have to be passed on together, in the manner of the buckets of water for the improvised extinction of a fire, before reaching our apprehension'.[43] His summing up is fairly brutal: ' "Chance" *is* an example of objectivity, most precious of aims, not only menaced but definitely compromised.'[44] By comparison, he praises Wharton for her 'artistic economy', her ability to give us the narrative, 'not in the crude state but in the extract'.[45] She shapes her expression 'into some sharp image or figure of her thought', suggesting that James favours the use of an 'objective correlative' to direct the narrative, over Conrad's network of storytellers, 'handling and fumbling and repointing' the story within an extensive narrative frame. Nevertheless, he goes on to admit that in spite of his criticisms of Conrad's novel, 'the sense of discomfort, as the show here works out, *has* been conjured away' by 'a miracle' of Conrad's artistic 'genius', leaving an example of 'a beautiful and generous mind at play'.[46] Indeed, in private, he actually recommended *Chance* to Edith Wharton herself as 'rather *yieldingly* difficult and charming'.[47] James's public remarks about *Chance*, at times caustic, but characteristically complex, may well have been cast in the light of an anxiety about Conrad attempting a 'Jamesian' subject, and no doubt reflect his own preoccupations at the time. As T. J. Lustig has remarked, 'The shift from seeing to knowing is part of a general tendency in later James to deal with centres of consciousness rather than points of view.'[48] James may have felt that in *Chance* Conrad overdid the number of 'points of view' of Flora de Barral at the expense of gaining greater access to her centre of consciousness. But because James had also experimented with 'points of view' in his presentation of women, his discomfort with Conrad's novel may arise in part from the

[42] Ibid. 149.   [43] Ibid. 151.   [44] Ibid. 150.
[45] Ibid. 154.   [46] Ibid. 150.
[47] Letter from Henry James to Edith Wharton, 27 Feb. 1914, in John H. Stape and Owen Knowles (eds.), *A Portrait in Letters: Correspondence To and About Conrad* (Amsterdam: Rodopi, 1996), 97.
[48] See T. J. Lustig's notes to Henry James, *The Turn of the Screw and Other Stories* (1898; Oxford: Oxford University Press, 1992), 263.

closeness of their aims. Furthermore, James's voice as critic in this instance bears some resemblance to that of the 'inscrutable' narrators of his fiction, whose own 'circumvalations' require a strenuous reader to unravel the utterances of the voice's often 'hidden' consciousness in order to guess the knowledge he has acquired. But however generous James intended to be, what he clearly does not concede is that Conrad's narratorial framework is, as it stands, fundamental to the design of *Chance*. The complexity of the construction foregrounds the isolation of the female protagonist, distanced as she is from the network of perspectives, plots, and agenda imposed on her, as the narrators attempt, but fail, to shape the heroine's story according to the conventions of a traditional romance.

James's emphasis on 'objectivity' in his review of *Chance* illustrates a fundamental aspect of his narrative theory that would prove highly influential for future literary critics. As I outlined in Chapter 1, this empiricist strain in criticism underlies a preference, eventually codified much later by Wayne Booth, for the Jamesian method of 'showing' over the tendency of writers like Conrad to 'tell'. James's preferences were taken up by subsequent critics, notably F. R. Leavis, who also privileged the precision of the writer who 'shows' the 'object' of the tale. In Leavis's remarks about 'adjectival insistence' in *The Great Tradition* (1948) we find the mistrust of the empiricist critic for the more phenomenological aspects of Conrad's writing (his inability to give adequate account of 'the mystery', 'the darkness', 'the unknown').[49] But Leavis goes further than James. He scores another point for 'objectivity' by associating Conrad's 'imprecision' in his mode of 'telling' with his presentation of women, whose indeterminate quality, Leavis argues, 'is of the same order' as the ill-defined 'mystery' of Kurtz's corruption. Thus a critical preference for James's 'showing' of the female consciousness, implying a greater understanding of the interiority of his women characters, emerges from the empiricist school of thought.

---

[49] See James M. Edie, Introduction, Pierre Thévenaz, *What is Phenomenology and Other Essays*, ed. and trans. James M. Edie (Chicago: Quadrangle Books, 1962), 19. In this case we can understand the term 'phenomenological' to refer, in Conrad's and James's writing, to that which 'does not concentrate exclusively on either the objects of experience or on the subject of experience, but on the point of contact where being and consciousness meet'.

If Leavis had found the 'phenomenological' aspects of Conrad's writing imprecise, then part of the difficulty of separating James and Conrad on this point centres on the fact that, as Paul Armstrong has shown, James's writing might also be appropriately termed 'phenomenological'. With reference to 'The Art of Fiction' (1884), for example, Armstrong explains how James's exploration of the perceptual implications suggested by a single 'glance' into the 'frame' anticipates early twentieth-century phenomenological thought about the relationship of vision and the attainment of knowledge.[50] In 'The Art of Fiction', James praises the accomplishment of 'an English novelist' (Anne Thackeray Ritchie) who had, in one tale, managed convincingly to give the impression of 'the nature and way of life of the French Protestant youth' from a momentary view through an open door, of some young men seated at a table round a finished meal.[51] James explains: 'The glimpse made a picture; it lasted only a moment, but that moment was experience . . . and she turned out her type.'[52] Although Armstrong writes only about James, his interpretation of this moment is significant not only for readers of James, but for those of Conrad, whose narrators constantly attempt to interpret the historical implications of a single glance into the frame.[53] Armstrong claims that James's account of perception here is close to that of Heiddegger (in *Being and Time*, 1927), who shows that understanding is always 'ahead of itself', teleologically, making explicit what appears to be implicit within the limitations, or horizons of ordinary observations. James's account also resembles Merleau-Ponty's theories, who, in *The Phenomenology of Perception*, uses Husserl's terminology to suggest that the *aspect*'s 'invitation to perceive beyond it' is a dynamic aid to interpretation, allowing the viewer to uncover potentialities delimited by the horizon of the view.[54] The phenomenologists' account of a relationship

---

[50] Paul B. Armstrong, *The Phenomenology of Henry James* (Chapel Hill and London: The University of North Carolina Press, 1983), 38–49.

[51] Henry James, 'The Art of Fiction,' (1884; New York: Library of America, 1984), 52.   [52] Ibid.

[53] Armstrong, *The Phenomenology of Henry James*, 42–3.

[54] See Maurice Merleau-Ponty, *The Phenomenology of Perception*, trans. Colin Smith (London: Routledge and Kegan Paul, 1962), 233. Merleau-Ponty's study of phenomenology in relation to painting explores the nature of the experience of looking—an experience consistently repeated in narratives of this period. See also,

between seeing and knowing, according to Armstrong, closely resembles James's perception of the creative process, where his authority arises from a transcendent experience generated by a single moment of vision.

The correspondences between James and Conrad can be identified, from a phenomenological perspective, in a common emphasis on the relationship between seeing and knowing. They are both concerned with the limitation of perspective as well as the process of revelation and attainment of knowledge. The closest analogy to James's emphasis on the revelatory power of vision arises in Conrad in the Preface to *The Nigger of 'The Narcissus'*, in his exhortation to the reader, 'before all, to make you *see*!' (p. xlii)—in which Conrad invokes the act of looking as an aid to understanding. His narrators frequently explore the fuller significance of a single glance into the frame—such as Marlow's attempts to 'fathom' his view of Jim or Flora. However, any comparison of the two writers needs to take into account their distinctive approaches to the relationship between vision and epistemology, an issue that arises with particular force in Conrad's presentation of the female protagonist of *Chance*.

The two authors explore similar problems of seeing and knowing in their novels, but they differ fundamentally in their attitude to the creative vision. Conrad is much more sceptical about the matter, the isolated moment of transcendent vision rarely occurring for Conrad himself with quite the same force that the experience has for James. He is considerably warier than James when describing *his* methodology, the *author*'s 'power to guess the unseen from the seen'. Nevertheless, he showed how acutely aware he was of Jamesian methods while composing *Chance*. While struggling with the early pages of *Chance* in December 1908, Conrad declared in a letter to James that he had read the 1907 Preface to the New York Edition of *The American*. At that time Conrad still perceived of this work as a 'sea novel' (CL 4, 59, 106), and it would shortly be put aside for a long period in favour of other projects. Yet when Conrad came to write his Author's Note for the novel in 1920, he echoed something of

---

Armstrong, *The Phenomenology of Henry James*, 42: 'each aspect of the thing which falls to our perception is still only an invitation to perceive beyond it, still only a momentary halt in the perceptual process.'

'The Master's' Preface, except that in the question of epistemology he took quite a different turn.

James declared, with the authority of one who possesses 'the power to guess the unseen from the seen', that in writing *The American*, 'the current must have gushed, full and clear, to my imagination, from the moment Christopher Newman rose before me'. James emphasises the 'felicity of the first glimpse'[55] of his subject for that novel, coupled with his capacity for imaginative observation that gave him the ability to see beyond, in time and space, the initial view. The role of the author, for James, relies on the question of 'perceived effect' and the skill of the artist depends on his ability to create 'effect *after* the fact',[56] as the process of creation itself takes on a narrative form. 'No painting of any picture', says James, 'can take effect without some form of reference and control.'[57] The writer must 'shape' the revelation that lies behind the initial 'reference' or 'glimpse' of his subject. Nevertheless, the 'fact' is something 'known', at least to the author. Conrad's relationship to his own creation is altogether more sceptical.

In *Chance*, Conrad enters into a debate with James over the issue of what can be 'known' to the author. He creates a role for Marlow that facilitates his critique of Jamesian narrative theory. Marlow's role as storyteller in this novel takes on a particular significance here because Conrad presents this narrator as someone who shows a Jamesian confidence in assembling the tale, and Marlow's remarks on the process of narrative construction sound at times remarkably close to those of James, at least the James of the Preface to *The American*. While the Marlow of *Heart of Darkness* had refused to pinpoint his knowledge, the Marlow of *Chance* frequently attempts to fix his image of the heroine in some way, even if he ultimately proves to be just as equivocal. Early in the novel he observes that 'it may be that a glimpse and no more is the proper way of seeing individuality' (85), and he creatively imagines a full picture of de Barral's psychology having experienced a view of the man himself on one isolated occasion. Like James's conception of

---

[55] Henry James, Preface to the New York Edition (1907), *The American* (1877; New York: W. W. Norton, 1978), 2.
[56] Ibid. 8.   [57] Ibid. 5.

Christopher Newman, Marlow makes the intellectual leap from 'glimpse' to full 'disclosure' (87), a complete characterisation of his 'type' proceeding from a brief glance. The story, Marlow claimed, was the reward of 'a moment of detachment from mere visual impressions' (87). Marlow here claims to reveal 'the secret of the situation' (261) by relying on a moment of highly perceptive vision. In effect, he claims for himself 'the power to guess the unseen from the seen'. Yet in practice, Marlow's control of his narrative wavers. His vision is not always as rewarding as the 'gushing current' of James's imagination, his glimpses of Flora generating only fragmentary moments of understanding, her complete history eluding his grasp. Moreover, by distancing himself as author from the chief narrator of the novel, Conrad appears sceptical of the storyteller's assumption of an overarching authority over the text.

Responding to the sentiments of James's Preface to *The American*, Conrad declares, in his Note to *Chance*, that he had likewise perceived a 'glimpse' of his subject. Yet he displays no great confidence in the view: 'At the crucial moment of my indecision Flora de Barral passed before me, but so swiftly that I failed at first to get hold of her' (p. vii). James's vision of Christopher Newman rises vertically before him. He effectively holds it with his gaze as it stimulates the workings of his imagination, whereas Conrad's 'spectre' moves more elusively on a horizontal plane, passing out of his field of vision before he can fully appreciate its presence. This insight into the enigmatic quality of Flora as she glides insubstantially through the net of the complex narrative structure of *Chance* contrasts dramatically with James's confident assertions. Conrad's remark suggests that he was initially less assured in his perception of Flora de Barral, but despite the implication that he did eventually 'get hold of her', I would suggest that his final presentation of her remains uncertain. His 'glimpse' of Flora de Barral during the creation of *Chance* produced for him an epistemological dilemma. In the Author's Note he suggests that latterly, unsure of his own grasp of her characterisation, he 'simply followed Captain Anthony', seeing the heroine through the eyes of the male protagonist. Yet Flora remains strangely incorporeal: 'each of us was bent on capturing his own dream' (p. viii). He leaves unanswered the question of his personal knowledge of his female protagonist, finally deferring to the reader's judgement. For Conrad, an 'objective correlative' eludes him because, for him, it is unknown or unknowable.[58] But the strength of Conrad's narrative lies in this very refusal to pinpoint the truth of his heroine's case. The 'interest' of his tale resides not in Conrad's ability to show how the woman *is*, but in his grasp of how easy, and how erroneous it is to *presume* to know her. Parodoxically, Flora de Barral nevertheless emerges as a striking figure, whose inner consciousness may be imaginatively reconstructed by the reader, and whose inner conflict is demonstrated by her struggles not only within the world of the text, but with those who narrate it. Conrad and James both emphasise the importance of point of view, an issue which arises especially in the presentation of their female characters. James's fascination with the framing of his figures and his scenes; the importance of the position of the observer; the effects of voyeurism and perspective, run parallel with Conrad's interest in the phenomenological relation between the subject who sees and the object viewed. Yet Conrad was less assured than James of the controlling power of the author who finally positions 'the frame' of the text. With regard to his own vision and its relationship to knowledge, he ultimately expresses a bleaker form of scepticism.

In fact Conrad may well have looked elsewhere for a suitable model for his treatment of the female protagonist. While we continue to appraise *Chance* as Conrad's most Jamesian novel, an unexpected echo of his friend John Galsworthy's narrative methods appears in Conrad's presentation of Flora de Barral. Galsworthy remarked in his Preface to *The Man of Property* that 'the figure of Irene' was 'never, as the reader may possibly have observed, present, except through the senses of other characters'.[59] Like Flora de Barral, Galsworthy's Irene Forsyte is seen predominantly from the outside, from others' perspectives. Irene's tragic return to her husband's home, following the death of her lover at the end of the novel, is described, not from her centre

[58] See James, Preface to 'The Turn of the Screw', l. Even in a narrative where James himself admits to the gap in information at the centre of the textual frame he nevertheless gestures towards his control of an 'objective': that is 'the study of a conceived "tone", the tone of suspected and felt trouble'.

[59] John Galsworthy, Preface, *The Man of Property* (1906; London: Heinemann, 1921), p. xii.

of consciousness, but from Soames Forsyte's point of view: 'he saw Irene sitting in her usual corner of the sofa . . . she did not move, and did not seem to see him.'[60] By presenting Irene's position through others' experience, Galsworthy achieved a stronger sense of her emotional isolation, a method which Conrad exploited with his use of multiple narrators in *Chance*. When tackling a female protagonist, Conrad may have perceived in Galsworthy's oblique presentation a method he could adopt to suit his equivocal and more sceptical point of view.

Conrad's complex narrative shows, in Marlow's presentation of Flora de Barral, the limitations of an author's capacity to discern the 'unseen from the seen'. He questions, on the one hand, the uneasy relationship between seeing and knowing, but he also explores the particular difficulty of 'knowing the woman', when the presentation of gender is so closely related to that of genre. By leaving us with Marlow's ultimately reductive pose of the woman seated in the 'rosy glow' of the lamp, he outlines some of the problems faced by the contemporary writer who attempts to liberate the female protagonist from the tyranny of both traditional generic assumptions *and* contemporary expectations of what it is to be a woman.

In this novel, Conrad recognises a problem of signification for the presentation of the woman. If he had imagined an expression of identity appropriate to his heroine, Flora would have had to surface from the stale plots and gestures which prevent her from flourishing and enter into an alternative linguistic framework. While James's explorations of the psychological life of his female protagonists emerge from a confidence in his authoritative position, Conrad's particular brand of scepticism makes him reluctant to assume full knowledge of the inner life of the woman. In the light of an enduring critical tradition that has privileged Jamesian claims for 'objectivity', Conrad's reticence has been consistently interpreted as a weakness. James even sneers at the fact that Conrad's complex methods are 'apparently what the common reader has seen and understood' (151). But the novel's appeal for contemporary women readers is hardly so surprising. Conrad's narrative accurately determines the extent to which a modern woman was exposed to the conflicting

---

[60] Galsworthy, *Man of Property*, 529.

demands of enduring patriarchal structures as well as radical ideologies that, in spite of their intention to liberate, might equally limit her individual sense of autonomy. Conrad's scepticism appears in his ironic questioning of his narrators' attempts to 'know' the woman, and impose a fixed role on the heroine according to traditional generic requirements. However inadequate his narrators, Conrad's glimpse of Flora de Barral enabled him to produce a compelling and perceptive reading of the dilemmas of the contemporary heroine embarking on an individual, but 'fine adventure' (444) of twentieth-century romance.

5

The Three Texts of *Chance*

Despite its economic success, *Chance* occupies an uneasy critical position in the Conrad canon. Critics have tended to regard the novel as an early instance of the author's decline, an example of the failure of his creative powers which ostensibly characterise the end of his career. This diagnosis has been advanced by Robert Siegle in his comparison of the serial text and the book version, 'The Two Texts of *Chance*'.[1] Siegle claims that the serial was, essentially, a more modernist text. He laments the book version's lack of the usual emphasis on 'the "perennial" issues of the fiction as read by J. Hillis Miller, Edward Said and Frederic Jameson'.[2] In Siegle's view, some of Conrad's extensive revisions from serial to book constituted errors of judgement, particularly the removal of passages in which the narrators discuss the nature and meaning of textuality, a theme which placed the serial in a more self-reflexive cast than that of the book. Siegle's argument supports the theory that Conrad now abandons, in the book version of *Chance*, the themes associated with his 'great' fiction, thus initiating the decline of his later career.[3]

Rather than follow Siegle's nostalgia for the modernist elements of the serialised *Chance*, I shall present Conrad's cuts for the book as evidence of a new direction in his fiction. From a different perspective the final version represents yet another form of experimentation, one in which Conrad responded directly to his new marketing contexts with the projection of *Chance* as a romance novel for women readers of popular fiction. The narratorial shift from the concerns of textuality to an emphasis on

---

[1] Robert Siegle, 'The Two Texts of *Chance*,' *Conradiana* 16:2 (1984), 83–101.

[2] Ibid. 83.

[3] On completion of the manuscript on 25 March 1912, Conrad had also tried to persuade Austin Harrison of the *English Review* to serialise *Chance*, a fact which suggests that the serial text was (at least to some extent) intended for a specifically literary audience (Frederick R. Karl, *Joseph Conrad: The Three Lives* (New York: Farrar, Straus, and Giroux, 1979), 713).

the role of the female protagonist reflects Conrad's new focus on the constructions of gender and identity within circumscribed generic forms. By taking into account a third, and earlier text of *Chance*, I shall also show that the revisions for the book version represented a necessary final stage in a much longer development of these interests from early sea story to mature experiment in gender and genre.[4]

In fact Conrad may have intended, from early in his career, to write a story centred on a female protagonist. Conrad first mentioned the idea for a short story 'Dynamite' in a letter of 1898 to Edward Garnett, where he discussed a prospective collection of short stories for *Blackwood's*.[5] Although set on board a ship carrying a cargo of explosives, Conrad had written to David Meldrum on 14 February 1899 that his 'dynamite ship' story was specifically 'the one about a captain's wife'.[6] This slender reference to Flora de Barral so early in Conrad's career suggests that Conrad had planned, yet never fulfilled, an earlier intention to try something new using a central female protagonist. Bearing in mind that the short story which became *Lord Jim* (1900) was conceived at the same time, the Marlow of that novel hints at the untold story of a captain's wife: 'marital relations of seamen would make an interesting subject, and I could tell you instances . . . However, this is not the place, nor the time, and we are concerned with Jim—who was unmarried' (156). We do not know how much, if any, of the original narrative about the married seaman was ever written in the late 1890s, for at this point in Conrad's career 'Dynamite' was never completed.

Conrad habitually responded to his literary crises with a strategy of delay and deferral. As new ideas took precedence in his imagination, uncompleted narratives were set aside in favour

---

[4] See also John Batchelor, *The Life of Joseph Conrad: A Critical Biography* (Oxford: Blackwell, 1994), ch. 8. Batchelor has undertaken extensive work on the variations from manuscript to book. However, by taking into account the interim stage of the serial text of *Chance*, we gain a fuller understanding of Conrad's final refinement of the text. In this chapter, all references to the book version of *Chance* are to the first English edition (London: Methuen, 1913), and page numbers quoted in the text.

[5] 28 May or 4 June, 1898, *CL* 2, 62. Conrad cited 'Dynamite' as a story of 5,000 words for a prospective collection, intended for publication, along with 'Jim', 'Youth', and 'A Seaman' in *Blackwood's Magazine* (London) and in the United States. The collection never materialised in this form, although 'Jim' became *Lord Jim* (1899) and 'A Seaman' probably became 'The End of the Tether', which was published with 'Youth' and *Heart of Darkness* in 1902.   [6] *CL* 2, 169.

of the next project, but eventually the early manuscript would be resurrected and restructured. The most striking example of this process occurred in the case of the late work, *The Rescue* (1923), which began as a short story 'The Rescuer' in 1896. Similarly, *Chance* (1913), the first of the late romances, underwent a process of textual expansion and revision as Conrad transformed the parameters of the narrative from short story to serialised novel to book. The finished work represents a literary enterprise spanning at least fifteen years, a fact which raises many questions about the development of the novel's elusive heroine.

The *Chance* Manuscript, now in the Berg Collection of the New York Public Library, provides a vital link between the earliest reference to 'Dynamite' and the finished novel.[7] Moreover, it provides us with some material signs of the problems Conrad encountered in the creation of his heroine. The finished portrait of Flora de Barral suggests that while he was sceptical about 'presuming to know' too much about her, he nevertheless imagined her predicament, even identifying with his female protagonist to a considerable extent. Several features of Conrad's biography confirm such a hypothesis. Elements of Conrad's childhood in Poland, and of his earlier life abroad, reappear in his depiction of Flora: the youth spent in isolation, the early loss of a young mother, the precarious relationship with a remote and preoccupied father, the crisis of 'identity' characterised by desire for annihilation of the self (Conrad attempted suicide at the age of sixteen in Marseilles), the hasty marriage to secure some form of emotional stability.[8] Given that *Chance* followed the painful creation of *Under Western Eyes*, which, with all its attendant memories of Poland had precipitated his psychological breakdown, the close correspondences with his frail, misunderstood heroine suggests one possibility for his earlier reluctance to explore the female role to the full.

Perhaps 'Dynamite' never got written simply because Conrad identified too closely with its subject. The manuscript provides some tantalising evidence in this respect, revealing marks of

---

[7] Conrad's note, attached to the first batch of the Berg MS, verifies that work on this version began in 1906, was laid aside, and not resumed until June 1911. The second batch of MS is dated in Conrad's hand: 'begun here on 3rd June 1911'.

[8] See Zdzisław Najder, *Joseph Conrad: A Chronicle* (Cambridge: Cambridge University Press, 1983), 3–39 for Conrad's early life in Poland.

Conrad's stress when writing about his female protagonist. David Smith's intriguing study of Conrad's manuscript of *Under Western Eyes* reveals that whenever the author was confronting self-referential moments that touched closely on the question of his identity, he would enter an elaborately doodled 'K' in the margin.[9] This could be 'K' for Korzeniowski, or Konrad, suggesting that Conrad was reasserting his Polish identity at these points. These curious signs cover the manuscript of *Under Western Eyes*. The manuscript of *Chance*, however, contains relatively few 'K's, except for the parts of the text in which Marlow's, or Anthony's relationship to Flora is under discussion. Flora's story, recounted in the text by Marlow, is dotted with these 'K's—usually at moments where he relates his own or Captain Anthony's perception of Flora, or where Flora's psychological state matched Conrad's own, given his recent illness: 'she with one foot in life and the other in a nightmare was at the same time inert and unstable and very much at the mercy of sudden impulses' (MS, 527). The 'K' hypothesis may at first seem unduly speculative. Yet the evidence of the manuscript becomes increasingly convincing as, without exception, the 'K's appear only at these moments where the fictional and autobiographical seem to merge (and where the gender of the subject is also conflated: Conrad's anxiety appears to converge with that of Flora, Marlow, Anthony at these points).[10] Conrad's creation of his female protagonist caused him some kind of psychological disturbance, and the history of *Chance* shows that he characteristically deferred the painful moment of expression.

Little remains of the original 'Dynamite' story in the finished *Chance*, and Conrad claimed in 1911 that the earlier parts (based on this short story), belonged 'to some other novel which will never now be written'.[11] Using the evidence of letters,

---

[9] David Smith (ed.), *Joseph Conrad's Under Western Eyes* (Hamden: Archon Books, 1991), 39–81.

[10] It is interesting to note that in the *Under Western Eyes* MS (in the Beinecke Library, Yale University), the majority of the Ks occur beside references to the women in the novel, particularly during the conversations between Razumov and Sophia Antonovna, when Razumov's identity is at stake. For example, when threatened with the possibility that Sophia will find out the truth about Haldin, a large 'K' appears in the margin beside the following words: 'he felt the need of perfect safety with its freedom from direct lying' (MS, 1079).

[11] Jean-Aubry, *Life and Letters*, ii. 146.

manuscript, the serial text, and the first edition we can reconstruct a history of this novel which shows that the role of the 'captain's wife' nevertheless continued to survive in Conrad's imagination, resurfacing throughout his career. Yet, while these sources suggest a much greater continuity in Conrad's interest in his female protagonist, they also point to a dramatic shift in her presentation, a shift that reflects Conrad's response to genre, readership, and publishing contexts during his lifetime.

The opening pages of the holograph is all that remains of the short story, in which the narrator refers to 'Archie' Powell's boat as *The Nellie*, thus linking the short story with the period of *Heart of Darkness* (1899). The first page bears the cancelled title 'Explosives, a Ship-Board Tale' (already changed from 'Dynamite'), which was replaced by the title eventually used for the serial version: 'Chance, a Tale with Comments'.[12] The change of title for the serial in 1912 suggests a major shift of emphasis during the creation of the novel. By dropping the reference to a 'shipboard tale' from the title, Conrad deliberately played down the nautical theme. While elements of the short story survive in the final text (the opening setting in the Thameside eating-house, the narrative of the young Powell's initiation into seamanship, his 'chance' encounter with his namesake, the older Powell), a number of details and incidents, later cut for both serial and book, suggest that the novel had already undergone some important changes of direction during the early stages of its creation.

The first pages of the manuscript show Conrad deliberately playing to the *Blackwood's* audience for which the story had been originally intended, a 'gentlemen' readership of a journal whose editorial preference was for tales of seamanship and imperial adventure.[13] Powell addresses his companions as 'gentlemen', and as 'yachtsmen', rather than as professional sailors, thus making an inclusive gesture towards the *Blackwood's* readers

---

[12] Conrad mentions the new title in a letter to J. B. Pinker of 12 May, 1905 (Berg Collection).

[13] For the pervading atmosphere of *Blackwood's*, see Mrs Margaret Oliphant, *Annals of a Publishing House: William Blackwood and His Sons* (Edinburgh and London: William Blackwood and Sons, 1897), i. 100. She remarks on the intention of its founder, 'to make his place of business a centre of literary society, a sort of literary club where men of letters might find a meeting-place'.

who may themselves have been 'week-end' yachters on the reaches of the Thames. At the same time Conrad established his narrator's authority over his readers, with the suggestion of a more professional form of seamanship from which they were excluded: 'You are but yachtsmen after all' (MS, 1).

The manuscript shows that the opening passages of 'Explosives' clearly emphasised the autobiographical element. Powell, identifying himself with the professional sailors whose trade had declined in the 1880s and 1890s with the advent of the steamship, invites his audience, both inside and outside the frame of the tale, to share in his memories of a former life (Conrad, too had suffered unemployment as a direct result of this technological development). Conrad drew attention to the use of the flashback to open the story, the eyes of the speaker: 'sparkling with the intoxication of a reminiscence coming up from the depths of memory' (MS, 1). The intensity of Powell's reminiscences of his youth suggests that 'Explosives' will develop as a 'rites of passage' narrative, in the manner of 'Youth' (written in 1898), with its strongly autobiographical component.[14] The style of Powell's narration sets the mood for a 'shipboard tale' and establishes the prominence and authority of his voice. We can presume that Conrad initially intended to extend Powell's character, establishing *him* as a main protagonist whose role we would expect to be given at least equal weight as that of the 'captain's wife'.

Yet the continuity between the opening of 'Youth' and the 'Explosives' manuscript of 1906 can be demonstrated by examining the short story 'Falk', which forms an intermediary link between the two. Written in 1901, later than 'Youth', Conrad had also prepared 'Falk' for *Blackwood's*, although it was rejected by that magazine due to its invocation of cannibalism.

---

[14] The serial opens with the second paragraph of the manuscript: 'He had seen us out of the window coming off to dine in an overloaded dinghy of a fourteen-ton yawl belonging to our host and skipper . . .' (Sunday Magazine, 21 Jan. 1912, 1–2). The frame narrator, who continues to emphasise the 'we', thus avoids the impression that this story is going to be primarily about Powell. In the first edition, Conrad achieves a further refinement: 'I believe he had seen us out of the window coming to dine in the dinghy of a fourteen-ton yawl belonging to Marlow my host and skipper . . .' (3). Conrad immediately establishes the presence of the two main narrators, whose combative dialogue—'we were always tilting at each other' (93)—will later emerge as the locus of so many conflicting images of women.

It was never serialised (appearing for the first time in *Typhoon and Other Stories*, 1902), but again its narrative framework anticipated a *Blackwood's* audience, establishing the exchange of seamen's tales in a Thameside restaurant as in 'Youth'.[15]

However, most significantly, the allusions to 'Falk' in the 'Explosives' manuscript strongly indicate a shift in the genesis of *Chance* towards the theme of human degeneration, a Darwinian motif which appears not only in 'Falk', but in another novel of this period, *The Secret Agent* (1907), and the later *Victory* (1915).[16] In 'Explosives' a comic preamble to the narrative describes Powell's altercations with a slovenly waiter. This appears neither in the serial nor in the book version of *Chance*.[17] As in 'Falk', the interlude introduces a Wellsian touch to the description of a lower-middle-class eating establishment, drawing attention to the sordidness and decrepitude of the scene and the use of the food metaphor to symbolise the degenerative condition of man in the survival of primitive instincts (also resembling the descriptions of Verloc's eating habits in *The Secret Agent*), as Marlow

levered about and sliced half-raw lumps of animal matter before him with masterful dexterity; but sinking back in the disenchanted weariness of a man who had dined badly, he left us to deal by ourselves with the specimens of vegetable refuse which the waiter (a greasy dingy servant in a tailcoat) classified learnedly as potatoes and cabbage. (MS, 8)

The correspondences between 'Falk' and 'Explosives' are explicit, as the frame narrator also emphasises the dingy setting, where there was 'a strange mustiness in everything', and where the

---

[15] See Norman Sherry, *Conrad's Eastern World* (Cambridge: Cambridge University Press, 1966), 296. Sherry identifies the 'small river hostelry' as either the Bull Inn, Chatham or the Lobster Arms, Hole Haven, where Conrad and G. F. W. Hope stopped during their trips on the Thames in Hope's yacht *Nellie*.

[16] For Darwin's influence on Conrad see Allan Hunter, *Joseph Conrad and the Ethics of Darwinism: The Challenges of Science* (London and Canberra: Croom Helm, 1983; Redmond O'Hanlon, *Joseph Conrad and Charles Darwin: The Influence of Scientific Thought on Conrad's Fiction* (Edinburgh: Salamander Press, 1984); Tony Tanner, 'Joseph Conrad and the Last Gentleman', *Critical Quarterly* 28 (1986), 109–42; George Levine, *Darwin and the Novelists: Patterns of Science in Victorian Fiction* (Cambridge, Mass.: Harvard University Press, 1988).

[17] Batchelor, *Life*, 207, remarks briefly on the similarity between the opening of the *Chance* MS and that of 'Falk'.

dinner, served by a 'decrepid' waiter, was 'execrable' (145). The occasion reminded the narrator of 'primeval man', who, 'evolving the first rudiments of cookery from his dim consciousness, scorched lumps of flesh at a fire of sticks in the company of other good fellows' (145–6). In 'Falk', the references to degenerative behaviour anticipates the revelation of Falk's cannibalism. Likewise, Powell's comic scene in the restaurant in 'Explosives' (cut for serial and book), in which he accuses the waiter of poisoning a fly with the Worcester Sauce, offers a presentiment[18] of the human poisoning later in the novel (de Barral's attempt on the life of Anthony): 'Do you mean to say the thing died a natural death—eh? From fright I suppose. The looks of some of the stuff you've the cheek to put before people are enough to frighten a fly to death' (MS, 1).[19]

Such a plot, conceived in a different setting, *had* been on Conrad's mind well before he made his first reference to 'Dynamite'. In 1894, Conrad wrote to Marguerite Poradowska describing the narrative on which he was currently working (thought to be the yet unnamed *An Outcast of the Islands*).[20] The plot he described was set in the Malay peninsula, but contained a situation of sexual 'enslavement' which led to both a poisoning through jealousy, followed by a suicide. Neither a poisoning nor a suicide occurs in the finished *Outcast*, but both occur in *Chance*. It is possible that Conrad subsequently decided to use this plot for 'Dynamite', transferring the scenario to a shipboard 'explosion' of passions over a captain's wife.

The *Chance* manuscript also demonstrates that Conrad had originally developed the 'degenerative' theme further through the role of Captain Anthony (surprisingly, given Anthony's final part as 'knight' in the book version of *Chance*). Anthony's observations are greatly extended in the manuscript. In a passage cancelled for both serial and book, Anthony extensively describes his encounter with Flora as an 'abduction', an impulsive 'capture of a woman', an act which he consciously recognises as the

---

[18] Paul Kirschner (ed.), *Typhoon and Other Stories* (Harmondsworth: Penguin, 1990), 299 n. 32, on Conrad's use of 'the device of a narrator telling his story to a small group of listeners, with a proleptic setting or prologue'.

[19] The page number here refers to the second batch of papers in the MS, which Conrad renumbered, starting again with the number 1. All references from now on refer to the sequence starting with number 1 of the second batch.

[20] 18? March 1894, CL 1, 171.

survival of primitive behaviour, having something of the 'age of caverns business' about it (MS, 847). His attitude is consistent with the preamble to 'Falk', in which the narrator talks of primitive man sitting back after a meal 'among the gnawed bones to tell his artless tales of experience—the tales of hunger and hunt—and of women perhaps!' (146).[21]

If the evolutionary motif of 'Falk' prefigured an important theme of an earlier version of *Chance*, we must remember that in 'Falk' it is still the behaviour of the *male* protagonist who occupies Conrad the most. Hermann's silent niece offers a powerful physical presence but her principal function is to provide a pretext for discussing the relationship between ethics and survival in the practice of seamanship. In 'Explosives' the woman's role may have originally functioned in a similar way (as a catalyst of the action), if the story was to focus on the overflow of male passions exacerbated by the presence of a woman on board ship (this element of the story survives most strongly in *Chance* in the Franklin episodes).

The leisurely tone of the opening paragraphs of 'Explosives' shows that initially Conrad was in no hurry to introduce the female protagonist, and Captain Anthony's extended role in the manuscript focuses on *his* actions, especially in his apologia for Flora's 'abduction', and in his long declaration of love. Many of these passages have been retained for the serial, where Flora's character remains somewhat obscured by Anthony's protracted speeches. Yet however self-critical Anthony appears in the earlier versions of *Chance*, the portrait of a decadent Anthony, following his lustful cravings, consistent with the theme of 'Falk', contrasts dramatically with the sea captain's ultimate self-image in the book version of *Chance* as the scrupulously chivalrous knight. In the book, Marlow describes Anthony as 'the rescuer of the most forlorn damsels of modern times, the man of violence, gentleness and generosity' (217) (but his behaviour in the novel is what we would now describe as 'passive-aggressive'). The final version allows for a far more ironic view of chauvinism, a portrait of male 'aggression' which is expressed, not

---

[21] See also Tony Tanner, ' "Gnawed Bones" and "Artless Tales": Eating and Narrative in Conrad', in Norman Sherry (ed.), *Joseph Conrad: A Commemoration* (London: Macmillan, 1976), 17–36. Tanner also describes the re-emergence of the theme in *Victory* (1915).

through physical brutality, but, paradoxically, through restraint. As I outlined in Chapter 4, it is Anthony's refusal to consummate the marriage which hurts Flora the most. In the absence, in the book version, of his extended declarations of love for Flora, we sense the pain of her abandonment far more acutely:

It was a rejection, a casting out; nothing new to her. But she who supposed all her sensibility dead by this time, discovered in herself a resentment of this ultimate betrayal. She had no resignation for this one. (310)

Conrad here provides a much subtler and more refined portrait of the heroine, one that is produced by a dramatic shift in theme. The emphasis on Flora's 'captivity' is still present, but the perspective has changed. The focus now falls on the woman and her entrapment on Anthony's ship. Conrad presents the 'abduction' as a trope of romantic fiction, as a means of showing the gap between Flora's equivocal sense of identity and her romantic representation, in which the storytellers make her into the victim of culturally defined assumptions about woman's passivity: 'one of those Redskin stories where the noble savages carry off a girl' (283).[22] It is no longer the atavistic male behaviour which is foregrounded in the narrative. Conrad now draws attention to the aesthetic constructions of a civilised world, to its artful, rather than 'artless' tales, to the narratives of chivalry and romance that imprison the female protagonist in her ivory tower.

The manuscript's emphasis on Anthony's role as more literally aggressive also left greater room for Powell's position as appropriate *moral* choice for Flora at the end of the narrative. Powell's moral outpourings in the early cancelled passages of the manuscript again closely resemble the narrator of 'Falk', who refers to those who have been 'pampered by the land' (145). This outlook is later inherited by Marlow, who becomes the moral arbiter of events in both the serial and book version of *Chance*. In the short story we feel that Conrad is building Powell's character on the basis of the young sailor's strong moral credentials, giving him a far more conventional position as 'hero' of the tale.

---

[22] Probably a reference to Mark Twain's satirical attack on Fenimore Cooper ('Fenimore Cooper's Literary Offences'). Marlow claims that he liked 'Redskin stories' (283).

As Conrad reduced Powell's character for the book version and
Captain Anthony's role increased in complexity, the suggestion
of a romance between Powell and Flora becomes less obvious
and more restrained. Ultimately the ending of *Chance* is uneasy.
But it is less schematic than the end of 'Falk', with its marriage
of two monumental, almost parodic representations of the masculine and the feminine. The final version of *Chance* sustains the
shift towards the novel's new presiding theme, one which both
questions and undermines the conventions of romance.

I

The major thematic changes probably occurred after 1909 with
Conrad's commission to write a woman's romance for *The
New York Herald*.[23] The new context demanded a reorientation
of the narrative to accommodate a new audience. The *New York
Herald* enjoyed a wide circulation that had been established
in the entrepreneurial spirit of the second half of the nineteenth
century. Moreover, new marketing strategies ensured that this
wider audience included women. In an early history of American journalism Willard Pleyer remarked that

with the rise of evening and Sunday papers and the increase in the amount
of display advertising, the importance of making special appeals to
women readers was more fully appreciated by newspaper editors and
publishers.[24]

As a result the large Sunday editions of the New York papers
gave considerable prominence to sections devoted to women
readers.

Conrad's earlier narratives had been serialised in sober contexts without illustrations, such as *Blackwood's Magazine* or *T.P.'s
Weekly*, where *Nostromo* was surrounded by advertisements for
tobacco and assurances that 'Alcoholic Excess *Can* be Cured

---

[23] See again letter of 2 June 1913 to J. B. Pinker, where Conrad suggested a rift
in continuity in the creation of *Chance*. He claimed that 'the rest of the novel' was
not written until 1911, and that the earlier parts belonged to 'some other novel' (Jean-
Aubry, *Life and Letters*, ii. 146).
[24] Willard Grosvenor Pleyer, *The History of American Journalism* (Boston:
Houghton Mifflin, 1927), 399.

under Direction'.[25] Instalments of *Chance*, however, appeared in the Sunday Magazine section of *The Herald* in 1912 flanked by articles on fashion, domestic matters, women's features, advertisements for Pear's Soap and the latest hairstyles. The publicity campaign for the serial confirmed the extraordinary transition in the marketing of Conrad's later novels. Prior to publication in *The Herald*, a full-page advertisement for the new serial was aimed at the women readers of the paper, who were assured that the 'World's Most Famous Author of Sea Stories' now 'Aimed to Interest Women Particularly' (see Fig. 1).[26]

Conrad's subsequent transformation of the text was considerable. To meet the demands of a wider audience, he made fundamental structural changes to his early 'Explosives' narrative. He altered the location, splitting it between sea and land, and, as the serial progressed, shifted the focus of the story from Powell's initial tale of the lonely sailor to the isolation of the young girl, alienated from a catalogue of received perspectives of 'the feminine'. He did, however, develop a 'modernist' role for both the frame narrator (a writer) and Marlow (a storyteller). As self-conscious mediators of the text they ruminate on the nature and meaning of the narrative act while, at the same time, they direct their subjective gazes towards the female protagonist, preserving what Marlow calls the 'hackneyed' illusions 'without which the male creature cannot get on' (86). Conrad retained the 'shipboard' element of the tale, but it was now subsumed within a larger frame in which the ship acted as a metaphor for the female protagonist's entrapment in a male construction of romance. It was presumably at this point in the development of the novel that Conrad introduced the additional female characters, the pernicious governess and an ardent 'feminist'. Aimed at the American readership, the narrative was now set against a background of recent topical issues including frauds in the financial world and a commentary on suffragist principles.

As we have seen in Chapter 4, *Chance*'s context reminds the reader not only of the psychological isolation of the female

[25] *T.P.'s Weekly*, 22 Jan. 1904, 119.

[26] *The New York Herald*, 14 Jan. 1912, Sunday Magazine Section, 8. See Cedric Watts on the marketing of *Chance* in Ian Willison, Warwick Gould, and Warren Chernaik (eds.), *Modernist Writers and the Marketplace* (Basingstoke: Macmillan, 1996).

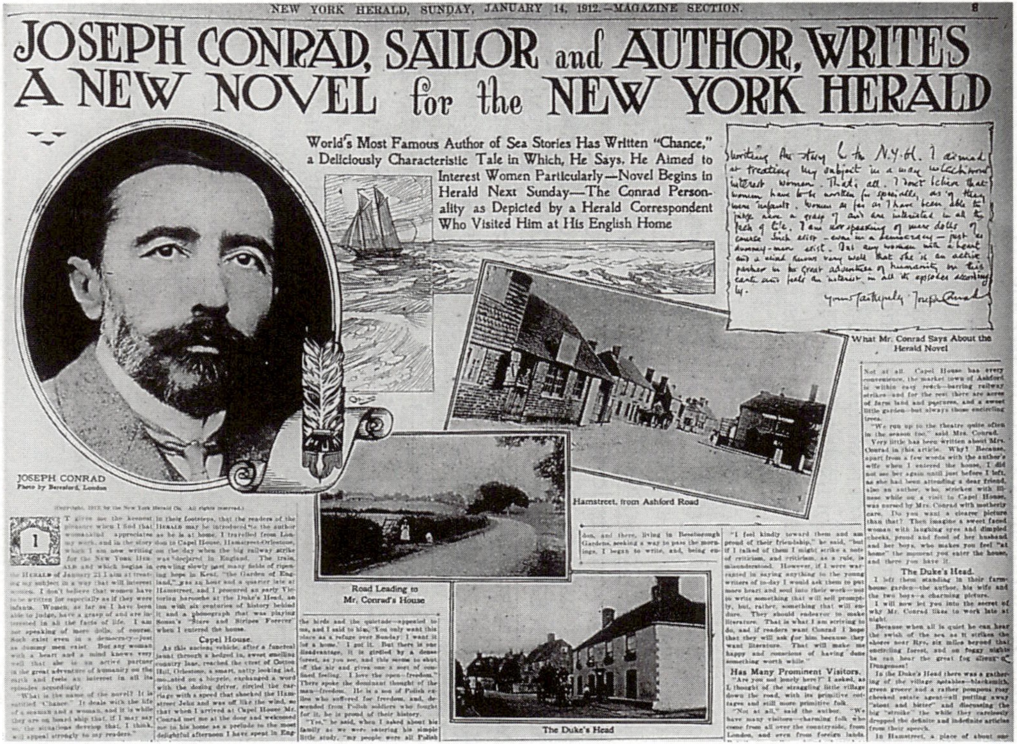

NEW YORK HERALD, SUNDAY, JANUARY 14, 1912.—MAGAZINE SECTION. 8

JOSEPH CONRAD, SAILOR and AUTHOR, WRITES A NEW NOVEL for the NEW YORK HERALD

World's Most Famous Author of Sea Stories Has Written "Chance," a Deliciously Characteristic Tale in Which, He Says, He Aimed to Interest Women Particularly—Novel Begins in Herald Next Sunday—The Conrad Personality as Depicted by a Herald Correspondent Who Visited Him at His English Home

JOSEPH CONRAD
Photo by Beresford, London

Writing the story for the N.Y.H. I aimed at treating my subject in a way which would interest women. That's all. I don't believe that women have to be written for specially, as if they were infants. Women as far as I have been able to judge have a grasp of and are interested in all the facts of life. I am not speaking of mere dolls of course. Such exist—even in a democracy—just as dummy-men exist. But any woman with a heart and a mind knows very well that she is an active partner in the great adventure of humanity on this earth and feels the interest in all its episodes accordingly.

Yours faithfully Joseph Conrad

What Mr. Conrad Says About the Herald Novel

Hamstreet, from Ashford Road

Road Leading to Mr. Conrad's House

The Duke's Head

Capel House.

Has Many Prominent Visitors.

The Duke's Head.

Fig. 1. 'World's Most Famous Author of Sea Stories . . . Aimed to Interest Women Particularly', interview with Conrad to promote *Chance*, *The New York Herald*, 14 January 1912, Sunday Magazine.

protagonist, but also of the endurance into the twentieth century of a widespread discussion about the ontological status of women. In 1867, E. L. Godkin had written in the *Nation* that 'woman's mind, body, social and political condition are now the subject of constant debate'.[27] By the turn of the century, queries about the 'nature' of women multiplied, accompanied by an increased demand for the vote. The themes discussed in *Chance* pervaded the journals and newspapers of the day. Marlow's voice on the subject of women is strikingly reminiscent of the dominant editorial tone of contemporary journals and newspapers, where women were frequently viewed through the lens of a Victorian reconstruction of chivalry. His remarks about a sense of 'honour' being a 'very fine medieval inheritance which women never got hold of' (56) suggest the kind of attitude expressed by 'The Spectator' of *Living Age*. This writer spoke of 'Women's Code of Honour' as something altogether missing from their sense of public life, a failing that could be used as evidence for denying women the franchise, since it might cause them to 'vote for persons rather than principles'.[28]

Such remarks were often accompanied by visual material that imposed further limitations on the range of available representations of women in popular publications. In 1912 *The Canadian Magazine* published a 'Study in Popular Aesthetics' entitled 'The Witchery of Woman's Smile', in which J. D. Logan gave a list of 'typical' feminine poses, flanked by illustrations: 'The seductive smile of the designing woman . . . the arch smile of the coquette . . . the supercilious smile of the élite.'[29] Even the eminent British Suffragist, Millicent Garrett Fawcett, could not resist the tendency to codify images of her sex when she spoke of the struggle to 'raise the ideal type of womanhood'.[30] Throughout *Chance* Conrad responded to the contemporary

[27] E. L. Godkin, *Nation*, 1867, quoted in Alfred Habegger, *Henry James and the 'Woman Business'* (Cambridge: Cambridge University Press, 1994), 9.

[28] Spectator, 'Women's Code of Honour,' *Living Age* 271 (Boston, 23 Dec. 1911), 762. Virginia Woolf also discusses the issue of women's honour in a late scene of *The Voyage Out* (1915; completed 1912).

[29] J. D. Logan, 'The Witchery of Woman's Smile: A Study in Popular Aesthetics', *The Canadian Magazine* 39 (Toronto, Oct. 1912), 522.

[30] Millicent Garrett Fawcett, 'Home and Politics', transcript of a speech delivered to the London Society for Women's Suffrage at Toynbee Hall, London (undated), 8. In Glasow University Library, Special Collection.

preoccupation with defining 'woman', exposing the dilemma of women who find themselves, as Jane Miller has observed, enticed into narratives 'which may reduce them by exalting them'.[31]

Thus the new publishing context presented a perplexing dilemma for Conrad, one that challenged and informed the direction of his late work. Unexpectedly, Conrad's text raises the question of how to determine the character and expectations of the prospective woman reader. Who was she? To what extent did she represent a construct of the marketing strategies of the newspaper?

Reading the serialised *Chance* in *The New York Herald* alerts us to the issue of gender and context in relation to reading practices. Kate Flint has written of the 'silence concerning woman as reader' which 'reverberates through almost all the reader-response criticism of the 1960s and 70s'.[32] Michael Riffaterre, Wolfgang Iser, and Hans Robert Jauss maintained that the text remains the dominant location of readers' expectations and responses.[33] Such theories are uncomplicated by the reader's gender, and unspecified in these cases. Amongst feminist critics who have addressed this issue, Diana Fuss clearly outlines the problem: to determine the gender of the reader invites a questioning of gender roles in a much wider frame, since, she states, 'readers, like texts, are constructed; they inhabit reading practices rather than create them *ex nihilo*.'[34] The serialised *Chance* shows how reading practices are constructed by the *context* of publication. *The Herald* encouraged a female readership with women's pages presenting topical issues and romance fiction alongside advertisements for fashion, beauty aids, and domestic appliances. But its projection of female images was nevertheless limited, carefully censored by a patronising editorial tone which endorsed woman's role as nurturer, idealising her beauty and domesticity.

[31] Jane Miller, *Seductions: Studies in Reading and Culture* (London: Virago, 1990), 2.

[32] Kate Flint, *The Woman Reader 1837–1914* (Oxford: Oxford University Press, 1993), 33.

[33] See Hans Robert Jauss, 'Literary History as a Challenge to Literary Theory', *New Literary History* 2 (1970), 14, who does at least suggest that a reader's response is to some extent dependent on historical period and 'horizon of expectations'.

[34] Diana Fuss, *Essentially Speaking* (London: Routledge, 1989), 35.

The text of *Chance*, read in this context, reflects the author's response to a new locus of publication for his work. The serialised novel draws attention, as we saw in Chapter 4, to the constructions of female identity imposed upon the heroine by the male narrators—the pure young girl, the innocent, tragic heroine of romance, the dutiful daughter and wife. It also encompasses a generic shift towards forms favoured by a popular readership: not just the romance, but the sensation novel, historical novel, and detective fiction. But in the context of *The Herald*, Conrad's oblique presentation of a woman's struggle to form an autonomous identity sustains a double irony. It plays on the reductiveness of conventional images of women propagated not only by the romance genre, but also by magazine advertisements and illustrations for popular fiction. Text and context often conflict in incentives, the female reader of *Chance* being offered a critique of the very images that construct her as reader of *The Herald*.

The context also demonstrates the contemporaneity of the text. *The Herald* ran pro- and anti-suffragist articles whose tones are reflected in the inconsistency of Marlow's view of women in the novel, and in his ironic presentation of Mrs Fyne the feminist, writing her tract on women's education. '1912 Is Year of Promise to the Suffragette Leaders' appeared in *The Herald* on 1 January 1912.[35] The following week a headline ran: 'Miss Shaw's Anti-Suffrage Sketch is produced at the Hotel Astor'.[36] Like the narrators of *Chance*, the editors gestured towards female emancipation. But they presented articles on this subject that continued to circumscribe woman's status. Under the title 'Man's Fair Counterpart and Stories of Her Doings of a Day', the reports on the 'New Woman' only covered 'suitable' professions—fashion, nursing, secretarial work. An article on a 'Nurse to Souls' (2 July 1911, 13) carried an illustration closely resembling the pose used to show Mrs Fyne caring for Flora in the instalment of *Chance* for 3 March 1912. The juxtaposition of text and illustration proves to be particularly ironic in this case since Mrs Fyne's relationship to Flora is ambiguous in the novel. In spite of her feminist principles, she ceases to support Flora's attempts to find independence when Flora elopes

---

[35] *New York Herald*, 1 Jan. 1912, 22.   [36] Ibid. 6 Jan. 1912, 20.

with her brother. Conrad presents his portrait of the 'feminist' as yet another construct, offering limited potential to his heroine. His emphasis on Mrs Fyne's masculinity, for example, with her 'ruddy out-of-doors complexion' wearing 'blouses with a starched front like a man's shirt, a stand-up collar and a long necktie' fits in well with *The Herald*'s most popular image of the 'liberated' woman, posing in walking boots and culottes (18 June 1911, 14). Again Conrad may have also been commenting on the 'New Woman' novel of the 1890s, whose heroines often provided a less radical image than we might assume from the popular image. As Tess Coslett has pointed out, these novels had frequently presented unthreatening or conventional images of women during this period, as in Annie Holdsworth's *Joanna Traill, Spinster*[37] whose heroine appears, 'not as a daring "Modern Woman", but as endearingly old-fashioned';[38] or caught between eras, as in Ella Hepworth Dixon's *The Story of a Modern Woman*, where the suggestion is made that the heroine had been 'born too late for the simple days of the fifties', when a woman expected no more than a good marriage, 'yet too soon' to expect her parents to 'equip a girl for the world as much as her brother'.[39] The tone of the *Herald* in 1912, on the subject of women's professions, suggests the endurance into the early decades of the twentieth century of this situation, and in his portraits of both Mrs Fyne and Flora, Conrad shows women who shift between conflicting expectations and assumptions about their role.

The Herald frequently vindicated the image of 'The Angel in the House', while, as we have seen, Conrad parodied its creator in his characterisation of the poet (and 'domestic tyrant') Carleon Anthony. His role produces further ironies in the context of the paper, where articles on how to iron your husband's shirts and training schools for marriage often appeared on the 'Woman's Page'. One report extols the virtue of a woman who nobly 'Gives up the Stage to Darn Socks', while an episode of *Chance* appears alongside an advertisement for 'Anthracite',

---

[37] Annie Holdsworth's *Joanna Traill, Spinster* (London: Heinemann, 1894).

[38] See Tess Coslett, *Woman to Woman: Female Friendship in Victorian Fiction* (Brighton: The Harvester Press, 1988), 143.

[39] Ella Hepworth Dixon, *The Story of a Modern Woman* (London: Heinemann, 1894), 14.

illustrating the domesticated woman poised over the stove (10 March 1912, 11). The juxtaposition is particularly jarring given Flora's need to provide for a dependent father. Moreover, the positioning of the illustration on the page meant that it could easily be mistaken for an illustration for *Chance*. The ambiguity is only partially removed by the insertion of the word 'Announcements' between serial text and advertisement illustration.

Conrad's narratorial strategy enabled him to exploit the context of the novel in his presentation of an isolated woman in search of an independent self. Flora, who resists interpretation within the text of *Chance*, is alienated both from the discussions of Marlow and his interlocutor over the nature of femininity, and from the editorial tone of the newspaper itself. Nevertheless, Conrad was to some extent restricted by his context, since he was forced to capitulate to the marketing incentives of the newspaper that reduced not only women, but even the authors of its fiction, to marketable images. The promotional article for *Chance* adopted a twofold strategy, pushing the image of Conrad as 'Famous Author of Sea Stories' as well as his new promise 'to Interest Women Particularly'. Readers' expectations had to be fulfilled. To show that Conrad was now a writer for women, his gallery of female characters were reproduced each week in the illustrations. Yet the widespread practice of syndication, which universalised illustrations for magazines and newspapers, produced homogeneous images of women.[40] Flora's wooden poses in the illustrations for *Chance* bear greater resemblance to the fashion advertisements that promise 'What Every Woman Wants', than to Conrad's elusive heroine.

Likewise the image of Conrad as author of the sea was sustained by recognisable, but often reductive iconographic tropes used to illustrate the text. In this respect, the early pages of the manuscript version of *Chance*, which promised, in its opening pages, a typical Conradian sea story from the era of 'Youth', appropriately fulfilled the thrust of the marketing campaign that relied on the well-known image of the author. The first

---

[40] See Mark Monmonier, *Maps With the News* (Chicago: University of Chicago Press, 1989), 77–84 for a discussion of the syndication of newspaper illustrations in the United States from 1884 onwards.

two instalments of the serial (21 and 28 January 1912) are almost solely devoted to Powell's tale and both carry illustrations of Powell's first ship. Given the importance of the visual component of serialised fiction their presence suggests the editorial decision to launch the novel on the basis of Conrad's established reputation, rather than on the new image of him as writer for women.

The illustration for 28 January 1912 presents Powell as a lone figure on board ship, leaning on the rail against a background of water, sail, and ships' chandlery. Magazine illustration for this period depended on recognition and repetition, and L. A. Shafer's drawings for *Chance* typically find their antecedents in the familiar disposition of figures in landscape or interior originating in seventeenth-century northern genre painting.[41] The illustration of Powell and his ship is even more derivative of a closer contemporary, Whistler, whose work on Thameside landscapes, such as the etching *Rotherhithe* or *Wapping on Thames* (1860) was also influenced by the genre tradition.

Powell's familiar pose also refers directly to his presentation in the text as isolated sailor. Conrad retained many passages for the serial from the manuscript (greatly reduced for the book), which express the young sailor's responses to the loneliness he experienced in boarding his first ship. The illustration bears a caption taken from the text of the serial: 'There wasn't anybody there to care whether he ever put foot on land again' (28 January 1912). The Powell of the serial strikes a fuller and more endearing figure than that of the book. The serial version includes Powell's terse portrait of an unsympathetic landlady, and his vivid expression of adolescent impatience with an elderly aunt who failed to understand his overwhelming passion for the sea. These autobiographical moments bear a resemblance to Conrad's own experience of Uncle Tadeusz Bobrowski's resistance to his desire to go to sea as a youth.[42]

Thus in the serial, illustration and story form an autonomous narrative unit in which the reception of a single instalment is mediated through the perspective of a familiar iconographic pose. Powell's story offers a poignant literary romanticisation

---

[41] See Anne Hollander, *Moving Pictures* (London and Cambridge, Mass.: Harvard University Press, 1991), 346–8. [42] Karl, *Three Lives*, 117–19.

of a received image of the lonely sailor and the sea, one which corresponds to a powerful visual tradition. With its autobiographical component the instalment as a whole appropriately fulfils the promotion of Conrad as 'Writer of the Sea'.

Yet Powell's story is largely redundant in the final narrative. The Powell of the serial offers a more satisfactory characterisation in its own right. But in this version, which still remains much closer to that of the short story, Conrad's portrait of the lonely Powell competes excessively with *Flora*'s isolation, pairing her too obviously with the innocent hero of romance embarking on his first quest. Conrad's strategy in the book is less conventional. Powell's presence in the final version is insubstantial, sketched thinly throughout the text, his status as hero replaced by that of Captain Anthony, whom Flora first marries. The shadowy, unformed figure of Powell in the book version, with his 'want of experience' (247) suggests a subtler parallel with the elusive Flora, who, as Marlow emphasises 'had nothing to fall back upon, no experience but such as to shake her belief in every human being' (217). Both characterisations are incomplete, both fail to come into being, neither reaching full expression of identity. Conrad hints at a further development, implicit in the fruition of their relationship when Anthony dies, but it is one that is never realised within the narrative, only projected beyond the limits of the text itself. Like the ultimate reorientation of Anthony's character for the book, the final changes in Powell's presentation from serial to book were essential for Conrad's more refined delineation of Flora. Moreover, Powell's voice in the serial, inherited from the short story, is too easily identifiable with Conrad's own, creating a flaw in the network of distancing viewpoints that isolate the heroine within the text.

II

Conrad's final revisions for the book reduced the remaining passages of the short story to its surviving remnant, where they do indeed seem almost to belong to a different novel. The digressive Powell plot had provided a valuable impetus for the serial, where it conveniently conformed to Conrad's best known and most marketable image. The publicity for the book, however, was now taken care of *outside* the text itself, so that Conrad was released to some extent from the limitations of marketing strategies. Here the dust-jacket, and not the illustrations for the text, combined the two marketing drives—Conrad as writer of the sea and writer for women—in an image depicting a woman on board ship (see Fig. 2). It was only after the revisions for the book, where Powell recedes as fully characterised hero, that Conrad's portrait of 'a captain's wife' finally emerged with greatest confidence.

Conrad also achieved his new focus for the book by tightening Marlow's garrulous narration. In the serial version he conformed to the editorial policy which ostensibly appeased the female readership, giving them, in Powell, a suitably heroic match for the heroine, offering drawn-out explanations of the moral structure of seamanship, and presenting Marlow's defensive apologies for his misogyny. While Marlow's voice swerves between the empathetic and the patronising, many of his more misogynistic remarks are followed, in the serial version, by a hasty retraction. When he relates Flora's response to the boarding of her husband's ship, he dilutes his acid tone 'it is lucky that small things please women' with a placatory remark: 'because without it their lot would be even harder than it is'.[43] Likewise, Marlow carefully explains the motives behind the story of the vindictive governess's behaviour in the serial: 'She had married very young, out of a suddenly impoverished and bereaved home, a man of promise who died at the end of six months, leaving her absolutely destitute'.[44] This kind of conciliatory remark is cut from the book version, removing all sense of apology for Marlow's rebarbative voice, and all superfluous explanations. Instead, Conrad now drew attention to the fluctuations of Marlow's narrative, allowing them to speak for themselves. Thus he threw the onus of interpretation back on the reader.

In the final version Conrad increased Marlow's dominance over the narration as a whole. Between parts one and two of the book version Conrad cut a protracted conversation between Marlow and Fyne on a train to London in which Marlow

---

[43] *New York Herald*, Sunday Magazine, 14 April 1912, 6.
[44] Ibid. 18 Feb. 1912, 6.

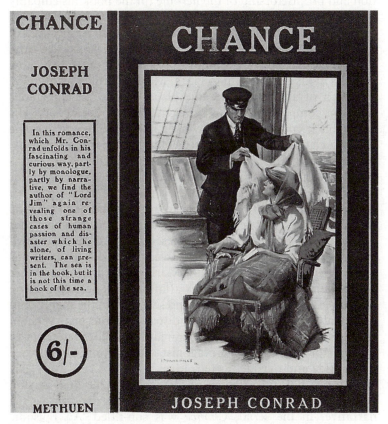

On the spine:

CHANCE

JOSEPH CONRAD

In this romance,
which Mr. Con-
rad unfolds in his
fascinating and
curious way, part-
ly by monologue,
partly by narra-
tive, we find the
author of "Lord
Jim" again re-
vealing one of
those strange
cases of human
passion and dis-
aster which he
alone, of living
writers, can pre-
sent. The sea is
in the book, but it
is not this time a
book of the sea.

6/-

METHUEN

On the front cover:

CHANCE

JOSEPH CONRAD

Fig. 2. Dust-jacket for the first English edition of *Chance*, London: Methuen, 1913.

implies Fyne's jealousy of Flora's relationship with Captain Anthony, suggesting that Fyne has learned 'in his seeing, solemn way . . . to care for the luckless Flora'.[45] Fyne's sexual interest in Flora conflicts with Marlow's own growing sense of affection and proprietorship of the heroine (in the book his empathy with Anthony suggests that Marlow is a *doppelgänger* for the 'knight'). In the final version Conrad unified all perspectives of the central female figure in Marlow's unreliable, possessive gaze.

Thus the full irony of Conrad's presentation of Marlow now emerges in his relationship to Flora. Marlow's role as storyteller in search of a romantic heroine places him in an ambiguous position, complicated by his subjective role in her history. His misogynistic comments about women and femininity undermine his own claims to a feminine sensibility, while Flora's increasing resistance to a conventional female role reduces his outrageous generalisations to an absurdity. His provocative claim for women's lack of a code of 'honour' is therefore unsettled by his dubious attraction to Flora in her role as 'victim' of a romantic tragedy. Besides, no one demonstrates a more actively chivalrous position than Flora herself, in her self-sacrifice for a dependent father. Thus Flora is caught between opposing assumptions about what it is to be a woman. Marlow tells Fyne that 'what your wife cannot tolerate in this affair is Miss de Barral being what she is' (171), yet he himself presents her in the highly conventional pose of the damsel in distress. In the final version, where the complex narration is united by Marlow's account of Flora's story, the female protagonist occupies an uneasy place both inside and outside his narrative.

Conrad's policy to tighten the structure of the final version is also reflected in the changes in subtitle and divisions of the narrative. In the serial, *Chance* was sub-titled 'An Episodic Tale, with Comments', implying a lack of structure, a whimsical and fragmentary dissemination of the text. The 'commentary' emerges in the didactic tone of the narration, and the narrators' diversions on moral and philosophical issues and the nature of literary form. Conrad dropped the didactic element of the title for the book, again restoring interpretative responsibility to the reader. The division of the book into 'A Tale in Two Parts',

[45] *New York Herald*, Sunday Magazine, 21 April 1912, 6.

that of 'Damsel' and 'Knight' introduces a sharper parody of the romance form, as well as drawing attention to the rhetorical jousting of Marlow and his interlocutor. The presence of a more rebarbative and more possessive Marlow means that the interlocutor's responses have a more dramatic effect on the reader. In the final version the first-person narrator's challenge to Marlow's outbursts—'Do you really believe what you have said?' (86)—more noticeably impedes the flow of his outrageous generalisations about women. When Marlow claims that 'compunction' is a sentiment 'rare in women', his interlocutor replies with an indignant 'Is it?' (144), undermining the authority of Marlow's voice with greater effect. The object of their dialogue is now to produce a definition of 'woman', while Marlow's sarcastic attribution of 'chivalrous feelings' to his sparring partner is undermined by his own adoption of a chivalrous role in relation to Flora.

Thus the book version also responded more effectively to the contemporary suffragist debate, and to the way in which the motif of chivalry had been appropriated as a potent signifier by the suffragette movement.[46] In Flora's ontological confusion, and in Marlow's ambivalent attitude to gender, his tendency to swerve between misogyny and identity with the female sex, we can see that Conrad's novel plays on the tension and ambiguity residing in a specifically contemporary conflict in the representation of gender.[47] Certainly within the woman's movement the denial

---

[46] In February 1912, for example, *The Common Cause*, the journal of the National Union of Women's Suffrage, adopted for its front cover an image of a female knight astride a horse, wielding a lance whose banner claims 'Justice to Women'. On 24 May 1912 the suffragist journal *Votes For Women* also carried an illustration of the female knight on its front cover. She is brandishing a banner inscribed with the words 'Prisoners of War'.

[47] See Lisa Tickner, *The Spectacle of Women: Imagery of the Suffrage Campaign 1907–14* (London: Chatto and Windus, 1987), 210–11. Tickner suggests that the appropriation of the figure of Joan of Arc during the final years of the Women's Social and Political Union campaign represents a defiance of order and convention 'in her virginity, transvestism and military vigilance', yet her subversion of femininity eluded the categories in which women traditionally held power ('in the domestic sphere, as courtesan, or as queen'). See also the abundant biographies in the period with such titles as Rosa Nouchette Carey, *Twelve Notable Good Women* (London: Hutchinson, 1901); C. C. Cairns, *Noble Women* (London and Edinburgh: T. C. and E. C. Jack, 1912); Henry Charles Moore, *Noble Deeds of the World's Heroines* (London: The Religious Tract Society, 1913). See also Ford Madox Ford, *Ladies Whose Bright Eyes* (first version, 1911), for a contemporary fictional ironisation of the female knight.

of romanticisations of 'femininity' existed alongside the militants' appropriation of a highly idealised image of transvestism, the usurpation of the traditionally male role of knight. Suffragette speeches drew attention to their resistance to received images of womanhood: 'when we speak of womanliness and the gentler qualities of the feminine nature, we must be careful not to mistake true for false'.[48] Yet Israel Zangwill's speech to the (militant) Women's Social and Political Union emphasised the adoption of a new, chivalric image by the women of the movement: 'self-sacrifice, fearlessness, endurance . . . these are the testimonies of your spirit, as they are the guarantees of your speedy and ineluctable victory.'[49]

While Conrad's final cuts for the book produced a keener ironisation of romance in a contemporary context, he simultaneously sacrificed many of the narrators' discussions about textuality and narrative dissemination. These passages from the serial version fall into a category of Conrad's work that can be more easily identified with his 'modernist' writing. The instalment for 18 February 1912 carries a suitable example of those cuts which, as I mentioned above, Robert Siegle regards as 'a loss to the Conrad canon'. The first-person narrator, himself a writer in this version, recognises in Marlow's account of de Barral's trial 'a fine subject for a short story . . . something for Edgar Poe—eh?' Marlow reprimands his interlocutor (a writer in the serial version) for his preferences for the printed story:

Oh! You are always on the watch for tales, tales to write. I must remark that this manner of looking on squirming humanity is somewhat heartless. But let that pass. For myself I prefer the tale one can watch, pursue, lose track of, pick up afresh and lose again, and then in the

---

[48] Millicent Garrett Fawcett, 'Home and Politics', transcription of a speech delivered at Toynbee Hall (London: London Society for Women's Suffrage, undated), in the University of Glasgow, Special Collection. Mrs Garrett Fawcett was unconvinced that militancy was the correct strategy by which to obtain the franchise.

[49] Israel Zangwill, 'The Sword and the Spirit', transcription of a speech given to the Women's Social and Political Union, 10 Nov. 1910, in the University of Glasgow Library, Special Collection. Zangwill, writer and Zionist, was famous for *The Children of the Ghetto* (1892). Conrad wrote to Jane Cobden Unwin on 22 February 1898 expressing his regret that he would miss meeting Zangwill at the Unwins (*CL* 2, 41).

silence, in the stillness of a tracker at fault listen to its distant sounds echoing in one's mind, or heart, or conscience. What to such an appeal can be the mere consecutiveness of the printed narration?[50]

In the exchange that follows Conrad mediates, through Marlow's scepticism, a variety of positions relating to the issue of oral versus written narration. Read in isolation, the discussion represents a stimulating modernist discourse on one of Conrad's predominant themes. We might indeed ask why he cut it from the book version of *Chance*.

One approach to understanding Conrad's final cuts is to take into account, not two, but three texts of *Chance*, with its development from rites of passage narrative, through its Darwinian motif, its ruminations on the conflicts of the male storyteller to its final emphasis on the frail, evanescent heroine. The serial version was moving towards a new direction in Conrad's work in which he closely responded to his new marketing contexts. But his confrontation of the gender issue was nevertheless limited by his retention of themes that belonged to an earlier period and were now inappropriate to the new emphasis on the heroine. Conrad unified the narration of the book by reducing the serial's tendency to wallow in digressions. He shifted the impetus for narration away from the somewhat abstract preoccupation of the male storyteller with his craft. These discussions would have gained greater impact, first in the context of the short story—the rites of passage narrative conveyed through the medium of seamen's reminiscences, then in the context of *The Herald*, where the interlocutor is himself a writer and the discussion takes place in a sea of print and reportage. But in the book version, where Marlow assumes the overarching control of a Jamesian author, the interlocutor's role as writer would compete too strongly with his position. The book shifts away from a discussion about different modes of storytelling (oral and written), focusing instead on the issue of how to tell a story about a woman when (male) expectations about women's roles limit her presentation within the genre of romance. In the final version it is Flora herself who has become the 'text', the location of endless interpretations of the 'damsel's' part.

[50] *New York Herald*, Sunday Magazine, 18 Feb. 1912, 6.

Yet her failure to inhabit fully the role of heroine simultaneously creates an ellipse at the centre of the narrative. Always viewed as a 'possible woman' (198), Flora has no means of realising her potential, since she is constantly entrapped in the plots imposed upon her. She resists Marlow's appropriation of a chivalrous role, and she also denies Anthony's role as knight, insisting that neither of them rescued her from suicide. She did not fear death, and was intent on marrying Anthony, not out of gratitude, but principally to save her father: 'If you will have it that you saved my life, then he has got it. It was not for me. Oh no! It was not for me that I—It was not fear!' (212). Characteristically, she never completes the statement, and the reader is left to discern her final meaning.

The shift in the narrators' concerns from textuality to gender implicitly draws attention to the close relationship between gender and genre.[51] As I remarked in Chapter 4, Marlow's difficulty in defining the identity of the female protagonist is extended to the classification of her story: 'The girl's life had presented itself to me as a tragi-comical adventure, the saddest thing on earth, slipping between frank laughter and unabashed tears' (282). It was 'not exactly a story for boys' (283), but neither is it exactly a romance. Rather than emphasising the narrators' 'modernist' preoccupations with the nature of textuality, Flora's evasions of the romance role, representing a gap in the narrative, now offer the final version of *Chance* its status as modernist text. Thus, as Conrad restored the focus of his early description of this story as one 'about a captain's wife', his final text gained from its sharper discussion of the question of 'being' a woman, inviting and challenging a more imaginative contemporary woman reader. This broader perspective of *Chance* enables us to view the novel in terms of Conrad's whole career rather than in the terms dictated by narrow critical assumptions about his contribution to modernism.

[51] For a theoretical perspective on the etymological relationship of gender and genre, see Jacques Derrida, 'The Law of Genre', trans. Avital Ronell, in W. J. T. Mitchell (ed.), *On Narrative* (Chicago: University of Chicago Press, 1981), 51–77.

6

Marketing for Women Readers

While revising *Chance* from serial to book in early June 1913, Conrad remarked on the importance of this novel's place in his career. Once he had spoken anxiously of *Chance*, but now he described it as 'the biggest piece of work I've done since Lord Jim'.[1] He was thinking of the novel in terms of a new theory of fiction developing during its creation. He wrote to Warrington Dawson that the 'sheer methods' constituted 'the only part of our art in which advance or at any rate novelty (of effects) is possible'.[2] In the final version of *Chance* Conrad experimented with a new degree of formal complexity while preserving something of his habitual scepticism in the treatment of the central figure and her relation to Marlow as principal narrator. Conrad's engagement with an unfamiliar publishing context had already, by his own testimony, prompted an innovative phase of his work.

Following the success of *Chance*, Conrad shaped his late career very deliberately. He wooed a wider audience, encouraged women readers, and paid close attention to the contexts of the serialisation of his novels. As we have seen, critics tend to dismiss this moment in his life as the signal of a steady decline, brought about by a failure of inspiration, an implicit lack of interest in his subject matter, and a distaste for the popular market. Yet his letters to publishers, editors, and illustrators of his work during this period offer a rather different story. Far from confirming the picture of Conrad's 'relaxed old age',[3] we glimpse instead a perspective of the writer embarking on a new phase of experimentation, to which he applied his habitual attention and professional rigour until the end of his life. In this chapter

---

[1] Letter to J. B. Pinker, 1 June 1913, *CL* 5, 229. Compare letter received by J. B. Pinker *c*.7 April 1913, before Conrad commenced revisions. *CL* 5, 208: 'It's the sort of stuff that *may* have a chance with the public'.

[2] Letter to Warrington Dawson, 1 June 1913, *CL* 5, 298.

[3] M. C. Bradbrook, *Joseph Conrad: Poland's English Genius* (Cambridge: Cambridge University Press, 1941), 11.

I shall discuss the new market, publishing contexts, and audience of the late work in the light of Conrad's serious remarks on what he identified as a radical shift in methodology during the later period of his career.

Conrad discussed the new direction of his fiction at length in a letter to F. N. Doubleday, written in December 1918. He expressed disappointment with Doubleday for failing to serialise *The Arrow of Gold* in the United States, since he was now shaping his fiction for a popular American market.[4] The letter offers more than a customary plea for publication. Here Conrad gives us a rare insight into the theoretical shift motivating the later fiction. First, he describes his latest work in terms of its innovative qualities, 'a method of presentation which was a new departure in Joseph Conrad's art'. He draws attention to both the visual and the retrospective elements of this text, claiming that its interest lay in 'so much portraiture of vanished years'. But while this might sound like a dismissive comment, he was anxious to emphasise the long gestation of the new method. He had completed *Arrow* rapidly—finishing it in ten months—but thought this might seem indecently short 'for a piece of creation depending on brush-strokes'. Although he had previously hesitated to take up the subject, nonetheless it was one that he had contemplated 'for some eighteen years'. 'Having found the mood', and with six years' experience of popularity with a wider market, Conrad now felt confident in a new medium.[5]

Conrad's reference to 'brush-strokes' intimates a style privileging the surface texture of the canvas, the immediacy of the visual effect. To some extent his remarks suggest a continuation with Walter Pater's influence, which had appeared in the *Preface* to The *Nigger of the 'Narcissus'*; Conrad also echoed Arthur Symons's description of Pater's *Imaginary Portraits*, where Symons refers to Pater's method as 'that of a very patient and elaborate brush-work' that gives 'concrete form to abstract ideas'.[6] But in addition Conrad expressed an understanding of popular serial publication in this letter. The new journals for which he was aiming, with their emphasis on the visual and the

---

[4] *The Arrow of Gold* initially appeared in *Lloyd's Magazine*, London, 1918–20.

[5] Letter to Doubleday, 21 Dec. 1918, Jean-Aubry, *Life and Letters*, ii. 213–14.

[6] Arthur Symons, 'Walter Pater', in *Studies in Two Literatures* (1897; New York: Garland Publishing, 1977), 173–4.

active, gave their readers immediate satisfaction in terms of pace and the anticipation of each new instalment. He claimed that the merits of a good serial could be reduced to 'the single point of "suspended interest"', a moment that represented a 'single feeling', combined with a 'certain form of action' (and here Conrad stresses the point: 'you'll notice I say *action*, not analysis'). This did not, however, preclude an adventure 'in which the deepest sensations (and not only the bodies) of the actors are involved'.[7] He cast the method in the terminology of drama rather than that of the novel, showing the need to hold the attention of the audience.[8] He emphasised action rather than explanation, the building of tension into a single 'scene', the conveyance of emotion through the disposition of figures within the movement of the plot. We may even discern in these remarks a deliberate courting of the burgeoning film industry.[9]

The tone of the letter contrasts dramatically with that of his earlier letters to Blackwood. In the late 1890s he had expressed his relief at not having to write for a market, and even as late as November 1911 he was still courting 'Maga' for 'Freya of the Seven Isles', implying, in a letter to Pinker, that he preferred the exclusivity of the journal, which 'had a good sort of public'.[10] But Conrad always kept one eye on the marketplace, and by 1918 he was ready to assure Doubleday that

I am sufficient of a democrat to detest the idea of being a writer of any 'coterie' of some small self-appointed aristocracy in the vast domain of art or letters. As a matter of feeling—not as a matter of business— I want to be read by many eyes and by all kinds of them, at that.[11]

We can only fully understand Conrad's accommodation of the new market by looking at the contexts and audience for which he was shaping the later novels. In fact Conrad had been testing out the popular market long before the publication of

---

[7] Jean-Aubry, *Life and Letters*, ii. 214.

[8] Conrad thought of the possibility of writing a dramatised version of *Arrow* (see letter to Eric Pinker, 8 Oct. 1922, TLS Berg).

[9] See letter of 23 May 1919 from Alice Kausner (dramatists' agent, New York) to J. B. Pinker, offering a contract for the cinema rights for several Conrad novels (including *Chance* and *Victory*) for 17,500 dollars; see also 24 May 1921 to J. B. Pinker for further comments relating to the film agreement (TLS Berg).

[10] *CL* 4, 506.   [11] Jean-Aubry, *Life and Letters*, ii. 214.

Chance or any of the later romances, experimenting with the potential of a highly visual medium, and above all, aiming to attract the wide, female readership of popular fiction. As far back as 1901, Conrad had sought this kind of context, when 'Amy Foster' appeared in the *Illustrated London News* with an illustration of Amy in a domestic setting, seated at table in a picture hat, as part of a 'conversation piece'. The story is flanked by illustrations of a royal colonial tour and full-page advertisements for 'Sunlight Soap'.[12] The illustrations for 'Gaspar Ruiz', in *Pall Mall Magazine* (July–December 1906), defining the setting as that of historical romance, anticipate the later context for *Suspense* in *Hutchinson's Magazine* (1925).

'A Smile of Fortune' in *London Magazine* in 1911 and 'Freya of the Seven Isles' for the *Metropolitan Magazine* in 1912 were also published in contexts that, like the *Herald*'s Sunday Magazine, offered Conrad the incentive for a new way of exploring a perennial issue of the fiction—the problem and implications of vision. He was now dealing with publications that increasingly drew on the importance of the image in the modern world of marketing, with its emphasis on photography, illustration, and design. 'Smile' appeared in *London Magazine* for February 1911, accompanied by a portrait of the sensuous Alice, lounging in her garden. The 'Wayfarer's Library' edition of *'Twixt Land and Sea* adopted this pose from 'Smile' to use as the frontispiece illustration, alerting the prospective reader to the role of the heroine, and signalling the genre of romance by placing her in an instantly recognisable pose seated in a secluded bower (in an adaptation of a *hortus conclusus*).[13] After *Chance*, *Victory* was promoted in *The Star* using a seductive illustration of a girl playing a violin.[14] *Victory* also appeared in *Munsey's Magazine* in 1915 (a prestigious New York 'story' magazine). The advance publicity advertised 'Conrad's new novel, "Victory—An Island Story"', as 'a romance, an adventure, and a love-story,' in

---

[12] 'Amy Foster', *Illustrated London News* 119 (July–Dec. 1901). The illustration, by Gunning King, is for the first instalment, 14 Dec. 915.

[13] *'Twixt Land and Sea*, 'Wayfarer's Library' (London: Dent, n.d.), frontispiece. Illustration by Herbert Cole (1914).

[14] Illustration, entitled 'The Girl with the Violin', for the *Star*, 24 Aug. 1915; *Munsey's Magazine* 53 [Jan. 1915], 906. For a discussion of *Victory* in the context of popular responses to the First World War, see Harold Orel, *Popular Fiction in England* (Lexington: The University Press of Kentucky, 1992).

which 'the heart of the woman . . . beats fastest', while the front cover of *Hutchinson's Magazine* (February 1925) advertised the new serialised *Suspense* with a glossy coloured illustration of a female bandit brandishing a pistol.[15]

The serialisation of *The Rover* in the leading American woman's magazine, *Pictorial Review* (September–December 1923), exemplifies the radical shift in context for Conrad's late works. According to the magazine historian Frank Mott, the *Pictorial Review* began in 1899 as 'the house organ of Albert McDowell's System of Dressmaking and Tailoring'.[16] It gained the reputation of being 'rather smart and clever in its notes on books and the drama'.[17] During the second decade of the twentieth century it entered into competition with *McCall's*, *Woman's Home Companion*, and *Ladies' Home Journal* for one of the biggest circulations of women's journals in the United States, developing a strongly visual component for its advertisements for fashion, beauty aids, and fiction (by 1923 illustrations were often in colour).[18]

In the context of periodical publication at the beginning of the twentieth century, readership was thus determined to some extent by the visual component of the text, which constantly aimed to create a predictable market. As Janice Radway has remarked, the fundamental relationship between marketing and readership depends on the fact that purchasing decisions 'cannot be reduced to a simple interaction between a book and a reader'. She shows that commercial success is partially dependent on a 'socially organised technology' (that included the visual marketing of the text), ensuring production and distribution.[19]

Responses to the text, as well as purchasing decisions, are controlled by a much wider body of contextual material with serial publication than with the sale of a book. The multiplicity of texts and illustrations filling the pages of *The New York Herald* Sunday Magazine in 1912 reflect an editorial policy that helped

---

[15] *Suspense* also appeared in the United States in 1935 in *The Saturday Review of Literature*. I am indebted to Gene Moore for pointing out to me the serialisation of *Suspense* in *Hutchinson's*.

[16] Frank Luther Mott, *A History of American Magazines, iv: 1885–1905* (Cambridge, Mass.: Harvard University Press, 1957), 362.　　　　　　[17] Ibid.

[18] Ibid. 770.

[19] Janice Radway, *Reading the Romance: Women, Patriarchy, and Popular Fiction* (Chapel Hill: University of North Carolina Press, 1984), 20.

to construct the readership of the women's romances published in the fiction section. Within the serialisations themselves illustrations usually conformed to a limited taxonomy, eliding any generic ambiguities residing within the text, but emphasising the conservative tendencies of popular fiction that shape its readers' desire and expectation for an immediately recognisable and infinitely re-saleable commodity. We have only to read *The Rover* in *The Pictorial Review*, or *Suspense* in *Hutchinson's Magazine* (February–August 1925), to recognise the extent to which Conrad's texts responded to this increasingly image-conscious market (see Fig. 3).[20] Moreover, by dropping Marlow as narrator, Conrad now suggests a much more immediate confrontation between the portraits presented within and without the text. In fact, he would often exploit the disjunction between the two, drawing attention to the reductive quality of received images. The coloured illustrations for *The Rover*, for example, are continuous in style and iconography with those of the fictional items placed either side of Conrad's story in *The Pictorial Review*. Illustrations for 'The Grand Woman', by Robert W. Sneddon, appearing adjacent to instalments of *The Rover*, clearly inform the reader of the specific genre we are to expect.[21] Likewise, illustrations for *The Rover*, presenting the swashbuckling poses taken by Peyrol, the period costumes, the carefully chosen romantic moments of Arlette and Réal, depicted in a lover's embrace, framed by the window space, all direct the reader to expect a deeply sentimental historical romance (see Fig. 4). Within the text itself Conrad draws attention to this context with his deliberate placing of Arlette in the poses of film stills: 'Peyrol . . . turned his head and saw the girl standing in the doorway' (38); 'he saw her appear, with nothing but the sky full of light at her back' (59); 'the rover had caught sight of Arlette's face at the open window' (230). There is no doubt that Conrad's ultimate aim was to attract lucrative film contracts for his fiction. As we can see from the presentation of romance in *The Rover*, Conrad shaped

[20] Nonetheless, Conrad's reputation as 'man of the sea' survived in this context. See *Pictorial Review*, Sept. 1925, 17, for an interview with Conrad, by Mary Austin, entitled, 'Joseph Conrad Tells What Women Don't Know About Men.' Austen recommended Conrad to women readers, 'because he is, more than any writer living, the prophet of the man's adventure,' and thus, she claimed, he offered women valuable insight into the 'man's world'.

[21] Robert W. Sneddon, 'A Grand Woman', *Pictorial Review*, Sept. 1923, 10.

Fig. 3. 'Introducing the Mysterious and Lovely Arlette . . .', opening page for the first instalment of *The Rover*, *The Pictorial Review*, September 1923.

"'SCEVOLA IS THIRSTING FOR YOUR BLOOD. HE'S THERE, YOU KNOW. DON'T TRUST PEYROL EITHER. I WAS LOOKING AT YOU TWO OUT THERE. I CAN TRUST HIM NO LONGER'"

Fig 4. 'Scevola is thirsting for your blood . . .', illustration to the third instalment of *The Rover*, *The Pictorial Review*, November 1923.

many passages of the later narratives with the medium of film in mind.[22]

On other occasions, however, Conrad undermines the traditionally romantic pose. His text comments on, rather than emulates, the highly stylised conventions of popular romance (such as 'The Grand Woman' which was published side by side with *The Rover*, and whose schematic and predictable closure of marriage does little to stimulate the imagination). Conrad first debunks the comic closure of his novel by sacrificing Peyrol, who ultimately dies to facilitate the romance plot of Arlette and Réal. But in the love scene between the two he also reverses the conventional gender roles of romance. Throughout the narrative Arlette poses passively in the frame of the window-space, and during the climax of the romance she occupies her usual place: 'he didn't see Arlette, who stood against the wall on one side of the window, out of the moonlight and in the darkest corner of the room' (240). But as Réal and Arlette declare their love, the woman takes the active role by proposing to Réal. She asks him to 'Come to the window so that I may look at you' (240), confronting him with 'a searching and appropriating expression' (241). She initiates the romance, not by entering the central locus of the text (where Réal is occupied in the adventure plot), but by inviting him to join her in the enframed space associated with her position throughout the narrative.

Conrad's correspondence with the editor of *Land and Water* about the illustrations for *The Rescue* shows his sensitivity to the visual context of his late work. The tone of *Land and Water*, an English publication with a strongly patriotic and imperialist bias (it was a forerunner of *Country Life*), was somewhat closer to some of his earlier publishing contexts. Yet the layout was moving towards the American style, with its abundant illustrations and photographs. However, Conrad objected strongly to Dudley Hardy's illustrations for the first instalment of *The Rescue*. He found Hardy's depiction of Lingard, the adventurer of the tropics, ludicrous: 'that face which says nothing, which suggests no type might belong to a hotel waiter or a stockbroker.'[23] He compared Hardy's drawings unfavourably with those of Maurice Greiffenhagen, who had illustrated 'Typhoon' in *Pall*

[22] See n. 9.   [23] 12 Dec. 1918, ALS Beinecke.

Mall Magazine (1902). Even though Greiffenhagen had probably never experienced a typhoon, Conrad thought he expressed the tone of the story appropriately: 'he had imagination enough to understand the words I had written.'[24] Conrad here demonstrates his awareness of the importance of illustration, the significance of interaction between the written and visual components of the text.

In fact, Greiffenhagen's illustrations for 'Typhoon' offer an exceptionally accurate visual counterpart to the modernist techniques of the narrative. The background of these drawings, showing the angular slant and patterning of ships' masts and ropes, or the interweaving pipes of the lower quarters, curiously anticipate Vorticist representations of mechanical and technical apparatus. The human figures possess a weight and solidity rarely found in magazine illustration in this period. Against this complex network of intersecting lines, appropriately conveying the lurching of a storm-tossed vessel, the characters look strangely destabilised, an effect that exactly matches MacWhirr's and others' experience in Conrad's text.

Eventually, after trying out a number of alternative artists, the editor of *Land and Water* secured Greiffenhagen for the remaining illustrations of *The Rescue*. This time Greiffenhagen capitalised not only on the plethora of references to 'gazes' and 'glances' in this novel, but also on the extraordinarily operatic quality of the scenes of Lingard's 'summit meeting' in the native enclosure. For one illustration he created a highly formalised pattern of 'stacked' heads and spears, positioned at right-angles to the roof of criss-crossed bamboo poles and leaves, with the principal figures, outlined in black, facing each other in profile. A blank space left at the centre of the scene creates an appropriate sense of drama (anticipating perhaps the gap in Lily Briscoe's painting in Woolf's *To the Lighthouse*, 1927), as the outcome of the meeting hangs in the balance. Greiffenhagen captured the theatrical tone of the later episodes of *The Rescue* while retaining something of the modernist resonances that linger in Conrad's handling of the 'unfathomable' in Lingard's relationship with Mrs Travers.

The trouble Conrad took over the illustrations provides an example of the care he afforded to the presentation of the text

---

[24] 12 Dec. 1918, ALS Beinecke.

within a highly visual medium. From a different perspective, he was also attending to the issue of the woman reader for whom the new publications were frequently marketed. The pervasive presence of male narrators and auditors within the texts of Conrad's fiction, particularly those of the middle years, has sometimes provoked an adverse response from feminists, and the issue continues to prove contentious. To conclude this discussion, I shall therefore turn again to Conrad's earlier work, comparing his anticipation of a predominantly male readership for *Heart of Darkness* with his treatment of the woman reader of *The Arrow of Gold*. In this novel I believe Conrad's narrative strategies arise partly from his continued attempts, in the later fiction, to engage with the woman reader of the illustrated serial magazines for which the later fiction was intended.

The earlier work, as we have seen, was published in contexts that supported a largely masculinist tone. To gain a sense of the exclusion some women readers have felt from the texts of Conrad's earlier narratives, Nina Pelikan Straus offers a useful reading of *Heart of Darkness*. She expresses the difficulties encountered by the woman reader of this novella, rightly observing that 'although [Marlow] speaks *about* women, there is no indication that women might be included among his hearers'.[25] However, far from vindicating the exclusion of women from the shared male knowledge revealed in the text, I believe that Conrad's presentation of the Intended offers a critique of patriarchal structures that marginalise the European women of the story. Conrad had written to William Blackwood at the end of May 1902, assuring him that the lie to the Intended constitutes the dramatic climax of Marlow's attenuated return from the abyss. Defending his methodology to Blackwood, Conrad remarks on the fundamental importance of the role of Kurtz's fiancée, where, 'in the light of the final incident', the whole story gains its real significance:

the last pages of Heart of Darkness where the interview of the man and the girl locks in . . . makes of that story something quite on another plane than an anecdote of a man who went mad in the Centre of Africa.[26]

[25] Nina Pelikan Straus, 'The Exclusion of the Intended from Secret Sharing in Conrad's *Heart of Darkness*', *Novel* 20:2 (1987), 124.

[26] William Blackburn (ed.), *Joseph Conrad: Letters to William Blackwood and David S. Meldrum* (Durham, NC: Duke University Press, 1958), 154.

By having Marlow protect her from the truth, Conrad exposes the patriarchal strategy that has traditionally excluded women from knowledge of male affairs. In *Heart of Darkness*, the European woman is denied access to the locus of Western power (the scene of imperial adventure), and also to its critique. The Intended is the only character within the text itself to whom the truth of 'the horror' is denied: the male auditors on the boat, for example, remain party to Marlow's confession of his lie. Outside the text, the reader (both male and female) may also reconstruct the truth. But Straus, like Chinua Achebe on the issue of Conrad's representation of the Africans,[27] raises an important question about reader-response, and whether Conrad's method does to some extent propagate the privileged status of the white European male by naturalising his position as reader within the text itself.

Once again *The Arrow of Gold* provides an example of the problems encountered by Conrad in his handling of his new audience, signalled, in this case, by the presence of the female reader to whom the male protagonist, M. George, addressed the 'manuscript' forming the main text of this novel. As if Conrad realised that he needed a greater emphasis on the gender of the reader to establish the novel as one directed towards a woman's eyes, he includes (in the book version), two framing 'Notes' explaining that M. George's text was written for a female childhood friend. Nevertheless, the frame narrator remains unspecified in terms of gender and identity. Moreover, in the book version of *Arrow*, Conrad's insistence on the mediation of the narrative occurs without giving us any real sense of the identity of the auditor. The narrator tells us in the first Note that all M. George's 'asides, disquisitions, and explanations addressed directly to the friend of his childhood' (4) have been edited out. The notion of a 'privileged reader' is much more shadowy than in Conrad's earlier works. In *Heart of Darkness* Marlow constantly alludes to his male companions on the boat during the course of his narrative, and, in *Lord Jim*, his after-dinner listeners interpolate in Marlow's monologue.

[27] Chinua Achebe, 'An Image of Africa: Racism in Conrad's *Heart of Darkness*', *Massachusetts Review* 18 (1977), 782–94.

By contrast, in *Arrow* we hear nothing of the relationship of the female reader to M. George's tale. We are merely tantalised by an unspecific reference to her. The tale itself emphasises the excessive aestheticisation of the central female protagonist, but the frame Notes introduce the first reference to the 'shaping' of women's lives (in this case the lives of the readers). M. George's nameless female auditor acts as a blank and unresponsive presence mediating between the readers and the story of his relationship with Rita. As if Conrad were responding to the social convention of the chaperone, M. George's auditor represents a formal intermediary whose female presence protects the propriety of the women readers who are about to enter into a risky tale of unlegitimised male romance. In the Marlow narratives, Marlow's sense of camaraderie with his listeners is strong (and in the case of *Lord Jim* the character of the auditor and 'privileged reader' largely corresponds to that of the implied *Blackwood's* reader, another 'one of us'). In *Arrow*, however, we gain no access to a potential 'club' of women who might receive Rita's story. On the contrary, Conrad's strategy deliberately isolates both protagonist and reader, to whom no female community of shared understanding or experience is available. Rita constantly confesses that she is unfamiliar with women and M. George's woman reader remains an elusive mystery.

Traditionally, critics have cited this novel as Conrad's worst attempt at a female portrait. Daniel Schwartz, for example, refers to the 'collapse of form' brought about by his failure to sustain the sharpness of irony exemplified by the male protagonists' trajectory from innocence to experience (in 'Youth', *Heart of Darkness* and *The Shadow-Line*). From the point of view of the woman reader, however, this novel's interest lies not so much with the rites of passage narrative of the young hero, but with Rita's equivocation and resistance of the romance role. She provides an alternative to the self-sacrificing Conradian heroine who resorts to despairing acts of murder, suicide, or, like Flora de Barral, sits uneasily in her pose of prospective bride at the close of *Chance*. As in *Chance*, Conrad creates a structure in which the woman's role resides at the centre of an economy predicated on male desire and expectations. Henry Allègre, the successor to a number of fictional 'collectors' of women (like

James's Gilbert Osmond in *The Portrait of a Lady*), initiates the worship of Rita as the image of 'the woman of all time', an idealisation which is repeated by each male protagonist in turn.[28] Conrad reveals the irony of Rita's position by showing her entrapment in this role. The brutal Ortega's possessive response to her amounts to much the same as the chivalrous mythologising of Captain Blunt or the passionate fantasy of M. George. Yet Rita herself denies the construction of a unified 'femininity' imposed on her by the men of the novel:

I have got to be what I am, and that *amigo*, is not so easy; because I may be simple, but like on all those on whom there is no peace I am not One. No, I am not One![29]   (300)

Her sense of a fragmented identity, represented in the novel by her refusal to command a definitive space, creates an unsettling dislocation at the centre of the romance plot. Continuously moving between Paris, Marseilles, and her native Tolosa, she behaves much more like the restless hero of romantic poetry, while her quest is not to pursue the idea of an essential self, but rather to escape from it. Her divided self is also represented by the *doppelgänger* figure of her sister Thérèse, whose nun-like appearance suggests the virginity that the men of the novel wish Rita had retained, but whose unlikeable character they all spurn. In this novel, the female protagonists, Rita and Thérèse, join the cast of Conrad's 'secret sharers' in the author's ongoing project to treat with scepticism the notion of a unified identity.

Rita's refusal to accommodate the comic closure of romance further disturbs the generic category of the novel, while it offers a wry comment on the context of its initial publication. In the

[28] This reference to the Mona Lisa is only one amongst many allusions to other art forms in this novel. See Pamela Bickley and Robert Hampson, ' "Lips That Have Been Kissed": Boccaccio, Verdi, Rossetti and *The Arrow of Gold*', *L'Époque Conradienne* (1988), 77–91, on the technical inventiveness of this novel in relation to painting and opera.

[29] See Andrew Michael Roberts, 'The Gaze and the Dummy: Sexual Politics in *The Arrow of Gold*', in Keith Carabine (ed.), *Joseph Conrad: Critical Assessments*, 4 vols. (Robertsbridge, East Sussex: Helm Information, 1992), iii. 546: 'Much radical feminist theory has seen the ideal of the unitary self as complicit with the oppressive imposition of male myths of rationality and identity.' In this context Roberts refers to Luce Irigaray, *This Sex Which is Not One*, trans. Catherine Porter with Carolyn Burke (1977; Ithaca, NY: Cornell University Press, 1985); Toril Moi, *Sexual/Textual Politics: Feminist Literary Theory* (London: Methuen, 1985), 10–15, 66–7.

serial version for *Lloyd's Magazine*, for which the two framing Notes were omitted, the reader is left with a view of the
leading characters resembling the soft-focus fade-out of early
romantic films. The lovers pose in the customary clinch, without any intimation of the drama's tragic closure: 'I shall seal
your lips with the thing itself . . . Like this' (336). In the final
version, where the Second Note describes the events following
the romantic union, we discover that Rita leaves M. George after
sharing six months of secluded bliss, and after his recovery from
the wound inflicted on him by his adversary, Captain Blunt, in
a duel. Part of the problem with the final presentation of the hero
is that Conrad fails to give him any real sense of progression in
the novel. He continues to idealise Rita and is forced to adopt
the position of Captain Blunt's rival, adhering to the absurd and
futile posturing of the chivalric code.[30] We are left feeling that
Rita's 'rite of passage' towards a fulfilment of identity has been
established more satisfactorily than that of the hero.

Conrad seemed to display an uneasiness in the closure of this
novel that is reflected in the responses of male readers. Letters
to Conrad frequently show that men in particular found the
endings of several of the later romances problematic. Bertrand
Russell said of *Chance* that he 'felt some qualms about the "happy
ending"' and Ford thought 'the end is odd, you know, old boy'.
Henri-René Lenormand was discretely critical of the closure
of *Arrow*: 'If certain readers feel disappointed . . . Perhaps their
sympathy for "Monsieur Georges" makes them wish to see him
happy sooner and for a longer time.'[31] Yet for a woman reader,
the ending of these novels offers an astute commentary on conventional assumptions about the position of the heroine in the
closure of romance.

[30] A striking comparison of Conrad's presentation of the duel in *Arrow of Gold*
can be made with that of the duel in Theodor Fontane's novel *Effi Briest* (1895).
In the contest between Effi's husband and lover, in which the lover, Crampas, dies,
Fontane expressed the futility of codes of behaviour which satisfy male conventions,
but ultimately resolve nothing. Given Conrad's debt to Flaubert, the parallel with
Fontane is of interest, since critics have also perceived a close analogy between the
work of Flaubert and Fontane. See Thomas Degering, *Das Verhältnis von Individuum und Gesellschaft in Fontanes 'Effi Briest' und Flauberts 'Madame Bovary'* (Bonn:
Bouvier, 1978).

[31] John H. Stape and Owen Knowles (eds.), *A Portrait in Letters: Correspondence
to and about Conrad* (Amsterdam: Rodopi, 1996): 22 Jan. 1914, 95; 19 Dec. 1916,
117; 26 March 1921, 177.

Constance Garnett's reading of *The Nigger of 'The Narcissus'*
in 1897 suggests the terms with which we might reconsider
Conrad's later experimentation with the genre. Her response to
Conrad's early novel alludes to the experience of the woman
reader entering the male dominion of the sea: 'being in a new
world . . . where I am picking up hints and glimpses at every
step.'[32] Likewise Conrad sometimes moved cautiously in his
presentation of the heroine of serial romance. Yet in *Arrow*, as
in *Chance*, his presentation of an enigmatic female protagonist
suggests a striking identification with the position of women
caught within a male construction of romance. Given the genre
and context, Rita's portrait of female independence offers the
woman reader a surprisingly refreshing critique of the narrators'
patriarchal strategies within this novel.

To the many explanations for the shift in content in Conrad's
late fiction we can add his response to the iconographic in a new
and wider publishing context. He took much greater account
of the visual impact of his work on a predominantly female
readership. During his later career, his works were being literally seen, for the first time, in the contexts of the women's pages
of newspapers and popular magazines, whose emphasis on illustrations, photographs, and advertisements bore witness to the
essential continuity of traditional modes of representation in
the early twentieth century. Conrad explored to great effect the
extent to which identity (especially female) was predicated on
such familiar images, in a context which reminds us that, within
the dominant culture, modernism produced only marginal alternatives, rather than overtaking conventional modes of seeing.

---

[32] Ibid. 30 Dec. 1897, 29.

7
Visuality and Gender in Late Conrad

Conrad's most famous critical dictum, 'before all, to make you *see*!' has ordinarily been construed in metaphorical terms. His fictional methods in this sense allude to an epistemological imperative, equating knowledge and insight. But there are grounds for reading this declared objective in a different way. In his later work, Conrad often interrogates more closely the outward presentation of events and relationships, inviting the reader of his final novels to engage with the physical act of looking, the physiology of vision itself. In other words, he also examines 'seeing' in a literal and in a technical sense. Without discarding the epistemological resonances of vision, he now places greater emphasis on what is actually seen, the aesthetic nature of the object in view, and the technical construction of the view. Like the Shakespeare of the late romances (especially *The Tempest*) Conrad turns finally to the questions of art and illusion, the ambiguities inherent in the process of structuring and framing the artefact itself.[1]

Of course Conrad had always been interested in these questions. But he made a transition towards a new method of addressing them. While he continued to concern himself with the modernist 'rupture', the presentation of dislocated consciousness and the fragmentation of identity, he moved towards a deeper investigation of surviving hegemonic codes of vision, the framing of the subject, and the physical as well as psychological effects of perspective, where the emphasis lay as much on outward appearances as on inward perceptions. The act of 'seeing' in these later works is as much constituted by the experience of constructing the frame as well as that of looking into it. Indeed, his new emphasis on these issues arises partly from his response to the publishing contexts in which he serialised the late work.

---

[1] See John Batchelor, 'Conrad and Shakespeare', *L'Époque Conradienne* 18 (1992), 121–51 on *Chance* and *Othello*, and *Victory* and *The Tempest*.

The popular marketing of his fiction in highly visual contexts elicited a fresh outlook on matters of spectacle, how we see things, what we see, how we respond to the surface of a text, to visual appearances and to the formal patterning of a narrative.

One contemporary reviewer of *Chance* astutely observed this shift in methodology when he suggested that 'the core of the story is, in one sense, like a picture within a frame which is itself painted—it is within a frame too, and that frame within another, again.'[2] Flora de Barral's portrait, ostensibly the 'core of the story', is presented as an image constantly receding from view, only momentarily glimpsed and then disappearing in the vanishing points of multiple perspectival constructions. Conrad's method in *Heart of Darkness* reveals the 'nothing' at the centre of Marlow's view, but in *Chance* Conrad uses Marlow to draw attention, as the early reviewer pointed out, to the framing devices of the narrative where Marlow and others constantly attempt to contain and often to diminish the identity of the female figure.[3]

Conrad's earlier methodology in 'Youth' and *Heart of Darkness*, as Ian Watt has shown, provides us with a modernist representation of Marlow's observations. His use of 'delayed decoding', for example, undermines the notion of immediate subject–object relations. In *Heart of Darkness*, Marlow initially perceives 'sticks' flying at him from the banks of the Congo, only understanding later that they are 'arrows'.[4] Conrad constructs Marlow's retelling of the event in such a way that the reader is made aware of the temporal gap between seeing and knowing, the 'narrative' of understanding that arises from the act of looking. The conventions of an illusionistic realism constructed within the frame of the novel are shattered by a method that

---

[2] C. E. Montague, Review of *Chance*, *The Manchester Guardian*, 15 Jan. 1914, 6.

[3] We have seen in Chs. 3 and 4 how Flora's body is gradually marginalised by successive characters. Psychologically damaged by the governess, physically rejected by her husband, petrified in Marlow's image of her as a 'carving of white marble', disappearing altogether 'behind the blank wall' of her husband's renunciation: only a 'possible', never an 'actual' woman.

[4] See Ian Watt, *Conrad in the Nineteenth Century* (Berkeley: University of California), 168–200 on impressionism and symbolism in Conrad. See Michael Levenson, *A Genealogy of Modernism: A Study of English Literary Doctrine 1908–1922* (Cambridge: Cambridge University Press, 1984), 91–9, on modernist artists who draw attention to the two-dimensionality of the picture-plane. Levenson cites Conrad's suggestion of formlessness in representing Marlow as a 'Buddha without a lotus flower' in *Heart of Darkness*.

draws attention, not to the authority of an image fixed in time and space, but to the flickering and transitory impressions created by the physiological and temporal phenomena associated with actual visual perception.

But in spite of the modernist revolutions in the visual arts, we find that the concept of the frame and the essentially mimetic codes produced by linear perspective still dominated the world of magazines, photography, and film in the early twentieth century. Jonathan Crary has pointed out that the 'myth of the modernist rupture depends fundamentally on the binary model of realism versus experimentation'.[5] While the work of impressionist and post-impressionist painters signalled a break with an older model of vision, 'loosely definable as Renaissance, perspectival, or normative'[6], the new technological inventions of photography, and later, the cinema, have reconfirmed 'the continuous unfolding of Renaissance-based modes of vision',[7] first theorised by Leon Battista Alberti in *On Painting*, 1435–6.

As Conrad's narratives begin to appear in contexts that reflect these new technological advances, they increasingly respond to the media's paradoxically conservative preference for traditional visual methods. However, we cannot readily assume new grounds for reading Conrad's late work without first establishing terms through which to evaluate his responses to these media. In this chapter I shall explore the ways in which Conrad frequently drew attention to the continuity of hegemonic codes of vision in the later fiction, alluding to the new technologies of photography, advertisement illustration, and film while simultaneously suggesting the conventionality of their structures of framing and perspective. In *Chance* he referred to the formality of the Fynes' pose: 'Fyne stood by her side, as in those old-fashioned photographs of married couples where you see a husband with his hand on the back of his wife's chair' (123). The first instalment of *The Arrow of Gold* in *Lloyd's Magazine* (December 1919) appeared alongside an illustration representing a formal portrait of Doña Rita, shown in its elaborate frame,

[5] Jonathan Crary, *Techniques of the Observer: On Vision and Modernity in the Nineteenth Century* (Cambridge, Mass.: MIT Press, 1990), 4. See also Suren Lalvani, 'Photography, Epistemology and the Body', *Cultural Studies* 7:3 (October 1993), 442–65.   [6] Crary, *Techniques of the Observer*, 3.
[7] Ibid.

her demure and seductive gaze inviting the reader to enter the narrative. In the book version, Conrad created a literary equivalent to the effects of a visual 'framing' device by framing his story with two notes in which his outer narrator shows how he intends to lead the reader (like the intercessors of a Renaissance religious painting) through the perspectives offered to them in his text.

Although we have no evidence that Conrad was aware of the scientific principles of one-point perspective, the number of studies of his modernist strategies available testify to the importance for him of 'point-of-view'.[8] In fact a brief outline of the workings of Albertian perspective reveals how a modernist such as Conrad depended on an understanding of the endurance of traditional codes of vision in order to create the dislocating effects of his narratives. Furthermore, contemporary visual theorists have suggested that Renaissance-based structures of perspective themselves produce an undermining effect on the identity of the viewer. We shall see that in his later career, Conrad emerges as an acute reader of visual conventions, exploiting the destabilising effects inherent within traditional perspectival constructions to explore the representation of identity and gender in the romance genre.

I

Alberti's theory of perspective invites the viewer to participate in the 'narrative' of the painting. The worlds of observer and observed are unified by a centric ray stretching from viewpoint to vanishing-point around which the illusion of three-dimensionality is constructed within the limits of a two-dimensional frame. Yet, as Norman Bryson has observed in his post-structuralist account of perspective, the experience of the viewer is often disconcerting:

[8] *Notes on Life and Letters*, 194. In this context see Frederick R. Karl, *Joseph Conrad: The Three Lives* (New York: Farrar, Straus, and Giroux, 1979), 397; John Batchelor, *The Life of Joseph Conrad: A Critical Appreciation* (Oxford: Blackwell, 1994), 68–9, for a discussion of the Preface to *The Nigger* and its association with Walter Pater's conclusion to *Studies in the History of the Renaissance* (1873) and the 'Essay on Style' in *Appreciations* (1889).

The viewpoint and the vanishing point are inseparable: there is no view-point without vanishing point, and no vanishing point without view-ing point. The self-possession of the viewing subject has built into it, therefore, the principle of its own abolition: annihilation of the sub-ject as center is a condition of the very moment of the look.[9]

The anxiety inherent in the transactions between self and world are built into the notion of the gaze. The construction of the Albertian pyramid, along whose orthogonals figures recede in gradually diminishing sizes, pulls the gaze towards the vanishing-point. The painting returns the gaze of the viewer from its infinitely receding vanishing-point, constantly reconstructing the viewer as a 'disembodied' subject—one that consists of a single physiological origin of vision. Thus the illusion of perspective challenges the identity of the observer. Moreover, the con-stricted gaze also anticipates the 'punctuality', or immediacy, in time and space, of the viewing subject, as well as the immedi-acy of subject–object relations (rather like the Cartesian con-struction of subjectivity). Conrad undermines the confidence of an immediate relation between subject and object by showing the way in which the body of the viewer is physically reduced by the act of looking. He describes Mrs Haldin's psychological deterioration in *Under Western Eyes* in terms of the physical deterioration associated with her gaze, through the frame of the window, onto the receding perspective of the Boulevard des Philosophes: '[she] turned her head away and looked out of the window for a time, with that new, sombre, extinct gaze of her sunken eyes which so completely made another woman of her' (114). Another striking example of this visual process exists in the reference to Jörgenson's native wife in *The Rescue*. The narrator identifies the process of memory as one of 'looking through' a frame upon the receding past (as on a portrait or a painting of a familiar landscape), remarking that 'all that was left of her youth was a pair of eyes, undimmed and mournful, which, when she was alone, seemed to look stonily into the past' (105).

Bryson's account clarifies Conrad's individual brand of scep-ticism, one that comes into play in his interpretation of the

[9] Norman Bryson, 'The Gaze in the Expanded Field', in Hal Foster (ed.), *Vision and Visuality: Discussions in Contemporary Culture* (Seattle: Bay Press, 1988), 91.

phenomenological aspects of vision.[10] Yet the Albertian model also carries important resonances for narrative theory, particularly in the case of a novelist like Conrad, who is primarily concerned with the destabilising effects of observation and the relationship between seeing and understanding. The frame negotiates between fiction and reality, just as the narrator mediates between the world of the story and that of the reader. Alberti's concept of *istoria*[11] or narrative in a painting includes his insistence on mediation, or the role of an intercessor. It reads like the description of the dramatised narrator of a Conradian novel:

I like there to be someone in the *istoria* who tells the spectators what is going on, and either beckons them with his hand to look . . . or by his gestures invites you to laugh or weep with them.[12]

In this context, the Florentine painter Masaccio, who put Alberti's theories into practice before they were transcribed in *Della Pittura*, provides a useful example in his painting *The Trinity* (1425–7). The figure of an intercessor, St Mary, who looks out at the viewer but gestures towards the crucifixion depicted within the central space of the painting, acts like the dramatised narrator of a novel, inviting the spectator to share the experience described within the frame.

Conrad's sceptical outlook led him to undermine the illusion built into what we consider to be quite ordinary ways of seeing. His fiction constantly denies the possibilities of gaining certain knowledge from a glimpse into the frame. Thus the encounter of observer and observed invariably results in disillusionment, a very different experience to that of the optimistic vision implied by the Renaissance creator of a window on the world. Far from possessing the object enframed, that which is seen constantly eludes the Conradian narrator or protagonist, who is instead drawn further into the vanishing-point that undermines the illusion of the

---

[10] See Ch. 4.

[11] Leon Battista Alberti, *On Painting*, trans. with an introd. and notes by John R. Spencer (1956; New Haven: Yale University Press, 1966), 70–85.

[12] Quoted in S. K. Heninger, 'Framing the Narrative,' Mark Lussier and S. K. Heninger (eds.), in *Perspective as a Problem in the Art, History and Literature of Early Modern England* (Lewiston, New York: The Edwin Mellin Press, 1992), 19. Heninger notes that Alberti borrows Ciceronian terms to state his theory. In the present context this suggests a movement from language and narrative to painting and, with a writer like Conrad, back to narrative.

perspectival construction. The gaze of the Conradian narrator, Marlow in *Heart of Darkness* and *Lord Jim*, or the English teacher in *Under Western Eyes*, is merely returned by an unfathomable view.

II

In the later novels, a shift occurred in Conrad's treatment of traditional structures of vision. He became increasingly intrigued by the hegemony of perspectival codes in constructing notions of identity within the text. He extended his interest in perspective to include a greater attention to the framing device itself, to the containment of identity within the frame, and to the disillusionment thus accorded to the viewer. In this context, Conrad frequently turns to the issue of gender and the way in which received assumptions about what it is to be 'male' or 'female' are often enframed, literally, within traditional visual constructions.

In 'A Smile of Fortune', a story from the period of *Chance*,[13] published initially in 1911 in *London Magazine*, the narrator defines Alice Jacobus as the 'sullen, passive victim' of his gaze. Entrapped in her father's house, 'the everlastingly irritated captive of the garden' (62), she is presented as the image of the frail Virgin of a medieval *hortus conclusus*. Yet Conrad emphasises the illusory nature of the framing device when the narrator discovers that Alice's actual demeanour, 'snarling and superb', is closer to a very different iconography—that of the African woman of *Heart of Darkness*. Indeed, she subverts the role represented by the white woman of that novella—the Intended —by refusing to adopt the image of idealised European femininity. As the narrator watches Alice, she awakens in him a sense of doubt and lack of confidence in his identity. The price of his 'cruel self-knowledge' is to lose hope of ever knowing the object of his desire. The power of the onlooker, predicated on implied possession of the viewed object, is diminished, while the image of Alice herself attains a startling presence as she resists her entrapment with palpable energy.

[13] Joseph Conrad, *'Twixt Land and Sea* (1912; London: Dent, 1947).

Conrad uses the female portrait on several occasions in *Victory* (1915), where he alludes to the traditional spatial ambiguities associated with Velasquez's *Roqueby Venus* (1650) in order to present the uneasy relationship between female privacy and a woman's expression of a public identity.[14] Mrs Schomberg is seen 'in a dim room upstairs' where she is 'elaborating those two long pendant ringlets which were such a feature of her hair dressing for her afternoon duties' (122). The 'toilet of Venus' pose is repeated by Lena, this time as her privacy is disturbed. Unconscious of being watched by Ricardo 'doing her hair with her bare arms uplifted', she is 'exposed and defenceless—and tempting' (288). Conrad's narrator (and by implication, his reader) enters into an ambiguous space in which the woman hovers between her private self and her public appearance. Ricardo's attempted rape accentuates the implied violation engendered in the act of watching. Since we also share Ricardo's (physical) point of view, Conrad unsettles the position of the reader as passive observer of events taking place in the text.[15]

Conrad's articulation of iconographic tropes in this novel allow for transformation and exchange of gender roles. Early in the novel, Heyst registers his uneasiness about a prospective relationship with Lena by contemplating his reflection in the mirror. His adoption of the 'toilet of Venus' pose signifies the disjunction between inward anxiety and outward appearance:

It was not a new-born vanity which induced this long survey. He felt so strange that he could not resist the suspicion of his personal

---

[14] See Jenijoy La Belle, *Herself Beheld: The Literature of the Looking-Glass* (Ithaca, NY: Cornell University Press, 1988), for the use of the 'female toilette' pose in literature; and Linda Nochlin, 'Women, Art, and Power', in *Women, Art, and Power and Other Essays* (London: Thames and Hudson, 1989), 26: 'On March 10, 1914 . . . a militant suffragist, Mary Richardson, alias Polly Dick, took an axe to Velazquez's *Roqueby Venus* in the National Art Gallery in London.' See also, Neville Williams, *Powder and Paint: A History of the Englishwoman's Toilet* (London: Longman's, Green, 1957), 113. Williams observed that the foundation statutes of Royal Holloway College for Women (1886) ensured that each girl's room was fitted with a mirror, so that 'even when immersed in her studies the young lady should not be negligent of her appearance'.

[15] By contrast, see Mrs Henry Wood, *East Lynne* (1861; London: Ward, Lock, 1910), 38, who, in her best-selling sensation novel uses the *heroine*'s voyeurism, to show *her* exclusion from a scene of domestic bliss, as Lady Isabel watches her former husband with his new love through the open door of the drawing-room. The scene was used to illustrate the frontispiece of the 1910 edition.

appearance having changed during the night. What he saw in the glass, however, was the man he knew before. It was almost a disappointment —a belittling of his recent experience. (90)

Conrad's use of the pose to express Heyst's unsettled psychological state in an intensely private moment takes full effect when the iconography recurs with the female characters of the novel—first Mrs Schomberg, and especially Lena, in relation to Ricardo's attack on her. The juxtaposition of these later scenes with Heyst's strictly un-erotic version of the pose draws attention to the way in which we read conventional representations of women. In this case, Conrad's use of the trope is dependent on the gender of the subject to convey its meaning. When Heyst looks in the mirror, his action signifies the soul-searching and self-contemplation of the hero; Lena's scene comments on her status, not as self-reflective woman, but as passive and tempting object of the male gaze. Heyst, on the other hand, insists on an isolated position of autonomy. Yet his pose of the Nietzschean philosopher is finally exposed as an empty gesture; his failure to 'see' Lena as she really is results in tragedy.

In *The Arrow of Gold* (1919) Conrad suggests the heroine's release from the fixed modes of representation imposed upon her throughout the novel. The painter Henry Allègre alludes to her, in her role as artist's model, as the Mona Lisa, 'the woman of all time' (59). Conrad's main protagonist, Monsieur George, also comments on the iconographic element of his first view of her, 'even the visual impression was more of colour in a picture than of the forms of actual life' (58). But later in the novel he is forced to modify his assumptions about her status as art object. Conrad again reverses the 'toilet of Venus' pose, conventionally taken by the female, as Monsieur George reflects upon Rita's feelings for him. He asks himself 'despairingly' whether she is in love with him while, he says, 'I brushed my hair before a glass' (163). Looking at his own mirror image in the bedroom of *her* house, he feels unsettled, seeking her (absent) gaze to complete his sense of identity. Yet, as with the example of Heyst in *Victory*, the reversal of gender roles does not necessarily imply the emasculation of the hero, rather the questioning of romance codes that fix the female in a conventionally passive position. Later in the novel, Rita herself takes up George's brushes to fix her hair in the same room, the fetishistic exchange signalling her transformation from the role of Roqueby Venus to that of autonomous 'hero', whose action precipitates the soul-searching of a figure closer to that of Heyst before the mirror.[16] Ultimately Conrad confirms the transformation by undermining the stock romantic closure. After an interlude of romance with M. George, Rita leaves him to follow an independent path.

Conrad's frequent reference to the framed image in the late novels could be viewed as an endorsement of the prescribed codes of romantic fiction. But the complexity of his response to the more pervasive presence of women in his later fiction demonstrates its experimental nature. Using the framing device to question the boundaries between private and public, between reader and text, the implications of power and exclusion from power ensuing from the act of looking, he moved towards an account of the construction of gender within the limitations and possibilities of romance.

III

Conrad's novel *The Rescue* offers one of the most appropriate examples of his shift in methodology to accommodate the visual world of his late marketing contexts. Like *Chance*, this novel also provides something of a paradigm of his career, since it began as a short story, 'The Rescuer' in 1896 during the period

---

[16] Conrad may also be responding to the way in which the *Roqueby Venus* pose frequently appears in illustrations for advertising in magazines and newspapers of this period. Advertisements for 'Pond's Vanishing Cream' in *The Pictorial Review* appear alongside instalments of *The Rover*, illustrating a woman gazing into a mirror. The reflection of her gaze, engaging directly with the reader, represents the vanishing-point of the image, luring the spectator to look at her displaying the product for sale. Of course the invitation to enter the realm of the advertisement is part of the rhetoric of the image, giving it its power to persuade. Yet an unsettling ambiguity resides in the presentation of the blank yet confident smile of the saleswoman. Such images so often demonstrate the essential paradox that Bryson referred to in his discussion of perspective. Ostensibly the framed image points to the power of the beholder who claims authority over the picture [he] owns. Yet its perspectival construction (which Velasquez exploited doubly with the use of the mirror) nevertheless destabilises and undermines the identity of the spectator, who is reduced to a punctual and disembodied subject. The framing of the scene (by camera's aperture, proscenium arch, spectator's eye) demands an interrogation not only of the object in view, but of the subjectivity of the observer.

of the great sea narratives, but was not finally published as a book until 1920. Having already experimented with popular contexts for *Chance*, *Victory*, and *Arrow*, instalments of *The Rescue* appeared in 1919 in *Land and Water*.[17] Published in the fiction section (aimed at the women readers of the journal), surrounded by abundant illustrations and photographs, Conrad's text demonstrates both the continuity and the development of his concern with the physiological manifestations of vision.

Forming a trilogy of Malay novels (with *Almayer* and *Outcast*), *The Rescue* tells the story of Tom Lingard ('King Tom' or 'Rajah Laut' of the Malay peninsula), a white adventurer whose prestige amongst the Malayan native tribes is unsurpassed. The plot follows Lingard's engagement in a chivalric quest to restore a royal Malayan brother and sister to their rightful lands; the complications that arise upon the arrival of Europeans, washed up on a nearby sandbank; the subsequent shift in the balance of power between whites and rival factions of the natives that ensues from the abduction of two European males; Lingard's complex negotiations with the natives; the mistimings of his rescue operation, and its final success, when the Europeans are restored to their vessel.

The extent to which Conrad's initial plan for the story places it in the context of 'boy's own' adventure is clear. He introduces his hero in the iconographic context of illustrations for this genre of popular fiction: a 'rough man' who moved about the deck of his yacht 'looking as if he had stepped out of an engraving in a book about buccaneers' (118). Yet in the revised book version, a second, romance plot achieves prominence, based on the attraction between Lingard and Mrs Travers, wife of the owner of the incoming European vessel. Their ultimately unattainable relationship constitutes the new focus of the novel, thus providing the romance requirement for the popular fiction section of *Land and Water*. The heroine, the upper-middle-class Edith

---

[17] See H. R. Fox Bourne, *English Newspapers: Chapters in the History of Journalism* (London: Chatto and Windus, 1887), ii. 320: '*Land and Water* was established in 1866, in the manner of "The Field"—a comprehensive repository of information on every sort of rural pastime'. It gave extensive war coverage from 1914–18, during which period the visual component of the journal increased, mainly with photographs of royalty at home and abroad. Latterly it possessed an extensive women's section with items on home management and fiction.

Travers, first appears in immaculate sailing attire lounging in a deck-chair on her yacht, a pose familiar to the readers of popular magazines and women's pages (it even constitutes the pose for the dust-jacket illustration for the 1913 Methuen first edition of *Chance*).

The novel covers familiar Conradian themes—the issues of loyalty, honour, and disillusion with the romantic quest. But a less familiar emphasis on visuality emerges in the presentation of the complex colonial encounter and in the 'unfathomable' bond of Edith Travers and Tom Lingard. These are described throughout in terms of a vast network of looks and glances, of observations and spectacularly theatrical scenes in which Conrad specifically investigates traditional visual structures and Western notions of representation.

As the novel progresses, Conrad increases his emphasis on seeing in terms of linear perspective, the look and the gaze. The question of the Europeans' disaffiliation from their familiar codes of behaviour is always at stake, and is recorded in their responses to visual appearances. Travers steadfastedly retains a British colonialist perspective throughout his trials, viewing the natives categorically as 'other'. D'Alcacer, the Travers's companion, represents an elegant, civilised but empathetic European who makes the most obviously 'painterly' observations that conform to Western patterns of representation. He imagines Mrs Travers in a European interior, 'in a luminous perspective of palatial drawing-rooms . . . in the throng at an official reception' (140).

Mrs Travers, however, is transformed by her experience, and we suspect that her disaffiliation from the moral structures of the mother country during the course of her stay in the Malay archipelago will problematise her return. In her case, Conrad uses the ambiguities inherent in the perspectival construction to denote her sense of unsettled identity as she regards the unfamiliar Eastern environment with a questioning gaze. He expresses her desire to lose herself in the distant horizons of a vast landscape, which she looks on as if through a gauze which obscures clear vision and meaning:

[Mrs Travers] answered him . . . as if she had spoken from behind the veil of an immense indifference stretched between her . . . and the meaning of events, between her eyes and the shallow sea which, like her gaze . . . seemed, far off in the distance of a faint horizon, beyond the reach of eye . . . to lose itself in the sky. (125)

The European woman's confrontation with a strange land and all its dislocating effects on her sense of self is represented as that of the observer of a perspective which draws her into the abyss of its vanishing-point. Her meeting with the Malay princess Immada is articulated in terms of the reciprocating gaze of 'the other': the 'dissimilar and inquiring glances' of the two women 'seemed to . . . hold each other with the grip of an intimate contact' (141). The intensity of the exchange is reaffirmed by its repetition, outside the text, in the illustration to the relevant instalment in *Land and Water* (20 February 1919).

On another occasion, Conrad uses the 'gaze' to refer to a nineteenth-century preoccupation with 'distraction'. Jonathan Crary has remarked on the prominence, from the 1870s, of the blank or distracted gaze in representations of women (Crary discusses Manet in particular). He traces the phenomenon to a growing emphasis, in psychological research of the period, with the notion of 'attentiveness'. Crary observes that 'the promin-ence of attention as a problem . . . is a sign of a generalized crisis in the status of a perceiving subject' (25), one which was seen to affect women in particular.[18] Conrad alludes to the phenomenon of distraction in *The Rescue*—but he reverses the gender roles. It is Lingard whom Mr Carter notices 'had not looked either at the sky or over the sea . . . not aloft, not any-where. He had looked at nothing!' (426). In *The Rescue* the male protagonist assumes the attitude of the 'distracted woman', while Mrs Travers's 'gaze' generates the sort of anagnorisis usu-ally reserved for the Conradian hero.

For what Mrs Travers experiences initially as the 'illusion' of the East actually puts her in touch with a greater sense of

---

[18] See Jonathan Crary, 'Unbinding Vision', in *October* 68 (Spring 1994), 21–44, on 'attentiveness', which he claims dominated the work of, amongst many others, Fechner, Ernst Mach, William James, Charcot, Alfred Binet, Théodule Ribot (23). Crary uses Manet's *The Conservatory* (1879) as the paradigm, where the woman gazes absently out of the picture frame, while the man leaning on her chair tries to attract her attention. See also Michael Fried, *Absorption and Theatricality: Painting and Beholder in the Age of Diderot* (Chicago and London: University of Chicago Press, 1980) on the 'significance of the alienating, distancing character of the chief female figure's frontal gaze in Manet's *Déjeuner sur l'herbe* and *Olympia*' (4), whose antecedents, Fried argues, can be traced to 18th-cent. art theory.

reality than she has ever known during her empty life of European salons. With Lingard she reaches an understanding that is confirmed during a transformational moment, as Mrs Travers dons native costume to enter the stockade where negotiations for her husband's release take place. Her identity is fulfilled during the performative act, as the self is literally seen to become another. Entering the stockade on Lingard's arm she 'had the sensation of acting in a gorgeously got up play on the brilliantly lighted stage of an exotic opera' (295).[19] As if she had entered the illusion herself, Lingard delights in her 'not as a living being but like a clever sketch in colours' (297). Their most intimate discussions focus on the subject of illusion, spectacle and drama. Lingard confesses that the one opera he had ever seen was to him 'more real than anything in life' (301), whereas Mrs Travers understands that the difference between them is that 'I have been living since my childhood in front of a show and that I never have been taken in for a moment by its tinsel and its noise or by anything that went on the stage' (305). Ultimately their relationship only exists in the space created by an illusory 'frame'. Moreover, Conrad's protracted use of the perspectival metaphor draws attention to the artificial nature of fiction itself. The anxiety caused by the couple's romantic desire to reach into oblivion, into the vanishing-point of the 'illusion' that has challenged their identities is repeated in the readers' desire for a happy ending. Edith's loyalty to her European life is put to the test, as is Lingard's loyalty to his native friends. Conrad offers a characteristically sceptical closure, leaving an open-endedness that requires a suspension of judgement. Both have been disillusioned by their attainment of knowledge, while at the same time accepting that they would not have changed the experience. The novel concludes literally with a clear picture of Lingard and

[19] See Batchelor, *Life*, 133, on Conrad's references to opera in the later fiction. He quotes Karl (*Three Lives*, 20), on Conrad's suggestion that *Victory* might make 'a libretto for a Puccini opera'. I would add that this is supported by the text of *Victory*, where Conrad gives Lena the line 'They call me Alma. I don't know why' (88), an echo of 'They call me Mimi. I know not why,' from the libretto (Giacosa and Illica) of Puccini's *La Bohème* (1896) based on the novel by H. Murger, *Scènes de Bohème* (1847–9). In *Nostromo* (90), Conrad makes 'His Provincial Excellency' refer incorrectly to *Lucia di Lammermoor* as a Mozart, not a Donizetti opera (1835). Perhaps Conrad was deliberately playing on the allusion to the title of Walter Scott's novel, *The Bride of Lammermoor* (1818).

Mrs Travers travelling across the sea in opposite directions, towards their separate horizons, Edith moving back towards her 'luminous perspective of palatial drawing rooms' away from her encounter with the 'man of infinite illusions' (466). Throughout the novel, Mrs Travers's relationship with Lingard has been recorded through the language of visuality. Her ultimate recognition and acceptance of the emptiness of her former life triggers a contemplation of the abyss. Overwhelmed by a sense of isolation, she looks into the 'finality in that illusion' (151). As the omniscient narrator enters Mrs Travers's centre of consciousness, Conrad this time gives the woman the encounter with the 'heart of darkness'.

As Conrad's novels moved into the world of glossy magazines, the age of photography, advertising, and the cinema, his texts both reflected and commented on the exigencies of this new context, in which both communication and commerce became increasingly reliant on the rhetoric of the image. His narratives move in and out of the conventions of the popular novel, his themes sometimes conforming and sometimes departing, with characteristic irony, from the generic expectations of their contexts. By reading these novels in terms of Conrad's response to the operations of perspective, we clarify his understanding of a new medium—one that called for immediate access to the (literally) visible, and to the question of how the woman is literally observed.

8
Suspense and the Novel of Sensation

Critics of Conrad have supplied us with an extensive record
of his literary sources, showing us the traditions, both philosophical and narratological, that sustained his fiction. We have
learned that he drew on sources ranging from Schopenhauer,
Darwin, Pater, French realism, impressionism, Dickens, Henry
James, the male adventure tradition, and the detective novel. What
has gone unnoticed, however, is Conrad's intriguing engagement
with women's writing. The female novel of sensation, pioneered
by such writers as Mary Elizabeth Braddon and Mrs Henry
Wood, has never been associated with Conrad's work. Initially
these women novelists had found a lucrative market for serialised fiction in the mainly female readership of the circulating
libraries of the 1860s and 1870s, but they continued to publish
successfully in the first decades of the twentieth century.[1]

As we have seen, Conrad also aimed to reach a female readership of popular fiction in his later work. His final, unfinished
novel, *Suspense*, for example, explores a Napoleonic theme,
accommodating the generic expectations of a wide market for
historical romance.[2] But this novel is not just a tale of male adventure set at the beginning of the nineteenth century. The romance
plot draws on a number of the conventions of an earlier
form of women's writing that had survived up to the time of
Conrad's late career. By focusing on the presentation of gender
and the narrative strategies of *Suspense*, and with particular reference to Mary Elizabeth Braddon's *Lady Audley's Secret*,[3] the

---

[1] See Elaine Showalter, *A Literature of their Own: from Charlotte Brontë to Doris
Lessing* (1977; London: Virago, 1982), 153–81; Jenny Taylor, *In the Secret Theatre
of Home: Wilkie Collins, Sensation Narrative, and Nineteenth-Century Psychology*
(London: Routedge, 1988); Lyn Pykett, *The 'Improper' Feminine: The Women's
Sensation Novel and the New Woman Writing* (London and New York: Routledge,
1992).   [2] *Suspense* was published posthumously in 1925.
[3] Mary *Elizabeth* Braddon, *Lady Audley's Secret* (1862; Oxford: Oxford Uni-

following discussion will show that Conrad's later fiction offers a sensitive commentary on the conventions of female sensationalism.[4]

Admittedly, these novels seem unlikely models of inspiration for Conrad. Indeed, he spoke deprecatingly of many popular contemporary women writers. He disparaged the works of Sarah Grand and Margaret Louisa Woods[5] and complained of the best-selling sensationalist, Marie Corelli, 'whose thought is commonplace, the style without distinction'.[6] But Ford Madox Ford pointed out that Conrad had cultivated a preference for some of the earlier popular women writers during his days at sea, particularly Mary Braddon and Mrs Wood, and he continued to read them in later life. Ford presents an image of Conrad that offers an alternative to the usual view of him as serious-minded man of letters, and provides us with a fresh glimpse of Conrad as reader, one that rarely appears in the biographies:

It was Conrad's good luck to be spared the usual literature that attends on the upbringing of the British writer. He read such dog-eared books as are found in the professional quarters of ships' crews. He read Mrs Henry Wood, Miss Braddon—above all Miss Braddon! . . . She wrote very good, very sound English; machined her plots inoffensively and well; was absolutely workmanlike, her best novels being the later and less-known ones. Long after this period of seamanship Conrad read *The Orange Girl*, a novel placed in the time of Charles II. He recognised in it, so he then said, all the qualities that he had found in the novelist's work when he had been before the mast.[7]

versity Press, 1987). All references are to this edition, and page numbers are quoted in the text.

[4] *Suspense* has received very little attention from scholars. For exceptions see: G. Jean-Aubry, 'The Inner History of Conrad's *Suspense*: Notes and Extracts from Letters', *The Bookman's Journal* 13:49 (Oct. 1925), 3–10; Tetsuo Yoshida, 'Joseph Conrad's Napoleonic Fiction,' *Studies in English Language and Literature* (Kyushu University) 33 (Jan. 1983), 65–94; Ugo Mursia, 'Notes on Conrad's Italian Novel: *Suspense*,' trans. Mario Curelli, in Gene Moore (ed.), *Conrad's Cities: Essays for Hans van Marle* (Amsterdam: Rodopi), 1992. For the only lengthy discussion of Conrad's creation of this novel, see Gene Moore, 'In Defense of *Suspense*', *Conradiana* 25:2 (Summer, 1993), 99–114. See also Robert Hampson, 'The Late Novels', in J. H. Stape (ed.) *The Cambridge Companion to Joseph Conrad* (Cambridge: Cambridge University Press, 1996), 140–59.

[5] 29 Oct. or 5 Nov. 1894, *CL* 1, 185; *CL* 2, 137.

[6] Letter to Aniela Zagórska, Christmas 1898, *CL* 2, 137. Marie Corelli was the pseudonym of Mary Mackay (1864–1924).

[7] Ford Madox Ford, *Joseph Conrad: A Personal Remembrance* (1924; New York: The Ecco Press, 1989), 96. In fact Ford confuses the title of Braddon's novel. *The Orange Girl*, whose title refers to Nell Gwynn, was written by Walter Besant.

The passage is remarkable for its suggestion that Conrad may have learned as much about writing from popular female authors of the period as he did from the great names usually associated with his work. While the numerous studies of influences on Conrad currently available draw attention to the fact that, whether consciously or not, 'intertextuality' became a way of life for this author, Ford's comment reminds us that Conrad read widely outside as well as inside the canon of his day. And while Conrad may have been critical of sensationalism, his own writing benefited from this tradition and commented on it. To assess Conrad's relationship to the traditions of female sensationalism I shall first review the conventions of the form, drawing principally on Braddon's strategies in her widely read novel, *Lady Audley's Secret*.

I

The sensation novel flourished from the 1860s onwards with plots focusing on the depiction of lurid, implausible, or sensational events. The action of these novels, concerned with the drama of concealed identities, conflicts over property and inheritance, and the unearthing of guilty secrets of disease and madness, takes place within the confines of the family in a domestic setting. Wilkie Collins established a number of the genre's conventions with *The Woman in White* (1860), but the sensation novel took a new impetus from writers such as Mary Elizabeth Braddon (1837–1915) and Mrs Henry Wood (1814–87), who continued writing in this vein, and whose novels, including their many dramatisations, attracted both a male and female audience until well into the twentieth century.[8]

The overriding characteristics of the female sensation novel fall into several overlapping categories. In terms of themes, they explore hidden identities, showing a preoccupation with the

It is much more likely, given Conrad's preference for Braddon, that Ford intended to cite Braddon's *London Pride* (1896; subtitled 'When the World Was Younger'), a novel set in the reign of Charles II that also touched on the life of the king's mistress.

[8] N. Donaldson, introduction to *Lady Audley's Secret* (New York: Dover Publications, 1974), p. vii. Braddon attributed her idea for the novel to Collins (*The Woman in White*), from whom she borrowed 'the signal device of a self-appointed detective'.

anxiety of inherited madness, as well as the suggestion of sexual ambivalence, presented through the covert plotting of incestuous and homosexual relationships. Stylistically, the sensational tone depends on a sense of theatricality and melodramatic excess, while representational methods include a strong iconographic element, reflected in the pervasive use of portraits. At the same time they borrowed from the Gothic novel the physical framing of figures within oppressive enclosures, like domestic interiors or walled gardens.

Braddon's novels are distinguished by a problematic representation of female identity. The main protagonists usually exhibit the ideal beauty and charm of the conventional romance heroine, but they are also intelligent, devious, resourceful, and treacherous, committing bigamy and contemplating murder to attain their desires. *Lady Audley's Secret*, for example, relates the story of Helen Talboys, who, having been abandoned by her husband George, falsifies her identity (posing as a governess, 'Lucy Graham'), and illegally marries a rich aristocrat to secure her future. However, during the course of the novel we learn that all Helen's dissimulations are primarily constructed in order to conceal a fear of inherited madness, passed down to her from her mother. When her first husband returns from Australia, hoping to be reunited with wife and child, 'Lady Audley' attempts to murder him, and subsequently poisons her second husband in order to conceal her 'secret'.

The notion of secrecy and concealment structures the plot of this novel. The narrative of *Lady Audley* resonates with references to the suppressed self—'every clue to identity burned and forgotten' (12)—and Braddon initially presents the heroine as a docile, impoverished governess, possessing the attributes of the Dickensian innocent (not unlike Marlow's most sentimental view of Flora de Barral in *Chance*). Beneath the surface, however, 'Lucy Graham' (Lady Audley) embodies the familiar image of the temptress, while her confession of bigamy, of appropriating a false identity, of attempted murder, show that all these crimes have been committed in order to maintain a fragile 'other' self, locked within the psyche.[9] Feminist critics have shown

---

[9] See Pykett, *The 'Improper' Feminine*, 90–1, who has remarked that the representation of Lady Audley raises the question of whether 'femininity is itself duplicitous'.

that the theme of insanity often provided an important signifier for female 'otherness' in the sensation novel of the period.[10] Yet Braddon daringly undermined the prevailing notion of 'inherited' madness by suggesting that insanity cannot account for Lady Audley's unstable behaviour, since she is in fact of sound mind (216).

Braddon's treatment of gender in *Lady Audley* is also problematic. The 'detective' of the novel, the barrister Robert Audley, initially appears as a listless, unmotivated figure (Braddon's character may have suggested itself to Dickens for Eugene Wrayburn in *Our Mutual Friend*, 1864–5). At first Audley displays complete indifference to female company. His interest in life is only reawakened when his old friend George Talboys, recently returned from Australia, mysteriously disappears. Subsequently, Audley's obsessive search for his friend generates a new self-awareness in which he re-examines the relationship. His reflections hint at the sexual undertones of their friendship: 'to think that it is possible to care so much for a fellow' (88–9). He later falls in love with George's sister Clara. But the romance plot offers little more than a mask for his true sexual inclinations, since Clara actually represents, for him, a substitute for George: 'What am I in the hands of this woman, who has my friend's face . . . ?' (258).

Meanwhile, Clara frankly confesses her incestuous feelings for her brother: 'I have stifled and dwarfed the natural feelings of my heart, until they have become unnatural in their intensity . . . I have no-one but my brother. All the love that my heart can hold has been centred on him' (200). Following the revelation that Lady Audley is in fact Helen Talboys, George's bigamous wife, George is finally rediscovered (having survived her attempt on his life). Both the homosexual and incestuous

---

[10] See Sandra M. Gilbert and Susan Gubar, *The Madwoman in the Attic: The Woman Writer and the Nineteenth-Century Literary Imagination* (New Haven: Yale University Press, 1978). See also, Elaine Showalter, *The Female Malady: Women and Madness and English Culture* (London: Virago Press, 1985), 68, for a discussion of the character of Bertha Mason in Charlotte Brontë's *Jane Eyre* (1847): 'The image of Bertha Mason haunts Connolly's book *Treatment of the Insane Without Mechanical Restraint* (1856), and supports his argument that insane women should be treated in asylums rather than at home.' John Connolly (1794–1866) was one of the most prominent Victorian psychiatrists, whose 'philanthropy' was later lampooned by Charles Reade in his novel *Hard Cash* (1863).

relationships are then neatly legitimized, as Robert marries Clara and they both settle down to live with George in a blissful triangular arrangement. Lady Audley takes on the role of the scapegoat in this harmonious closure, as she is cast out, doomed to spend the rest of her days in an asylum.

As Lady Audley confesses, Robert saves his friend George, and the men unite in a happy 'threesome' with Clara, the final melodrama is played out in a series of theatrical gestures. The histrionic tone characterises Braddon's style throughout the novel, in spite of the narratorial emphasis on the secret, inward life of its protagonists. Furthermore, Braddon describes her heroines, literally, as consummate actresses. The impulse to conceal exerts an overwhelming force over the life of the heroine, as we see on one occasion when the detective figure of *Lady Audley* closes in on the protagonist's 'secret'. Lady Audley sits alone, contemplating her past crimes and her present fate, when her thoughts are interrupted by a continuous knocking at the door. Instinctively she grasps a book, assuming a pose that belies her inner turmoil:

Insignificant as this action was . . . it spoke very plainly of ever-recurring fears—of fatal necessities for concealment—of a mind that in its silent agonies was ever alive to the importance of outward effect. It told more plainly than anything . . . how complete an actress my lady had been made by the awful necessity of her life. (298)

Braddon employs a number of specific representational devices to reveal the implicitly performative nature of her heroine's actions. Her female protagonist is often 'presented' theatrically, 'enframed' in a window space or doorway, visually enclosed by the architectural limits of the house or garden, as if contained by a proscenium arch. The inclusion of iconographic references also provides a network of signs conveying the disjunction between seeing and knowing, emphasising the importance of masking and disguise in ensuring the heroine's survival. A portrait in oils of Lady Audley, for example, shows something of the character to which the ordinary observer has no access.[11]

[11] See Kate Flint, *The Woman Reader 1837–1914* (Oxford: Oxford University Press, 1993), 293, on the abundance of complex references to paintings and literature of the period in these novels, a phenomenon that 'goes some way towards giving the lie to the dangerously uncritical mindlessness' often assumed to have been fostered in the women readers of sensation fiction.

Its exaggerated style suggests the key to the female protagonist's identity. The narrator comments on the painter's 'lurid' effects, which gave 'a sinister light to the deep blue eyes': 'it was so like and yet so unlike' (70) the appearance of the sitter. Braddon is gibing at the Pre-Raphaelites here—whose theories ostensibly privileged naturalism, yet whose style strongly influenced the exaggerated designs of contemporary theatre.

Elaine Showalter rightly suggests that these novels have been underrated. She observes that their treatment of female identity not only expressed the underlying instability of an ostensibly repressive Victorian society, but that they also provided one of the few imaginative outlets for women. With a gesture of defiance against patriarchal authority, the heroine of Mrs Wood's *East Lynne* (1861) exchanges family and duty for a lover and a new identity. And if Lady Audley's secret turns out to be suppressed rage rather than madness, then her violence consolidates a social threat, a warning of potential anarchy that might accompany woman's 'release' from her conventionally passive status.[12] Thus Showalter emphasises these novels' subversive power to disturb conventional social categories.

However, while Showalter attempts to recover these texts for a feminist cause, some of Braddon and Wood's apparently radical strategies ultimately fail to liberate the female figure from her limited position. The closure of the novel is perhaps less satisfactory to the feminist reader than might be supposed. The narrator of *Lady Audley* condemns the destructive power of the heroine, her potential 'madness' (the secret of the novel), controlled by her confinement to a private asylum. Likewise the heroine of *East Lynne* describes herself as an 'interloper, a criminal woman who had thrust herself into the house', then dies tragically in her newly adopted role of the solitary governess, unrecognised by her own son.[13] The heroines in both cases are left isolated, outcasts of society, the predominant role of the male prevails. Moreover, the presence of covert plots suggesting sexual deviance undermines the strict conventionality of the romance closure, yet offers no positive alternative to the

---

[12] Showalter, *A Literature of Their Own*, 158.
[13] Mrs Henry Wood, *East Lynne* (1862; London: Ward, Lock and Co., 1910), 378.

frustrated heroines. Although Braddon deftly incorporates subversive strategies into the domestic arrangements at the end of
Lady Audley's Secret, the final status of the heroine remains
unchanged.

Thus the sub-plots of the novel reveal some intriguing vacil-
lations of gender, daring in their suggestion of alternatives to
marriage, yet the privileged status of the male bond is emphasised throughout. In fact the narrator is so careful to reproduce
stereotypical views of the feminine threat that it is sometimes
difficult to imagine the consolation women might have found
in these texts. The rhetorical strategies therefore control a complex moral structure in which traditional ideologies are maintained while the reader is persuaded both to empathise with the
protagonist and condemn her.

II

Conrad responded to the complexity of issues raised by these
novels with characteristic irony. In fact his creative impulse
had always relied, to some extent, on a subversive treatment
of popular genres, and his responses to them act as a structuring principle throughout the fiction. He frequently constructed
complex narrative strategies and time-frames to undermine
popular conventions, and used the static poses of traditional
nineteenth-century literary portraits to explore the relationship
between seeing, being, and knowing. Thus Marlow's inquiring
(but uncomprehending) gaze rests on the pale romantic figure of
Flora de Barral in *Chance* (1913), just as he had once watched
Lord Jim fade from view against the glitter of the sea, 'fated never
to see him clearly' (241).[14]

Conrad also shows how traditional values are perpetuated
by literary forms such as adventure stories, sensation novels

---

[14] See John Batchelor, Introduction to *Lord Jim* (1900; Oxford: Oxford University Press, 1983), pp. xxi–xxii: 'Jim's Patusan adventures seem to break down into
separate short stories, one for each *Blackwood's* number, each presenting Jim as
a courageous hero, the Victorian ideal notion of the good British imperialist. One
may note that stories of imperial adventure were much more to the taste and reading habits of *Blackwood's* readers than the concentrated and subtle psychological
exploration which occupies the first twenty chapters of Conrad's novel.'

and detective fiction. Marlow's equivocal position at the end of *Heart of Darkness* (1899) undermines the comfortable 'return' to the mother country of the protagonist of popular travel tales. The tragic dimensions of Winnie Verloc's role in *The Secret Agent* question the traditional resolution of detective fiction and sensation novels of the period. The box-office closure of *Chance* is deflected by the destabilising effects of the novel's narrative strategies that constantly unsettle the reader's assumptions about the romance genre.

Similarly Conrad reproduced the devices of sensationalism while questioning its less than radical strategies. He frequently drew on the genre's patterns of representation, particularly exploiting its use of visual and dramatic effects, its suggestions of sexual ambivalence, its exploration of secret identities, locating patterns of instability within conventional plots of romance and the family. His first attempt at a domestic drama, 'The Return' (1898) bears some resemblance to the enclosure of Ibsen's *The Doll's House* (1879).[15] But it also alludes to the frustration of the unfulfilled heroines of sensation novels, entrapped in their restricted domestic situations. 'The Return' depicts a crisis in the marriage of an upper-middle-class English couple in which the woman attempts, unsuccessfully, to leave her husband. Mrs Hervey, 'intensely bored with her home', felt as if she were 'packed in a tight box', where 'her individuality—of which she was very conscious—had no play' (120). Like the domestic settings of the sensation novel, the Herveys' house possessed its share of secrets: 'Heavy curtains, caught back, half concealed dark corners' (123), just as Marlow in *Chance* later alludes to the unearthing of the de Barral secret from within the concealed spaces of the house in Brighton, in his 'sensational' portrait of the 'criminal' governess.

In *The Secret Agent*, Conrad juxtaposes private and public lives in his treatment of Winnie Verloc's 'sensational' murder of her husband.[16] With her brutal solution to the discovery of her

---

[15] 'The Return' in *Tales of Unrest* (London: Dent, 1947). Following Edmund Gosse's 1889 review of *A Doll's House* (1879), the play was successfully produced in London. For another dramatic source for 'The Return' (in *Lady Windermere's Fan*, 1892), see Paul Kirschner, 'Wilde's Shadow in Conrad's "The Return"', *Notes and Queries* 40:4 (Dec. 1993), 495–6.

[16] See Wendy Moffat, 'Domestic Violence: The Simple Tale within *The Secret Agent*', *English Literature in Transition 1880–1920*, 37:4 (1994), 465–89.

husband's treachery in involving her brother in the anarchist plot, Winnie literally 'brings home' the instability and corruption at the heart of London society. Conrad negotiates the textual spaces within the novel, presenting Verloc's pornography store as the intermediary between the 'slimy aquarium'[17] of the outer London streets and the inner sanctuary of jaded comfort in his domestic milieu. By drawing on the methods of the sensation novel, with its melodramatic representation of domestic conflict, Conrad illustrates the interdependence of public and private life in a society which ostensibly idealised the notion of home and domestic duty (presented in such essays as Ruskin's *Sesame and Lilies*, 1865, 1871), as a sacrosanct and enclosed world protected from the public sphere.

Conrad's frequent allusions to ghostly presences in the fiction function in the sensational mode, undermining the characters', and the readers' assumptions about the security of identity or domestic well-being. The juxtaposition of aural and visual images in *The Secret Agent* creates a suitably disturbing sense of anticipation and horror. Having drawn attention to the ticking clock throughout the novel, and by using an undramatised narrator who enters Winnie Verloc's consciousness at the moment of the murder, Conrad skilfully enforces the contrast between clock time and felt time, or Bergsonian durée.[18] He simultaneously presents the clock's ticking with the 'trickling' of Verloc's blood, while Winnie, in her altered psychological state, perceives the time in which it takes to kill her husband as artificially distended (265).

In *Victory*, Conrad undermines the structures of Victorian Gothic in his ironic presentation of Schomberg's terror, after the arrival of Jones and his party at his hotel. The threat of murder at the hands of degenerate desperadoes hangs over him, and Davidson tells us that he 'had been overpowered, as it were, by his imagination' (148). Conrad alludes to the sexual subtexts of the sensation novel in his description of Schomberg's 'sensational' association of sex and death. His desire for Lena is juxtaposed against his fear of the intruders, and is undermined by

---

[17] See Owen Knowles, 'Fishy Business in Conrad's *Secret Agent*', *Notes and Queries*, 37:4 (1990), 433–43, for a discussion of the fish imagery in the novel.

[18] Henri Bergson (1859–1941) explored this phenomenon in *Essai sur les données immédiates de la conscience* (1888).

the fact that Jones's homosexuality challenges his self-image of manliness (his 'Officer of the Reserve' pose).

In *The Arrow of Gold*, Thérèse irrationally fears that a murder might be committed in the house in the Avenue of the Consuls. Her appearance resembles that of the spectre-nun from Charlotte Brontë's *Villette* (1853), while she glides through the house, a Gothic figure with lighted candle, transfixed in silent poses on landings and in doorways, fleetingly appearing and mysteriously disappearing from sight into the darkened spaces of the house. The melodramatic presentation of Mrs Travers's extra-marital relationship in *The Rescue* offers a wry comment on the tired poses of sensationalism. The narrator describes the heroine watching Lingard 'with bated breath as at a great actor on a darkened stage in some simple and tremendous drama' (282). And in *The Rover*, Arlette's Gothic figure moves insubstantially throughout the spaces of the text. Her visual presentation associates her with the tragic memories of a childhood during the French Revolution, and suggests a further continuity in Conrad's reference to the Gothic allusions of the sensation novel.

However, Conrad's use of multiple narratorial perspectives enables him to question the ultimately conservative, and predominantly moral closure of these novels. The male narrators' constant interrogation of the female 'threat' in *Chance*, and of the 'ideal' woman in *The Arrow of Gold*; his complex presentation of the deaths of Winnie Verloc in *The Secret Agent* and of Lena in *Victory*, remind us that women's roles have been limited rather than liberated by the conventions of a form that confine them ultimately to the status of *femme fatale*.[19] In *Suspense*, where Conrad allows his heroine to speak for herself, we shall see that he continued to explore the issue by drawing on the sensationalist tradition right up to the end of his career.

III

Suspense appeared posthumously in *Hutchinson's Magazine*, a story magazine for popular tastes, alongside titles such as Eden

---

[19] See Rebecca Stott, *The Fabrication of the Late Victorian 'femme fatale': The Kiss of Death* (Basingstoke: Macmillan, 1992).

Phillpotts's 'A Voice in the Dark',[20] or 'The Madonna's Hand',
by John Home, described by the editor as a 'story of tender
romance, passion, and jealousy set in a Sicilian atmosphere'.[21]
In his final novel, Conrad discussed the topic of suppressed
identities within a context that supported a specifically melodramatic presentation.

Most of the action of *Suspense* takes place *circa* 1815,
around the time of Napoleon's incarceration on Elba, and tells
the story of a young English gentleman, Cosmo Latham. In his
travels to Italy Latham encounters a revolutionary group plotting to release Napoleon. There he also meets and falls in love
with Adèle de Montevesso, daughter of an old family friend.
Adèle confesses to Cosmo that she is trapped in a loveless marriage. She has only married Count Helion de Montevesso in order
to save her parents, exiled during the French revolution, from
penury. Conrad hints that, unknown to Cosmo and Adèle, they
are in fact half-siblings, Adèle being the illegitimate daughter of
Cosmo's father. In the same way that Conrad combined elements of the detective and political novel in *The Secret Agent*,
he characteristically used a hybrid genre with *Suspense*, borrowing from sensation narratives to create the romance plot of
Adèle and Cosmo, and from the adventure story for the tale of
Cosmo's encounters with the rebels and the Napoleonic theme.
Thus the plot suggests that the identity of both male and female
protagonists will be partly circumscribed by the requirements
of the genre. Adèle belongs to the romance plot, but Cosmo is
divided between the locus of historical romance and that of
'boy's own' adventure.

Suspense integrates various elements of sensation fiction in
its attention to suppressed female identity; the Gothic device
of enclosure in the domestic scene; the suggestion of sexual
deviance in the incest plot; the use of an animated painting of
the heroine to generate terror; and the affirmation of male
bonding in the final remaining chapter. Nevertheless, the heroines differ in one fundamental respect. Unlike the dissimulating
'Lucy Graham', Adèle's motives are entirely self-sacrificing, since

---

[20] *Hutchinson's Magazine* (Feb. 1925), 137–8. *Suspense* was also serialised in *The
Saturday Review of Literature*, June–Sept. 1925.
[21] *Hutchinson's Magazine* (July 1925), 57.

she married to save her family, rather than herself, from destitution. But she resembles the heroines of the sensation novels
in that she is compelled to conceal her 'true' identity to survive
this scenario. For Adèle's entrapment in marriage constitutes
her lack of selfhood. The young hero Cosmo detects early in
his relationship with Adèle that 'marvellous as she was, she was
not her own mistress' (96). Adèle repeatedly confesses to him
that her husband 'could never forgive me for being what I am'
(142). With echoes of Turgenev's Lisa, and James's Madame
de Cintré in *The American*, she claims that after accepting de
Montevesso's proposal, she felt 'as though I had done with the
world, as though I had taken the veil' (135). But also Like Clara
Talboys in *Lady Audley*, she had 'learned early to suppress
every expression of feeling' (150). Conrad also alludes to the sensation novel's preoccupation with psychological instability as
Adèle's situation, like that of Lady Audley, leads her to surmise
that 'there have been times when I felt as if I were mad' (152).
Moreover, Conrad's presentation of a secondary female figure,
Clelia, niece of the Count de Montevesso, who spies on Adèle
for her uncle, offers further confirmation of the novel's debt
to sensationalism. The narrator observes that the young girl's
sudden infatuation for Cosmo suggested 'the manifestation of
some inherited lunacy' (186).

The limitation of the heroine's movement within the domestic
sphere represents a recurring trope in both novels, as if the
symbol of the house signifies her imprisonment in a false identity. Lady Audley is rarely pictured outside, and when she does
appear in the garden of Sir Michael Audley's residence, the
setting expresses the gloom of Gothic enclosures: 'the lonely
garden was as quiet as some solitary graveyard, walled in and
hidden away from the world of the living' (274). While this setting is reminiscent of the 'hortus conclusus' in which Conrad's
Alice is entrapped in 'A Smile of Fortune', we find that Lady
Audley is more frequently presented in a Pre-Raphaelite interior
—'faint shadows of green and crimson fell upon my lady's face
from the mullioned window by which she sat' (120).

Similarly, the heroine of *Suspense* never appears outdoors,
or in a landscape. In all the scenes depicting the relationship of
Adèle and Cosmo, Conrad carefully reproduces the theatrical
devices of the sensation novel, creating an atmosphere of heavy,

dark interiors, richly textured furnishings, and dramatic lighting effects. Adèle's pose is constantly fixed by the narrator's gaze,
framed by the artificial extremities of enclosed spaces, where she
moves, between rooms, between furniture, glimpsed in doorways
and window seats, as if gliding through countless tableaux behind
an invisible proscenium.

Cosmo's first meeting with Adèle in the Palazzo Brignoli[22]
demonstrates the narrator's highly voyeuristic, but also specifically theatrical treatment of interiors. First, after picking his way
along dark corridors Cosmo himself steps onto the 'stage', signalled by a combination of visual and aural effects:

he heard the door shut behind him, leaving him as it were alone with
the heavy screen of figured velvet and three windows through which
sunshine poured in a way that almost blinded him after his long experience of half-lights. (83)

His initial view of Adèle represents the familiar northern-style
female portrait, 'a lady seated at a writing-table' (84), while
her demeanour is strikingly dramatised by the 'composed nobility of her attitude' (92). When the two are joined by another
woman, the narrator describes a notably theatrical tableau: 'for
a moment the three persons in the room preserved an absolute
immobility' (89). Later in the scene Adèle herself appropriates
a theatrical metaphor to describe her perception of her failed
marriage: 'the play is over, the stage seems empty' (90).

These moments in Conrad's novel constitute a striking reference, not only to the iconographic traditions and melodramatic
style of the sensation novel, but also to their many dramatisations, in which each scene invariably ended with a frozen
tableau, where the actors held their poses for several seconds as
the curtain fell. The dramatisation of Braddon's novel *Aurora
Floyd* (1863; first adapted for the stage by C. H. Hazlewood in
1864), offers a pertinent example of the 'sensational' climax
of Victorian melodrama, so often coinciding with the exposure
of the heroine's marriage as a sham. Act 1, scene 3 of the play
ends with the stage direction 'Tableau, Music', as the heroine
Aurora, contentedly married to her second husband (her first

---

[22] For an identification of the settings of *Suspense*, see Mursia, 'Notes on Conrad's
Italian Novel', 269–81.

having 'died'), has been exposed as a bigamist. Aurora breaks into hysterical laughter, as she is watched by her 'resurrected' first husband, himself a bigamist, and a couple of unscrupulous servants who have plotted her demise. Hazlewood's stage directions for the tableau are worth quoting since they illustrate perfectly the heroine's transformation from habitual actor to repository of others' gazes:

[. . . at this moment MRS POWELL appears at the window and looks in exultingly—STEVE points exultingly to the certificate he holds in his hand, regarding AURORA with looks of hate as he stands by door, R.—JAMES with his hands in his pockets, and one leg coolly crossed over the other, looks on with indifference. Tableau—Music][23]

The visual disposition of the scene, with its multiple viewpoints focused on the seemingly unknowable female character (while the audience looks on from the other side of the proscenium arch), emphasises the predominantly voyeuristic character of the genre. We may be reminded here of Conrad's rhetorical tactics in *Chance*, as the reader experiences a variety of narratorial perspectives directed towards the enigmatic Flora.[24]

In *Suspense*, however, where the female protagonist is given long passages of direct speech, Conrad manipulates the melodramatic component using a rather different strategy. Here he gives his heroine a voice, an opportunity to relate her autobiography to a sympathetic auditor. The melodramatic flourishes repeat all the outward signs of the sensation novel and drama. The heroine's dilemma of identity and the breakdown of her marriage are presented with familiar references to 'stagey' effects. Yet the essential departure from the genre resides in Adèle's voluntary confession. Unlike the heroines of Braddon's novels, whose crimes are dramatically exposed and whose confessions

[23] Colin H. Hazlewood, *Aurora Floyd* (drama in 3 acts), or 'The Dark Deed in the Wood' (London: Lacy's Acting Edition of Plays, 1864), quoted in Nina Auerbach, *Private Theatricals: The Lives of the Victorians* (Cambridge, Mass.: Harvard University Press, 1990), 33.

[24] For Conrad's relationship to the theatre see Batchelor, *Life*, 123, 149, 272, 275, on the dramatisations. See *Three Plays: Laughing Anne, One Day More, The Secret Agent* (London: Methuen, 1934). Macdonald Hastings adapted *Victory* for the stage. See Miss Lilian Hallowes's (Conrad's secretary's) notebook, Bodleian Library MS Eng. Misc. e. 578: *Victory* ran at the Globe Theatre, 26 March–14 June 1919. Miss Hallowes also records that Conrad started a film script of 'Gaspar Ruiz' on 14 September 1920. The typed copy was finished on 29 October 1920.

are elicited by persistent 'detectives', Conrad's heroine freely offers a description of her marriage to Count Helion as an 'empty stage'. Conrad liberates her from the conventions of the genre by allowing her the integrity of a willing delivery of her story.

Other plots, however, remain concealed in *Suspense*. Unfortunately we shall never know how Conrad intended to complete the novel—as Jessie Conrad bluntly put it: '*Suspense* remains just suspense.'[25] But one unreconciled plot line is suggested strongly by comparison with the novel of sensation—that of the unknowingly incestuous relationship of Cosmo and Adèle, and the hint of a homosexual bond between Cosmo and Attilio, the Napoleonic sympathiser. We can only speculate on Conrad's allusion to the type of subtext contained in the narrative of *Lady Audley*, where Clara Talboys and Robert Audley both express excessive affection for her brother George. However, the existing text of *Suspense* reveals some evidence of covert plotting. At the outset of the novel we learn that the young Cosmo, like Robert Audley, had shown little interest in women. During his European travels he had embarked on only one very superficial liaison with a woman, and, on meeting Attilio on his first night in Genoa, she is soon obliterated from his mind: 'was it possible that a shabby fellow . . . could have got between him and Lady Jane about the time of sunset?' (93). His next encounter, with Adèle de Montevesso, holds greater promise of heterosexual romance, but it is partly doomed by the suggestion of incest that hovers over the text. Cosmo and Adèle shared part of their childhood at Latham Hall, Cosmo's family home when his father gave shelter to Adèle's parents, the Marquis d'Armand and his wife. But the narrator frequently hints at Sir Charles Latham's former intimacy with Adèle's mother, the Marquise (18, 22, 36). While the d'Armands are residing at Latham Hall in exile, Sir Charles shows a distinct preference for the Marquise over his wife. As for Adèle, he demonstrates a particularly 'fatherly' affection for her: 'it was not difficult' for Sir Charles to love her 'as though she had been another daughter of his own' (36). Much later he encourages Cosmo to visit her abroad, as a member of the family. Cosmo subsequently falls in love with Adèle, but Conrad never concluded the romance plot. The existing final chapter in the book describes Cosmo's return to the company of the Napoleonic rebels and Napoleon's messenger, Attilio, the man with whom he had felt such an affinity at the outset of his adventures.

If we look into the history of *Suspense*, Ford Madox Ford provides a clue to the implied incest plot. *Suspense*, like *Chance* and *The Rescue*, developed in Conrad's imagination over a long period of his career. Conrad first mentions his 'Mediterranean novel' in a letter to William Blackwood in 1902. He wrote of 'another work to try my further luck', which he described as 'a novel of intrigue with the Mediterranean, coast and sea, for the scene'.[26] A possible collaboration with Ford on this novel never came to fruition, but Ford himself published a 'Napoleonic' novel, *A Little Less Than Gods* (1928), which in many ways acts as a sequel to *Suspense*. The protagonists' situations are almost identical in both novels, although Ford deals with a later date in history (the time of General Ney's legendary survival of his own 'execution'), an event that follows those described by Conrad in *Suspense*. But in Ford's novel the revelation that the protagonists, who have fallen in love, are brother and sister, constitutes the dramatic climax of the narrative. Ford implies that the dénouement has been anticipated by the heroine: 'there was no surprise: the thought, she was aware, had been for ever at the back of her mind.'[27]

According to Ford Conrad had been considering the subject of incest when he wrote *The Sisters* (1895), the unfinished fragment discussed earlier in relation to Poradowska's *Pour Noémi*. In his introduction to *The Sisters*, published posthumously in 1928, Ford claimed that Conrad wanted:

---

[26] William Blackburn (ed.), *Letters to William Blackwood and David S. Meldrum* (Durham, NC: Duke University Press, 1958), 158. Conrad did extensive research for this novel. The Beinecke Library, Yale University, holds Conrad's admission card and call slips for the British Library reading room for 7 June–7 Dec. 1920, during which time he ordered (amongst others), the following books: T. Bosworth, *The Island Empire*, 1855; Thiers, *Le Retour de l'île d'Elbe*, 1873; *Le Registre de l'île d'Elbe*—lettres et ordres inédits de Napoleon 1er–28 mai 1814–22 février 1815; *Correspondance de Napoléon de 1804 à avril 1815*; Norwood Young, *Napoleon in Exile* (in Elba), 1914.

[27] Ford Madox Ford, *A Little Less Than Gods* (London: Duckworth, 1928), 206.

to render the emotions of a shared passion that by its nature must be most hopeless of all. At the end of his life when he felt his position secure he began upon this task . . . it was his ambition to write of the passion between a couple who were, unknowingly, brother and sister. That, in *Suspense*, he was going to risk.[28]

Ford commented on the history of Conrad's interest in this subject: 'In Poland he had been brought into contact with a number of tragico-romantic instances of unconscious unions that were within the limits of the Canon Law.' He claimed that the first of their published collaborations, *The Inheritors*, 'has a faint and fantastic suggestion of—unrequited—love between brother and sister', and that *The Sisters* was an early attempt at the same thing: 'The pensive Slav painter was to have married the older sister and then to have had an incestuous child by the other.'[29]

While neither the existing texts of *The Sisters* nor *Suspense* demonstrates conclusively that Conrad was about to reveal incestuous relationships, Conrad gives us enough hints to validate Ford's claim. Ford goes on to say that in 1906, 'when desperately casting about for "subjects" ' Conrad had thought about reviving *The Sisters* again. Shortly afterwards, however, he arrived at Ford's house with the first chapter of the first draft of *Chance*. Conrad's customary creative patterns show how themes overlap from novel to novel, as he broke off one work to begin something new. Frequently a major theme of one will appear as a ghostly repetition in another. It is possible that certain ideas associated with *The Sisters* found their way into *Chance* in this fashion. For in this novel, where Mrs Fyne responds jealously to her brother's elopement with Flora ('they are so utterly unsuited for each other', 143), the relationship of Mrs Fyne and Captain Anthony carries with it the suggestion of an excessive attachment between brother and sister.

Moreover, at this point in *Chance*, Mrs Fyne behaves very much in the manner of the wronged sister of the sensation novel. Like Clara Talboys in *Lady Audley*, she will do anything to preserve her brother from the wicked feminine wiles of the heroine. Of course problematic sexual relationships had to be

---

[28] Ford Madox Ford, Introduction, *The Sisters* (New York: Crosby Gaige, 1928), 5.   [29] Ibid., 5–6.

treated guardedly in the sensation novel, for reasons of propriety and censorship. But the methods outlined in *Lady Audley* show that such restraint did not undermine the sense of passion with which such relationships were handled. The strategy of covert plotting merely gave them a forbidden quality, adding dramatic impact to their presentation.

Conrad exploited this feature of the sensation novel in his treatment of the protagonists of *Suspense*. His omniscient narrator adopts an equivocal tone, making oblique references to Adèle de Montevesso as a substitute sister (as well as potential lover), for Cosmo. During their first meeting in Italy Cosmo tells Adèle of his inability to communicate with his 'real' sister: 'what could one write to a young girl like Henrietta?' (91). Whereas, he adds, 'I think perhaps you could understand me' (92).[30]

While the 'forbidden' relationships of *Lady Audley* are, ironically, sanctioned at the end of the novel by the domestic arrangements of three of its protagonists, it seems unlikely that Conrad intended such a cosy closure for *Suspense*. Moreover, a strategic shift from the romance plot to the adventure plot, occurring at the end of the penultimate chapter of Part III, suggests that Conrad may have been uneasy with the way he had been shaping the love story. In this scene, Conrad articulates this anxiety using one of his most striking references to the sensationalist tradition.

The scene occurs after Cosmo's second daytime visit to Adèle. Returning to his bedroom at the Genoan inn where he is staying, Cosmo later that night sees the heroine in a vision of a painted martyr. He subsequently runs in terror from the inn. The final part of the novel describes how, in his late-night wanderings by the harbour, Cosmo resumes his acquaintance with

---

[30] It seems that Conrad then makes a sly autobiographical reference to his earlier relationship with Marguerite Poradowska when Adèle replies: 'That would be because I am so much older' (92). In spite of the biographical speculation over the extent of Conrad's intimacy with Poradowska, the evidence shows that, as a distant relation and an older, more experienced woman, she represented something of the 'forbidden' to Conrad. See letter from Tadeusz Bobrowski to Joseph Conrad, 18/30 July 1891, in Zdzisław Najder (ed.), *Conrad's Polish Background: Letters to and from Polish Friends*, trans. Halina Carroll (London: Oxford University Press, 1964), 148. Uncle Tadeusz Bobrowski had warned him to stay away from her, writing to him in 1891 that a relationship with Poradowska 'would be a stone round your neck'.

Attilio. Cosmo is once more embroiled in the rebels' adventures as he is first arrested, then rescued by Attilio and his friends. In the closing chapter Conrad's heroine disappears from the narrative. There is no further reference to Adèle once Cosmo becomes caught up again in the relationship with Attilio and in the male plot.

Conrad's strategy leaves the outcome of relationships and the direction of the plot unresolved. However, the vision scene provides some hints, where Adèle makes her final, ghostly appearance as a spectre-like painting, reminiscent of the lurid effects of Braddon's use of portraiture in *Lady Audley*. The painting of Adèle, as described by Cosmo, leaps out at the hero—one might say—straight from the sensationalist tradition. Cosmo recounts his experience as something that

must have been foretold to him in some picture he had seen in Latham Hall, where one came on pictures (mostly of the Italian school) in unexpected places, on landings, at the end of dark corridors, in spare bedrooms. A luminous oval face on the dark background—the noble full-length woman, stepping out of the narrow frame with long draperies held by jewelled clasps and girdle, with pearls on head and bosom, carrying a book and pen (or was it a palm?), and—yes! he saw it plainly with terror—with her left breast pierced by a dagger. He saw it there plainly as if the blow had been struck before his eyes. The released hilt seemed to vibrate yet, while the eyes looked straight at him, profound, unconscious, in miraculous tranquillity.

Terror-struck, as if at the discovery of a crime, he jumped up trembling in every limb. He had a horror of the room, of being alone within its four bare walls, on which there were no pictures, except that awful one which seemed to hang in the air before his eyes. (195–6)

This extraordinary scene recreates an atmosphere of Gothic melodrama, recalling the terror released in Braddon's novels by the revelation of female identity and 'feminine' power. The composite iconography suggests a type for a number of different Christian martyrs (St Lucy, St Agnes, St Justina of Padua[31]), yet the flimsy dress and presence of the dagger through the heart most convincingly allude to the classical 'martyrdom' of Lucretia, an image assimilated into Christian iconography in

---

[31] See George Kaftal, *Saints in Italian Art: Iconography of the Saints in Tuscan Painting* (Florence: Sansoni, 1952), 606, 646; see also S. Baring-Gould, *The Lives of the Saints* (London: Nimmo, 1907).

the Renaissance, and which was revived in the nineteenth century as an exemplum of female sacrifice. (Lucretia is raped by her husband's kinsman and, after entreating her father and husband to avenge the deed, commits suicide.[32])

While Cosmo's vision of Adèle appears to function as a Gothic trope, generating fear in the beholder and implying unsettled emotions in the heroine, it also suggests a deliberate reference more specifically to the sensation novels of the 1860s. One of the first parodies of Braddon and Wood, for example, was entitled *Lucretia; or, The Heroine of the Nineteenth Century*. Appearing in 1868, *Lucretia* was written by a Tractarian, Francis Paget, who railed against what he considered to be the cheap degradation of love expressed in these women's work.

Yet Conrad's allusion to Lucretia as a sensationalist vision also resembles the trope of self-sacrifice used frequently by his younger contemporaries to represent women in their novels.[33] Marjorie Bowen, for example, a prolific writer of historical novels conceived in a sensationalist manner, whom Conrad possibly read, frequently presented her heroines in this way.[34] Given the initials of her name, she may have been one of the novelists whom Ford had confused with Mary Braddon, since she wrote several novels about the life, not of 'The Orange Girl', but of the family of William of Orange. If Conrad had read her, she would certainly have provided him with contemporary source material for a historical novel such as *Suspense*, aimed at the popular market. In Bowen's *Prince and Heretic* (1914), which describes the marriage of the elder William Nassau to

[32] See Ian Donaldson, *The Rapes of Lucretia: A Myth and its Transformations* (Oxford: Clarendon Press, 1992) for a discussion of the literary versions by Livy (27–25 BC), Dionysius of Halicarnassus (*c*.7 BC), Ovid, a few years later, and Plutarch as well as the history of the iconography of the myth. For a further discussion of the Lucretia myth see Sylvana Tomaselli and Roy Porter (eds.), *Rape: An Historical and Social Enquiry* (Oxford: Blackwell, 1986), ch. 8. Conrad may also have been thinking of Shakespeare's *The Rape of Lucrece* (1594).

[33] See Moore, '*Suspense*', 107–8, for a discussion of Conrad's extensive borrowings from the *Memoirs* of the Comtesse de Boigne (published 1907) for this novel. Moore does not draw attention to Lady Hamilton's 'tableaux vivants', described by the Comtesse as 'attitudes'. See *Mémoires of the Comtesse de Boigne*, trans. and abridged by Sylvia de Morsier-Kotthaus (London: Museum Press, 1956); in this context it may be useful to note a suggestive reference: 'I turned round in surprise and even a little fear, for she [Lady Hamilton as Medea] was brandishing a dagger!' (56).

[34] Marjorie Bowen was the pseudonym of Gabrielle Margaret Vere Campbell (1886–1952).

Anne of Saxony, the heroine, Renée, whose love for William is unattainable, imagines that a painting depicting a female martyr speaks to her as a metaphor of her own situation: 'It was a Flemish painting, perhaps a hundred years old, and represented a young saint, Agnes, Barbara, or Cecilia, being led out to martyrdom.'[35] Her novel *Because of These Things* (1915), set in Bologna in the fifteenth century, at one point describes the hero's vision of a woman, which had appeared as if from a painting he has recently removed from his room:

He thought that a woman grew up from the darkness, formed rapidly, and came to instant perfection out of a swirl of fire, jewels, and flowers. She was dressed like one of those Italian ladies he had lately met, in full vanity of brocade and velvet, lace and gems . . . she had a look of the Madonna he had lately flung from his room . . . the room was certainly full of vague horror; reality was mingled with his vision.[36]

Again, in *The Carnival of Florence* (1915), Bowen describes 'a fine work by some early master representing the dolorous Virgin wearing a heavy gilt crown and gazing upwards with eyes red with tears, while seven swords were thrust into her heart'.[37] Bowen's novels were frequently serialised in *Hutchinson's Magazine*, in which *Suspense* appeared in February 1925, after Conrad's death. Her serial novel 'The Gorgeous Lovers' appeared beside an instalment of *Suspense* in the issue for April 1925, in which she refers to pictures of the heroine dressed as a variety of mythological figures: Hebe, Diana or Minerva.[38] Although Conrad never saw his own novel published, and may not have read this particular Bowen story, we can see how closely he accommodated his fiction to this type of serial context.

However, Conrad's narrative strategies differ considerably from those of Bowen, whose narrators wield a relatively uncomplicated authority over the story. Conrad, on the other hand, uses the omniscient narrator to move between limited and unreliable perspectives, creating an uneasy tension between the main plots of the novel (that of Cosmo, whose position shifts

---

[35] Marjorie Bowen, *Prince and Heretic* (London: Methuen, 1914), 152.
[36] Marjorie Bowen, *Because of These Things* (London: Methuen, 1915), 9.
[37] Marjorie Bowen, *The Carnival of Florence* (London: Methuen, 1915), 226.
[38] Marjorie Bowen, 'The Gorgeous Lovers', in *Huchinson's Magazine* (April 1925), 359.

awkwardly between the locus of romance and adventure, and that of Adèle, who is enclosed in the domestic plot).

But if Conrad was looking for models for his final presentation of the heroine, a far more personal allusion may have suggested itself to him. Recalling the impact of *Pour Noémi* on Conrad's unfinished *The Sisters*, it is worth noting that Poradowska, like many contemporary writers of romance fiction, used literary portraiture throughout her romance, in the manner of the sensation novel, to suggest hidden identities in the heroine, as well as to imply the hero's fixed assumptions about her role both as idealised woman and as victim. As with Cosmo in *Suspense*, Noémi reminds the artist André of the subject of an Italian Renaissance painting: '[elle] lui était apparue, semblable à certaines figures mystérieuses de la Renaissance italienne' (155:89). However, André paints her in the costume of a Polish heroine of the sixteenth century, 'la reine Barbe Radziwiłł', who had probably been poisoned by her mother-in-law (Bona Sforza) in 1547.[39] Like Cosmo's spectral vision of Adèle dressed as a Renaissance martyr, Noémi impersonates the dead woman at the moment at which she appears in a vision to King Sigismond: 'le spectre de sa femme morte' (155:68). Her costume closely resembles, in its details, that of Conrad's martyred heroine:

la jeune femme . . . se laissait vêtir de souple drap . . . sa taille gracieuse était enserée dans une ceinture enrichie de gemmes précieuses, ses lourds cheveux aux chauds reflets s'échappaient en tresses serrées de la caracteristique coiffure royale: un véritable casque de perles qui encadrait divinement son fin visage.[40]

[the young woman . . . allowed herself to be dressed in yielding cloth . . . her graceful waist encircled by a belt adorned with precious jewels, her heavy hair with its warm tones escaping in tight plaits from the characteristically regal head-dress: a veritable helmet of pearls that divinely framed her delicate face.]

Conrad's echoing of *Pour Noémi* in *Suspense* supports Ford's suggestion of a link between *The Sisters* and this novel, and adds further evidence of the surviving influence of Poradowska

---

[39] See Norman Davies, *Gods Playground: A History of Poland* (New York: Columbia University Press, 1982), i. 145.

[40] *Pour Noémi*, *Revue des Deux Mondes* 155 (1 Oct. 1899), 524.

in Conrad's late career.[41] However, Conrad undermines, in his novel, some of Poradowska's implied narratorial strategies. While the protagonist of *Pour Noémi* (who may have been modelled on Conrad himself[42]) sustains his authority as the romantic artist with visionary powers, Cosmo questions the authority of his vision. André's painting memorialises his subject as murder victim, at the same time alluding to his metaphorical possession of her. On the other hand, Cosmo's portrait of the heroine as martyr represents a projection of his imagination, a subjective reconstruction of *his* fears rather than an objective insight into the woman's identity.

In fact Conrad delivers an expressly sceptical response to the methods of the sensation novel. In Braddon's novel, for example, Lady Audley's stepdaughter Alicia pays tribute to the artist's ability to read character accurately: 'a painter is in a manner inspired . . . is able to see, through the expression of the face, another expression that is equally part of it, though not to be perceived by common eyes' (71). And at first Conrad echoes Braddon directly in *Suspense* with an almost identical assertion that 'such visions were for artists, for inspired seers' (195–6). In *Suspense*, however, Conrad later makes Cosmo doubt the validity of his vision, as well as the authority of the artist to 'read' character:

[Cosmo's] superstitious mood had left him. An old picture was an old picture . . . A copyist is not an inspired person; not a seer of visions. He felt critical, almost ironic, towards the Cosmo of the morning, the Cosmo of the day, the Cosmo rushing away like a scared child from a fanciful resemblance, that probably did not even exist. (250)

In an earlier version, collected in the Ashley Manuscript (the First Copy of *Suspense* was a typewritten script with Conrad's alterations by hand[43]), Conrad had extended Cosmo's rational

---

[41] Conrad may also have read an article by M. F. Ponsard, 'La Première Représentation de *Lucrèce*' in the *Revue des Deux Mondes*, 155 (1 Sept. 1899), 168–86, the issue in which the second part of Poradowska's *Marylka* was published. Ponsard, son of the French playwright François Ponsard, recalled how his father had been inspired to write a drama about Lucretia (1843) by the memory of a painting that had been hanging in the family home, 'sous les yeux depuis son enfance', and that depicted the moment when 'elle enfonce le poignard dans son sein'. The son remarked on the visionary effect it had had on his father's dreams.

[42] See Ch. 3.   [43] Ashley MS 2958, British Library.

explanation for his vision. The unpublished version is less equivocal, giving the 'Cosmo of the morning' full responsibility for imagining the vision. The narrator tells us that the 'vision' is merely the impression that Adèle's face habitually produces in him. As the romantic hero of the male adventure plot, Cosmo's 'vision' confirms his conventional view of the heroine as a self-sacrificial, passive, and dutiful woman. The final version leaves room for a more ambivalent reading, placing greater emphasis on the novel's self-reflexive tone and its questioning of the sensation form.

Thus Conrad's use of the portrait device to question female identity places him in a rather different context relative to his contemporaries and to his received image. He also appears in consequence to be more indebted to popular conventions, in tune with his broad experimentation with visuality and 'framing' in the later works. In this context, we might look briefly at the position occupied by Conrad and other contemporary writers of 'literary merit', who often expressed an uneasy ambiguity with regard to the presentation of female identity. Novels of the period frequently refer to a form of visual representation where, within the text itself, the female figure is not only seen *by* the narrator, but also seen *as* another, described as the subject of a painting, a sculpture, striking a well-known pose or viewed as a traditional image.[44] In other words, her representation is subject to a form of metaphorical substitution, her identity only completed by association with another. As if her autonomy were always in question, she is made present to the reader only through a performative act in which she must assume an already identifiable role.

The device of the female portrait was adopted during this period by both 'literary' writers and writers for a wide readership of popular tastes. It was used in a variety of contexts as a means of expressing women's precarious ontological status, as well as suggesting the difficulties writers themselves encountered in defining the female presence within their texts.[45] After all,

[44] See Margaret Anne Doody, ch. 17, 'Ekphrasis: Looking at the Picture', in *The True Story of the Novel* (London: Harper Collins, 1997), 387–404.

[45] Dozens of examples of this device can be found in nineteenth- and early twentieth-century literature. See George Eliot, *Middlemarch* (1871–2; Harmondsworth: Penguin, 1965), 692, who expresses a moment of psychologial disturbance

a popular novelist like Marie Corelli described her heroine in *The Murder of Delicia* as someone who 'studied the art of dressing perfectly', an occupation that 'made her look like a Greuze or a Romney picture'.[46] Five years later, Henry James used the same strategy as that of his best-selling contemporary, albeit with a greater degree of sophistication, to distinguish the identity of one of the female protagonists of *The Sacred Fount*: '[Mrs Server] might have been herself—all Greuze tints, all pale pinks and blues and pearly whites and candid eyes—an old dead pastel under glass.'[47] Later still, in *The Wings of the Dove*, the terminally ill Milly Theale recognises herself in the strained, elong-ated, but sumptuously adorned subject of a Bronzino painting of a Venetian princess. Milly understands that 'I shall never be better than this', but that is nevertheless, 'dead, dead, dead.'[48] While Corelli exploits a commonplace literary device overtly to draw attention to the beauty and desirability of the heroine, James explores a more complex relationship of female iden-tity and representation. As his heroines occupy a framed space, their beautified form physically idealised by the image, he hints on the one hand at the empowerment of the woman evoked by such a performative gesture, but on the other hand, he suggests her 'mortification' as she is contained by the physical limitations of the frame. Moreover, Mrs Server's 'candid eyes', and Milly Theale's anagnoris both suggest the self-knowledge of those women whose precarious identity is paradoxically shaped, yet rendered impermanent by the act of representation.

James's methods are suggestive of Conrad's strategies in the later works, where he draws attention to the implications ensuing from the enframing of the heroine as portrait. Flora de Barral assumes the suicide pose associated with the fallen women of nineteenth-century painting. Conrad comments on traditional

---

in the heroine: '[Dorothea] never looked towards him any more than if she had been a sculptured Psche modelled to look another way'; George Meredith, *Diana of the Crossways* (1885; New York: The Book League of America, 1931), 3: '[Mrs Warwick] might pose for a statue'; Arnold Bennett, *The Roll Call* (London: Hutchinson, 1918), 9, where the narrator describes the heroine as a 'luminous living picture, framed by the window'.

[46] Marie Corelli, *The Murder of Delicia* (London: Skeffington, 1896), 6.

[47] Henry James, *The Sacred Fount* (1901; Harmondsworth: Penguin, 1994), 32.

[48] Henry James, *The Wings of the Dove* (1902; Oxford: Oxford University Press, 1984), 157.

iconography as he presents Lena in *Victory*, and Rita in *The Arrow of Gold* in the pose of the 'toilet of Venus' or the *Mona Lisa*. Conrad's response to the framing device is perhaps most developed in *Arrow*, where, with its somewhat fin-de-siècle tone, Rita is aestheticised throughout. The male narrator even describes his initial acquaintance with her through the stories of two other male figures as a 'visual' presentation: 'to me she was only "presented" elusively, in vanishing words' (31). He hints at the ineffectiveness of all their efforts to 'frame' her identity, limit her autonomy. She was further 'presented' to him, he says, in the Rue de Bologne, where 'that side of the frame in which that woman appeared to one down the perspective of the great Allée was not permanent'(32). In *The Rover*, Arlette is identified most frequently as a Gothic figure enframed in the window space. In *Suspense*, where Conrad also borrows the methods of the sensation novel, Adèle de Montevesso appears as the 'sensational' visionary painting of a Renaissance martyr. Here Conrad makes a similar point to James as the image suggests the beauty and transcendence of the saintly figure, her pose 'frozen' in the painting at the moment of death, a dagger pierced through the heart.

The reference to Lucretia suggests further important resonances. The image, bolting from its frame, causes the familiar 'terror' of the sensation novel in the observer. Cosmo's vision follows his intimate interview with Adèle, one of those rare occasions on which Conrad gave his heroine a voice, with which she confesses the failure of her marriage. Conrad could also be implying that, by 'stepping out of the narrow frame', Adèle rejects a fixed identity, resisting the self-sacrificial status imposed on herself and by others: by her husband Count Helion, for whom she was 'the latest acquisition' (137); by Cosmo himself, or by the reader of romance who recognises the significance of the painting.

In fact, Elisabeth Bronfen's psychoanalytic analysis of literature and painting might seem to offer an appropriate explanation of the operations occurring in Conrad's novel (although Bronfen never mentions Conrad specifically). She responds to Freud's lecture 'On Femininity' (1933) in her discussion, with reference to the case of Edith Wharton's Lily Bart, the heroine of *The House of Mirth* (1905), who finds her ideal expression of identity for the only time in the novel while taking part in a performance of *tableaux vivants*, impersonating Joshua Reynolds's portrait of *Mrs Lloyd* (1776). Bronfen sees the status of the woman 'enframed' being inscribed by the rhetoric of *Unheimlichkeit*: 'death's figure in life'.[49] Yet her emphasis is on the mortification of the heroine, her transformation into the position of a dead woman as she appears as a painting—'it was as though she had stepped, not out of, but into Reynolds' canvas'. She fails to account fully for the transcendence of Lily Bart's action as she embodies 'the person represented without ceasing to be herself',[50]—an action resembling Edith Travers's attainment of identity as she dons native costume in *The Rescue*.

Conrad's representation of his heroine in *Suspense* as the portrait of a martyr seems at first a more promising example of the process described by Bronfen in her Freudian analysis. But again, the paradigm does not explain some of the complexities of the generic signalling at work in Conrad's text. Cosmo's attempt to force tragic closure by imagining the heroine enframed as martyr is foiled by Adèle's active rejection of the pose, 'stepping', not 'into', like Lily Bart, but 'out of the narrow frame'. The scene marks the movement of the hero from the locus of romance to that of the adventure plot. But however terrifying his vision, the shift occurs, not as Adèle perishes in a moment of identification with the dead, but, paradoxically, at the moment of resurrection.[51]

Indeed, Cosmo's terror arises 'as if at the discovery of a crime' (196). Since the pose of Lucretia carries an implication of incest among the Tarquins,[52] could Conrad be suggesting here

[49] Elisabeth Bronfen, *Over her Dead Body: Death, Femininity and the Aesthetic* (Manchester: Manchester University Press, 1992), 269–81.

[50] Edith Wharton, *The House of Mirth* (1905; New York: Berkeley Books, 1981), 135.

[51] Alternatively, Conrad's use of a painting to represent the heroine might be considered from a phenomenological perspective. In its title alone, Paul Ricoeur's *Oneself As Another* (1992) suggests a continuity with the operations at work in Conrad's novel. However, unlike Bronfen, Ricoeur suggests the positive character of his brand of hermeneutics with the use of the term 'attestation'. Conrad's scepticism hardly allows for such a positive account. His representation of the heroine as 'another' draws attention to the slippery relationship of the female self to the other in a context where the term 'female' already presupposes a notion of alterity, and where the act of viewing generates such a disturbance in the male subject.

[52] See Donaldson, *Rapes of Lucretia*, 19.

that the 'crime' refers to the incestuous relationship of Cosmo and Adèle, and Cosmo's vision a traumatic anagnorisis?

If this is the case, then neither the earlier Ashley Manuscript version nor the published version adequately accounts for the almost indecent haste with which Adèle represents a flight from himself, a failure to confront her refusal of a fixed identity, and a return to the familiar territory of the male adventure story. The episode represents one of the most tantalising and unsettling moments in Conrad's treatment of gender since it leaves the issues unresolved. It also suggests that, after experimenting with the representation of women in the romance genre, Conrad himself retreated back into the scenarios of his earlier work—into the narratives of men and male bonding.[53]

Nevertheless, the surviving text demonstrates Conrad's continued preoccupation with popular forms, and with the problematic issue of the presentation of the romance heroine. Whatever Conrad intended for the ending of *Suspense*, the above discussion has shown that, in his treatment of the female role, and the relationship between the main protagonists, Conrad was indebted to the novel of sensation. As Gene Moore has observed, 'after thirty years it is time for a critical reassessment of the assumptions underlying the achievement-and-decline thesis',[54] one that has sanctioned critics' neglect of the late works and consequently some of Conrad's most stimulating discussions of women in his fiction. The case of *Suspense* shows that right up to the end of his career Conrad was, contrary to our traditional assumptions, exploring the representation of female identity and responding to the popular genres that have both questioned and propagated conventional roles for women.

---

[53] For a discussion of male-bonding in literary contexts, see Eve Kosofsky Sedgwick, *Between Men: English Literature and Male Homosocial Desire* (New York: Columbia University Press, 1985).   [54] Moore, '*Suspense*', 99.

Conclusion

In 1937, an entry for Joseph Conrad appeared in the *Dictionary of National Biography*'s supplement for the years 1922–30. His career was summarised for posterity in the following terms:

Conrad's moment of emergence as one of the great novelists of the day came quite suddenly with the publication of *Chance*, a book far less adapted to ready popularity than some of its predecessors and, it must be confessed, more characteristic of its author's affectations than of his qualities. The fact that *Chance* made Conrad's larger reputation is an ironic comment on the power of concerted publicity in modern life.[1]

The biographer concluded that only the earlier work represented Conrad's true achievement: 'the sea was always his real love; and as worshipper, interpreter, and prose-laureate of the sea his name will endure.'[2] Thus Conrad's fear, registered near the end of his life, that he would be remembered principally for his 'sea stuff', was already being fulfilled by the late 1930s. Furthermore, we see that *Chance* was established in the public memory as an example of Conrad's weakest work, whose unfathomable success could only be explained by the power of modern marketing methods.

Combined with his lasting image as man of the sea, and writer for men, Conrad's association with women and women readers has been discretely elided from his public image. This book has argued against the prevailing view by addressing the reductive critical paradigm that sustains such a perspective. Conrad created women characters throughout his career, displaying the sceptic's reticence about inhabiting the feminine consciousness in the way that was so readily available to someone like Henry James. The study of his early childhood in Poland, and the later allusions to his mother's memory in his writing, his responses to the female characterisations of Polish romantic drama, his letters to Poradowska, and his response to

---

[1] Michael Sadleir, entry for Joseph Conrad, *Dictionary of National Biography* 1922–1930, ed. J. R. H. Weaver (London: Oxford University Press, 1937), 208.
[2] Ibid. 209.

Poradowska's romantic fiction, have shown that we cannot so easily dismiss Conrad's complex and elusive relationship to women in his life and in his work.

Ultimately, Conrad negotiated his difficulties by experimenting with genre. By taking the late works seriously, in which he explored the relationship of gender and genre in the romance form, we can trace a continuity in his work. In the very early Malay novels Conrad responded to the genre of exotic romance, but these works have also been selectively excluded from the canon. Conrad continually exploited and questioned the popular traditions throughout his fiction, showing a strong relationship to the genres of the adventure story, detective fiction, and the female sensation novel.

Despite his conflicting opinions about the production of 'popular' fiction, he also sought a wide audience throughout his career, adjusting his self-image to accommodate the market. But the neglect of Conrad's interest in writing for and about women has been perpetuated by a bifurcation of his work into eras of decline and achievement. This too overlooked the continuity that existed in his creative practices. Throughout his writings, Conrad explored the theme of 'appearances', the relationship of observer and observed, to illustrate the range of human perception and misunderstanding. In the early Malay novels the male protagonists perceive the heroines' looks as a locus of female strength and sexual power. The Intended remains something of an enigmatic, peripheral figure in *Heart of Darkness*, but our limited view of her is presented in the form of Kurtz's painting, and in Marlow's idealised evocation of her. In *Lord Jim*, Marlow's view of Jim fades into the horizon, emphasising the narrator's unfulfilled attempts to match 'seeing' in the ordinary sense and 'seeing' in the sense of 'knowing', while in *Chance* an interlocutor questions the authority of Marlow's observations. Conrad's presentation of *Nostromo* gives us multiple perspectives, and the narrative of *Under Western Eyes* is mediated through the limited perspective of the English teacher.

We have seen that the later works show an even stronger concern for the visual, where the reader's gaze is more frequently turned towards the women of the narratives. *The Arrow of Gold* is replete with visual symbols, references to paintings, the aestheticisation of the heroine as she assumes (and resists) the poses imposed upon her by the men of the novel. In the later passages of *The Rescue*, Mrs Travers's uneasy encounter with the East is expressed principally as an exchange of meaningful and enigmatic glances. Arlette repeatedly takes her position at the window in *The Rover*, while the reader gains a privileged view of her as if positioned before a proscenium arch or film screen, where the rapidly unfolding events resemble the sequential patterning of entrances and exits in a play, or shots in a film.

Increasingly, Conrad explored the construction of female identity within the visual contexts in which his later work was published. The allusions to the self-sacrificing mother-figure and the female knight of Polish romantic literature, and the enduring influence of Marguerite Poradowska's work, provided him with sources for the presentation of women throughout his career. In *Chance* Conrad produced an arresting portrait of female isolation, one whose development spanned a substantial part of his career as a writer. Furthermore, we can interpret the actions of Rita, Arlette, and finally Adèle, who rejects her self-sacrificing pose of the martyr, as Conrad's attempt to liberate his heroines from their peripheral positions within the structures of male plots.

The mystery surrounding the outcome of Adèle's narrative in *Suspense* offers an appropriate conclusion to Conrad's treatment of women in the fiction, which remained reserved, and ultimately more complex than has often been assumed. In the light of the evidence, Conrad's identification with his heroines undermines the view of him as misogynist. The mediation of his narratives, in which he distances himself from the pronouncements of his male narrators, suggests a characteristically sceptical view.

This book has challenged the separation of Conrad's work into early and late novels by placing greater emphasis on continuities, his constant experimentation rather than decline, especially in his confrontation with the issue of presenting women in fiction. New perspectives on the biography, on readership, and contexts of publication have made it possible to situate Conrad in a different critical context, one that recovers the whole Conrad corpus for a wider readership.

Bibliography

I. MANUSCRIPTS

Bodleian Library, Oxford
  MS Eng. Misc. e. 578
British Library, London
  MS Ashley 2958. Suspense
New York Public Library, The Berg Collection
  MS Chance (1912)
Yale University, Beinecke Library
  Joseph Conrad, Letters to Marguerite Poradowska
  MS Under Western Eyes

II. NEWSPAPERS AND MAGAZINES

Daily News. London. 1895.
The Bookman. New York. 1895–1914.
Blackwood's Magazine. Edinburgh and London. 1897–1900.
The Savoy Magazine. London. 1896.
The Saturday Review. London. 1896.
Cosmopolis. London. 1897.
The Cornhill Magazine. London. 1897.
Illustrated London News. London. 1901.
Glasgow Evening News. Glasgow. 1903.
Pall Mall Magazine. London. 1902–13.
T.P.'s Weekly. London. 1904.
London Magazine. London. 1908–12.
The New York Herald, New York 1910–13.
Living Age. Boston. 1911.
The Canadian Magazine. Toronto. 1912.
The Manchester Guardian. London. 1914.
Nation. London. 1914.
The Observer. London. 1914.
The Star. London. 1915.
Munsey's Magazine. New York. 1915.
Lloyd's Magazine. London. 1918–20.
Land and Water. London. 1919.
Pictorial Review. New York. 1923.

The New Statesman. London. 1923.
Hutchinson's Magazine. London. 1925.

III. PRINTED SOURCES

ACHEBE, CHINUA. 'An Image of Africa: Racism in Conrad's *Heart of Darkness*.' *Massachusetts Review* 18 (1977), 782–94.

ALBERTI, LEON BATTISTA. *On Painting* (1435–6), trans. with an Introduction and Notes by John R. Spencer. 1956. New Haven: Yale University Press, 1966.

AMBROSINI, RICHARD. *Conrad's Fiction as Critical Discourse*. Cambridge: Cambridge University Press, 1991.

ARMSTRONG, PAUL B. *The Phenomenology of Henry James*. Chapel Hill and London: The University of North Carolina Press, 1983.

——. Misogyny and the Ethics of Reading: The Problem of Conrad's *Chance*', in Keith Carabine, Owen Knowles, Wiesław Krajka (eds.), *Contexts for Conrad*. Boulder, Colo.: East European Monographs, 1993, 151–74.

ATLEE, H. FALCONER. *A Woman of Impulse*. London: F. V. White, 1898.

AUERBACH, NINA. *Private Theatricals: The Lives of the Victorians*. Cambridge, Mass.: Harvard University Press, 1990.

AVELING, ELEANOR MARX and EDWARD. *The Woman Question*. London: Swan Sonnenschein, 1886.

BACHELARD, GASTON. *The Poetics of Space*, trans. Maria Jolas. Boston: Beacon Press, 1964.

BAINES, JOCELYN. *Joseph Conrad: A Critical Biography*. London: Weidenfield and Nicholson, 1960.

BARING-GOULD, S. *The Lives of the Saints*. London: Nimmo, 1907.

BATCHELOR, JOHN. Introduction. *Lord Jim*. Oxford: Oxford University Press, 1983.

——. 'Conrad and Shakespeare.' *L'Époque Conradienne* (1992), 124–51.

——. *The Life of Joseph Conrad: A Critical Biography*. Oxford: Blackwell, 1994.

BENDER, TODD K. *et al. Concordances to Conrad's Works*. New York and London: Garland, 1976– .

BENNETT, ARNOLD. *The Old Wives' Tale*. 1908. London: Grosset and Dunlap, 1911.

——. *The Roll Call*. London: Hutchinson, 1918.

BERTHOUD, JACQUES. *Joseph Conrad: The Major Phase*. Cambridge: Cambridge University Press, 1978.

BESANT, WALTER. *The Orange Girl*. London: Chatto and Windus, 1899.

BICKLEY, PAMELA, and HAMPSON, ROBERT. ' "Lips That Have Been Kissed": Boccacio, Verdi, Rossetti and *The Arrow of Gold*.' *L'Époque Conradienne* (1988), 77–91.

BLACKBURN, WILLIAM (ed.), *Joseph Conrad: Letters to William Blackwood and David Meldrum*. Durham, NC: Duke University Press, 1958.

BLAND, LUCY. *Banishing the Beast: English Feminism and Sexual Morality 1885–1914*. Harmondsworth: Penguin, 1995.

BLOOM, HAROLD (ed.). *Joseph Conrad: Modern Critical Views*. New York: Chelsea House, 1986.

BOHLMANN, OTTO. *Conrad's Existentialism*. Basingstoke and London: Macmillan, 1991.

BONNEY, WILLIAM W. *Thorns and Arabesques: Contexts for Conrad's Fiction*. Baltimore: Johns Hopkins University Press, 1980.

BOOTH, WAYNE C. *The Rhetoric of Fiction*. 1961. Harmondsworth: Penguin, 1987.

BOURNE, H. R. FOX. *English Newspapers: Chapters in the History of Journalism* (2 vols.). London: Chatto and Windus, 1887.

BOWEN, MARJORIE (Gabrielle Margaret Vere Campbell). *Prince and Heretic*. London: Methuen, 1914.

——. *Because of These Things*. London: Methuen, 1915.

——. *The Carnival of Florence*. London: Methuen, 1915.

——. 'The Gorgeous Lovers'. *Hutchinson's Magazine*, April 1925.

BRADBROOK, M. C. *Joseph Conrad: Poland's English Genius*. Cambridge: Cambridge University Press, 1941.

BRADBURY, MALCOLM, and MCFARLANE, JAMES (eds.). *Modernism: A Guide to European Literature 1890–1930*. Harmondsworth: Penguin, 1976.

BRADDON, MARY ELIZABETH. *Lady Audley's Secret*. Leipzig: Tauchnitz, 1862.

——. *London Pride; or, When the World was Younger*. London: Simpkin, 1896.

BREBACH, RAYMOND. *Joseph Conrad, Ford Madox Ford, and the Making of Romance*. Ann Arbor: UMI Research Press, 1985.

BRODIE, SUSAN LUNDVALL. 'Conrad's Feminine Perspective'. *Conradiana* 16:2 (1984) 141–54.

BRONFEN, ELISABETH. *Over Her Dead Body: Death, Femininity and the Aesthetic*. Manchester: Manchester University Press, 1992.

BRYSON, NORMAN. *Vision and Painting: The Logic of the Gaze*. New Haven and London: Yale University Press, 1983.

——. 'The Gaze in the Expanded Field', in Hal Foster (ed.), *Vision and Visuality: Discussions in Contemporary Culture*. Seattle: Bay Press, 1988.

BUSZA, ANDRZEJ. 'Conrad's Polish Literary Background and Some Illustrations of the Influence of Polish Literature on his Work'. *Antemurale* 10 (1966), 109–255.

CAIRD, MONA. 'Marriage', in *Westminster Review* 130 (August 1888).

——. 'Ideal Marriage', in *Westminster Review* 130 (November 1888).

CAIRNS, C. C. *Noble Women*. London and Edinburgh: T. C. and E. C. Jack, 1912.

CARABINE, KEITH. 'From *Razumov* to *Under Western Eyes*: The Dwindling of Natalia Haldin's "Possibilities".' *The Ugo Mursia Memorial Lectures*. Milano: Mursia International, 1988.

——. (ed.). *Joseph Conrad: Critical Perspectives* (4 vols.). Mainfield, East Sussex: Helm Information, 1992.

——. 'From *Razumov* to *Under Western Eyes*: The Case of Peter Ivanovitch.' *Conradiana* 25:1 (1993), 3–29.

CAREY, ROSA NOUCHETTE. *Twelve Notable Good Women*. London: Hutchinson, 1901.

CAVE, TERENCE. *Recognitions*. Oxford: Clarendon Press, 1988.

CIXOUS, HÉLÈNE, and CLÉMENT, CATHERINE. 'Sorties: Out and Out: Attacks/Ways Out/Forays', in *The Newly Born Woman*, trans. Betsy Wing. Manchester: Manchester University Press, 1986.

CLIFFORD, JAMES. *The Predicament of Culture: Twentieth-Century Ethnography, Literature and Art*. Cambridge, Mass.: Harvard University Press, 1988.

COLBRON, GRACE ISABEL. 'Conrad's Women.' *Bookman* 38 (January 1914), 476–9.

COLLINS, WILKIE. *The Woman in White*. 1859–60. Harmondsworth: Penguin, 1974.

COLVIN, SIR SYDNEY. Review. *The Observer*, 18 January 1914.

CONRAD, BORYS. *My Father: Joseph Conrad*. London: Calder and Boyars, 1970.

CONRAD, JESSIE. *Joseph Conrad as I Knew Him*. London: Heinemann, 1926.

——. *Joseph Conrad and his Circle*. London: Jarrolds, 1935.

CONRAD, JOHN. *Joseph Conrad: Times Remembered*. Cambridge: Cambridge University Press, 1981.

CONRAD, JOSEPH. 'The Lagoon'. *Cornhill Magazine*, January 1897, 59–70.

——. *Chance*. London: Methuen, 1913.

——. Interview with Marian Dabrowski. *Tygodnik Illustrowany* 1917, in Zdzisław Najder (ed.), *Conrad Under Familial Eyes*, trans. Halina Carroll. Cambridge: Cambridge University Press, 1983.

——. *The Secret Agent, Laughing Anne, and One Day More*, with an Introduction by John Galsworthy. London: John Castle, 1924.

CONRAD, JOSEPH. *Tales of Unrest.* 1898. New York: Doubleday, 1926.

——. *The Sisters*, with an Introduction by Ford Madox Ford. New York: Crosby Gaige, 1928.

——. *Three Plays.* London: Methuen, 1934.

——. The Collected Edition of the Works of Joseph Conrad. London: Dent, 1946–55.

——. *Almayer's Folly*, ed. David Leon Higdon and Floyd Eddleman with an Introduction by Ian Watt. 1895. Cambridge: Cambridge University Press, 1994.

——. and FORD MADOX FORD. *The Nature of a Crime*, in *Congo Diary and Other Uncollected Pieces*, ed. and with Comments by Zdzisław Najder. New York: Doubleday, 1978.

——. *The Inheritors.* 1901. Stroud, Gloucestershire: Sutton Publishing, 1991.

CONROY, MARK. *Modernism and Authority: Strategies of Legitimation in Flaubert and Conrad.* Baltimore: Johns Hopkins University Press, 1985.

CORELLI, MARIE. *The Murder of Delicia.* London: Skeffington, 1896.

COSSLETT, TESS. *Woman to Woman: Female Friendship in Victorian Fiction.* Brighton: The Harvester Press, 1988.

COX, MARIAN. *The Crowds and the Veiled Woman.* New York and London: Funk and Wagnalls, 1910.

CRANKSHAW, EDWARD. *Joseph Conrad: Some Aspects of the Art of the Novel.* London: John Lane, 1936.

CRARY, JONATHAN. *Techniques of the Observer: On Vision and Modernity in the Nineteenth Century.* Cambridge, Mass.: MIT Press, 1990.

——. 'Unbinding Vision.' *October* 68 (Spring 1994), 21–44.

CURLE, RICHARD. *Joseph Conrad: A Study.* London: Kegan Paul, Trench, Trübner, 1914.

——. *The Last Twelve Years of Joseph Conrad.* London: Sampson, Low, Marston, 1928.

CURELLI, MARIO. 'Napoleone all'Elba in Conrad e Hardy.' *Rivista Italiana di Studi Napoleonici* 17:1 (1980), 63–77.

CZOSNOWSKI, STANISŁAW. 'Conradiana'. *Epoka* 136 (Warsaw, 1929), repr. in Zdzisław Najder (ed.), *Conrad Under Familial Eyes*, trans. Halina Carroll. Cambridge: Cambridge University Press, 1983.

DAICHES, DAVID. 'Joseph Conrad', in *The Novel and the Modern World.* Chicago: University of Chicago Press, 1939; revised edition, 1960.

DALESKI, H. M. *Joseph Conrad: The Way of Dispossession.* London: Faber and Faber, 1977.

DAVIDSON, ARNOLD E. *Conrad's Endings: A Study of the Five Major Novels.* Ann Arbor: UMI Research Press, 1984.

DAVIES, LAURENCE. 'Conrad, *Chance* and Women Readers', in Andrew Michael Roberts (ed.), *Conrad and Gender*. Amsterdam: Rodopi, 1993.

DAVIES, NORMAN. *God's Playground: A History of Poland* (2 vols.). i: *The Origins to 1795*. New York: Columbia University Press, 1982.

DE BOIGNE, COMTESSE. *Mémoirs of the Comtesse de Boigne*, trans. Sylvia de Morsier-Kotthaus. London: Museum Press, 1956.

DE LAURETIS, TERESA, and HEATH, STEPHEN (eds.). *The Cinematic Apparatus*. London: Macmillan, 1989.

DEGERING, THOMAS. *Das Verhältnis von Individuum und Gesellschaft in Fontanes 'Effi Briest' und Flauberts 'Madame Bovary'*. Bonn: Bouvier, 1978.

DERRIDA, JACQUES. 'The Law of Genre', trans. Avital Ronell, in W. J. T. Mitchell (ed.), *On Narrative*. Chicago: University of Chicago Press, 1981, 51–77.

DIXON, ELLA HEPWORTH. *The Story of a Modern Woman*. London: Heinemann, 1894.

DODSON, SANDRA. '*Lord Jim* and the Modern Sublime.' *The Conradian* 18:2 (1994), 77–101.

DONALDSON, IAN. *The Rapes of Lucretia: A Myth and Its Transformations*. Oxford: Clarendon Press, 1992.

DONALDSON, NORMAN. Introduction. *Lady Audley's Secret*. 1862. New York: Dover Publications, 1974.

DOODY, MARGARET ANNE. *The True Story of the Novel*. London: Harper Collins, 1997.

DUNCAN-JONES, E. E. 'Some Sources of *Chance*.' *Review of English Studies* 20 (November 1969), 468–71.

DYBOSKI, ROMAN. 'Z Mlodoski Jozefa Conrada.' *Czas* (Cracow) December 1927, in Andrzej Busza, 'Conrad's Polish Literary Background.' *Antemurale* 10 (1966), 109–255.

EDIE, JAMES M. Introduction to Pierre Thévenaz, *What is Phenomenology and Other Essays*, ed. and trans. James M. Edie. Chicago and London: University of Chicago Press, 1972.

ELBERT, MONIKA. 'Possession and Self-Possession: The "Dialectic of Desire" in '*Twixt Land and Sea*', in Andrew Michael Roberts (ed.), *Conrad and Gender*. Amsterdam: Rodopi, 1993.

ELIOT, GEORGE. *Middlemarch*. 1871–2. Harmondsworth: Penguin, 1965.

ELIOT, T. S. 'Short Reviews: Jessie Conrad, *Joseph Conrad As I Knew Him* (1926).' *Criterion* 5 (January 1927).

ERDINAST-VULCAN, DAPHNA. *Joseph Conrad and the Modern Temper*. Oxford: Clarendon Press, 1991.

FAWCETT, MILLICENT GARRETT. 'Home and Politics'. Suffragist Pamphlet. London, n.d.

——. *The Women's Victory—and After: Personal Reminiscences, 1911–18*. London: Sidgwick and Jackson, 1920.

FINCHAM, GAIL, and HOOPER, MYRTLE (eds.). *Under Postcolonial Eyes: Joseph Conrad After Empire*. Rondesbosch: University of Cape Town Press, 1996.

FLEISHMAN, AVROM. *Conrad's Politics: Community and Anarchy in the Fiction of Joseph Conrad*. Chicago: University of Chicago Press, 1967.

FLINT, KATE. *The Woman Reader 1837–1914*. Oxford: Oxford University Press, 1993.

FOGEL, AARON. *Coercion to Speak: Conrad's Poetics of Dialogue*. Cambridge, Mass: Harvard University Press, 1985.

FOLLETT, WILSON. *Joseph Conrad: A Short Study of His Intellectual and Emotional Attitude Toward His Work and of the Chief Characteristics of his Work*. Garden City, NY: Doubleday, Page, 1915.

FONTANE, THEODOR. *Effie Briest*. 1895. Trans. Douglas Parmée. Harmondsworth: Penguin, 1967.

FORD, FORD MADOX. *Joseph Conrad: A Personal Remembrance* 1924. New York: Ecco Press, 1989.

——. Introduction, *The Sisters*. New York: Crosby Gaige, 1928.

——. *A Little Less Than Gods*. London: Duckworth, 1928.

——. *Ladies Whose Bright Eyes*. 1935. Manchester: Carcanet Press, 1988.

FORD, JANE. 'James Joyce and the Conrad Connection: The Anxiety of Influence', *Conradiana* 17:1 (1985), 3–17.

FOUCAULT, MICHEL. *The Order of Things: An Archeology of the Human Sciences*. 1966. London: Routledge, 1991.

FRASER, GAIL. *Interweaving Patterns in the Work of Joseph Conrad*. Ann Arbor and London: UMI Research Press, 1988.

——. 'Mediating Between the Sexes: Conrad's *Chance.*' *Review of English Studies* 43 (February 1992), 81–8.

——. 'Empire of the Senses: Miscegenation in *An Outcast of the Islands*,' in K. Carabine, O. Knowles, W. Krajka (eds.), *Contexts for Conrad*. Boulder Colo.: East European Monographs, 1993.

FRIED, MICHAEL. *Absorption and Theatricality: Painting and the Beholder in the Age of Diderot*. Chicago and London: University of Chicago Press, 1980.

FRIES, MAUREEN. 'Feminism—Antifeminism in *Under Western Eyes*'. *Conradiana* 5:2 (1973) 56–65.

FUSS, DIANA. *Essentially Speaking*. London: Routledge, 1989.

GALSWORTHY, JOHN. *The Man of Property*. 1906. London: Heinemann, 1921.

——. *Strife.* 1909. *Great Modern British Plays*, ed. J. W. Marriot. London: Harrap, 1929.

——. *Joy: A Play on the Letter 'I' in Three Acts.* 1909. New York: Scribners, 1916.

——. *The Dark Flower.* 1913. London: Heinemann, 1923.

——. *Castles in Spain and Other Screeds.* London: Heinemann, 1927.

GARNETT, EDWARD. *The Breaking Point.* London: Duckworth, 1907.

——. *Turgenev*, with an Introduction by Joseph Conrad. London: Collins, 1914.

——. Review. *Nation* 24 January 1914, 720–2.

——. (ed.) *Letters from Joseph Conrad.* New York, 1928.

——. *Conrad's Prefaces to His Works* (with an introduction by Edward Garnett). London: J. M. Dent, 1937.

GEDDES, GARY. *Conrad's Later Novels.* Montreal: McGill-Queen's University Press, 1974.

GEE, JOHN A., and STURM, J. (eds. and trans.). *Letters of Joseph Conrad to Marguerite Poradowska: 1890–1920.* New Haven: Yale University Press, 1940; repr. Port Washington, NY, and London: Kennikat Press, 1973.

GILBERT, SANDRA M., and GUBAR, SUSAN. *The Madwoman in the Attic: The Woman Writer and the Nineteenth-Century Literary Imagination.* New Haven: Yale University Press, 1978.

——. 'Sexual Linguistics: Gender, Language, Sexuality', in Catherine Belsey and Jane Moore (eds.), *The Feminist Reader: Essays in Gender and the Politics of Literary Criticism.* Basingstoke and London: Macmillan, 1989.

GILLON, ADAM. *The Eternal Solitary: A Study of Joseph Conrad.* New York: Bookman Associates, 1960.

——. 'Conrad in Poland'. *Polish Review* 19:3–4 (1974), 3–28.

GIROUARD, MARK. *The Return to Camelot: Chivalry and the English Gentleman.* New Haven and London: Yale University Press, 1981.

GODWIN, EDWIN LAWRENCE. 'Random Collections.' *Evening Post* (New York), 30 December 1899.

GOGWILT, CHRISTOPHER. *The Invention of the West: Joseph Conrad and the Double-Mapping of Europe and Empire.* Stanford, CA: Stanford University Press, 1995.

GOODMAN, ROBIN TRUTH. 'Conrad's Closet', *Conradiana* 30:2 (1998), 83–124.

GORDAN, JOHN. *Joseph Conrad: The Making of a Novelist.* Cambridge, Mass.: Harvard University Press, 1940.

GRAND, SARAH (Frances Elizabeth McFall). *The Heavenly Twins.* New York: Cassell, 1893.

GUERARD, ALBERT J. *Conrad the Novelist*. Cambridge, Mass.: Harvard University Press, 1958.

HABEGGER, ALFRED. *Henry James and the 'Woman Business'*. Cambridge: Cambridge University Press, 1989.

HAGGARD, RIDER. *She*. 1887. Harmondsworth: Penguin, 1994.

HAMNER, ROBERT D. (ed.). *Joseph Conrad: Third World Perspectives*. Washington, DC: Three Continents Press, 1990.

HAMPSON, ROBERT. *Joseph Conrad: Betrayal and Identity*. Basingstoke and London: Macmillan, 1992.

——. '*Chance* and the Secret Life: Conrad, Thackeray, Stevenson', in Andrew Michael Roberts (ed.), *Conrad and Gender*. Amsterdam: Rodopi, 1993.

——. 'The Late Novels', in J. H. Stape (ed.), *The Cambridge Companion to Joseph Conrad*. Cambridge: Cambridge University Press, 1996.

HARPER, IDA HUSTED (ed.). *The History of Woman Suffrage* (6 vols.). New York: National American Woman Suffrage Association, 1922.

HARPHAM, GEOFFREY GALT. *One of Us: The Mastery of Joseph Conrad*. Chicago: the University of Chicago Press, 1996.

HAWTHORN, JEREMY. *Joseph Conrad: Language and Fictional Self-Consciousness*. London: Edward Arnold, 1979.

——. *Joseph Conrad: Narrative Technique and Ideological Commitment*. London: Edward Arnold, 1990.

HAY, ELOISE KNAPP. *The Political Novels of Joseph Conrad: A Critical Study*. Chicago: University of Chicago Press, 1963.

HEILBRUN, CAROLYN. *Towards Androgeny*. London: Gollancz, 1973.

HENINGER, S. K. 'Framing the Narrative', in Mark Lussier and S. K. Heninger (eds.), *Perspective as a Problem in the Art, History and Literature of Early Modern England*. Lewiston, New York: The Edwin Mellin Press, 1992.

HERVOUET, YVES. *The French Face of Joseph Conrad*. Cambridge: Cambridge University Press, 1990.

HEWITT, DOUGLAS. *Conrad: A Reassessment*. Cambridge: Bowes and Bowes, 1952.

HOLDSWORTH, ANNIE. *Joanna Traill, Spinster*. London: Heinemann, 1894.

HOLLANDER, ANNE. *Moving Pictures*. Cambridge, Mass.: Harvard University Press, 1991.

HOUGH, GRAHAM. *Image and Experience: Studies in a Literary Revolution*. London: Duckworth, 1960.

HUGHES, KATHRYN. *The Victorian Governess*. London: Hambledon Press, 1993.

HUGHES, LINDA K., and LUND, MICHAEL. *The Victorian Serial*. Charlottesville and London: University of Virginia Press, 1991.

HUNTER, ALLAN. *Joseph Conrad and the Ethics of Darwinism: The Challenges of Science*. London: Croom Helm, 1983.

INGRAM, ALLAN (ed.), *Joseph Conrad: Selected Literary Criticism and The Shadow-Line*. London and New York: Methuen, 1986.

IRIGARAY, LUCE. *This Sex Which is Not One*. 1977. Trans. Catherine Porter with Carolyn Burke. Ithaca, NY: Cornell University Press, 1985.

JAMES, HENRY. *The American*. 1877. New York: W. W. Norton, 1978.

——. 'The Art of Fiction'. 1884; New York: The Library of America, 1984.

——. *The Portrait of a Lady*. 1881. Oxford: Oxford University Press, 1981.

——. *The Turn of the Screw and Other Stories*. 1898. Oxford: Oxford University Press, 1992.

——. *The Sacred Fount*. 1901. London: Penguin, 1994.

——. *The Wings of the Dove*. 1902. Oxford: Oxford University Press, 1984.

——. 'The Younger Generation'. *Times Literary Supplement* 2 April and 19 March 1914.

——. 'The New Novel' (1914), in *Henry James: Essays, American and English Writers*. New York: The Library of America, 1984.

JAMESON, FREDRIC. *The Political Unconscious: Narrative as a Socially Symbolic Act*. Ithaca, NY: Cornell University Press, 1981.

JAUSS, HANS ROBERT. 'Literary History as a Challenge to Literary Theory.' *New Literary History* 2 (1970).

JEAN-AUBRY, G. 'The Inner History of Conrad's *Suspense*: Notes and Extracts from Letters.' *The Bookman's Journal* 13:49 (October 1925), 3–10.

——. *Joseph Conrad: Life and Letters* (2 vols.). New York: Doubleday Page, 1927.

——. *Vie de Conrad*. Paris: Gallimard, 1947. Translated as *The Sea Dreamer: A Definitive Biography of Joseph Conrad*. London: Allen and Unwin, 1957.

JED, STEPHANIE A. *Chaste Thinking: The Rape of Lucretia and the Birth of Humanism*. Bloomington: Indiana University Press, 1989.

JOHNSON, BRUCE. *Conrad's Models of Mind*. Minneapolis: University of Minnesota Press, 1971.

JONES, MICHAEL P. *Conrad's Heroism: A Paradise Lost*. Ann Arbor: UMI Research Press, 1985.

JORDANOVA, LUDMILLA. 'Linda Nochlin's Lecture: "Women, Art, and Power" ', in Norman Bryson, Michael Holly, Keith Moxy (eds.), *Visual Theory: Painting and Interpretation*. Cambridge: Polity Press, 1991.

JUDD, ALAN. *Ford Madox Ford*. Cambridge, Mass.: Harvard University Press, 1990.

KAFTAL, GEORGE. *Saints in Italian Art: Iconography of the Saints in Tuscan Painting*. Florence: Sansoni, 1952.

KARL, FREDERICK R. *Joseph Conrad: The Three Lives*. New York: Farrar, Straus, and Giroux, 1979.

——. and DAVIES, LAURENCE (eds.). *The Collected Letters of Joseph Conrad* (8 vols.). Cambridge: Cambridge University Press, 1983– .

KEATING, PETER. *The Haunted Study: A Social History of the English Novel 1875–1914*. London: Secker and Warburg, 1989.

KELLY, MYRA. 'Her Little Young Ladyship.' *New York Herald* Sunday Magazine, June 1911.

KIRSCHNER, PAUL. *Conrad: The Psychologist as Artist*. Edinburgh: Oliver and Boyd, 1968.

——. (ed.). *Typhoon and Other Stories*. Harmondsworth: Penguin, 1990.

——. 'Wilde's Shadow in Conrad's "The Return".' *Notes and Queries* 40:4 (December 1993), 495–6.

KLEIN, KAREN. 'The Feminist Predicament in Conrad's *Nostromo*', in John Hazel Smith (ed.), *Brandeis Essays in Literature*. Waltham, Mass.: Department of English and American Literature, 1983, 101–16.

KNOWLES, OWEN. *A Conrad Chronology*. London and Basingstoke: Macmillan, 1989.

——. 'Fishy Business in Conrad's *Secret Agent*.' *Notes and Queries* 37:4 (1990), 433–43.

——. 'Conrad's Correspondence: A Literary Dimension.' *Conradiana* 23:1 (1991), 19–27.

——. *An Annotated Critical Bibliography of Joseph Conrad*. Hemel Hempstead, Hertfordshire: Harvester Wheatsheaf, 1992.

KRASIŃSKI, ZYGMUNT. *The Un-divine Comedy*. 1833. In Harold B. Segel (ed. and trans.), *Polish Romantic Drama*. Ithaca, NY: Cornell University Press, 1977.

KRENN, HELIÉNA. *Conrad's Lingard Trilogy: Empire, Race, and Women in the Malay Novels*. New York and London: Garland, 1990.

——. 'The "Beautiful" World of Women: Women as Reflections of Colonial Issues in Conrad's Malay Novels', in Keith Carabine, Owen Knowles, Wiesław Krajka (eds.), *Contexts for Conrad*. Boulder, Colo.: East European Monographs, 1993, 105–19.

KRYŻANOWSKI, JULIAN. *The History of Polish Literature*. 1972. Warsaw: PWN-Polish Scientific Publishers, 1978.

LA BELLE, JENIJOY. *Herself Beheld: The Literature of the Looking-Glass*. Ithaca, NY: Cornell University Press, 1988.

LALVANI, SURIN. 'Photography, Epistemology and the Body.' *Cultural Studies* 7:3 (1993), 442–65.

LEAVIS, F. R. *The Great Tradition: George Eliot, Henry James, Joseph Conrad.* Harmondsworth: Penguin, 1962.

LERNER, DANIEL. 'The Influence of Turgenev on James'. *The Slavonic and East European Review* 20 (Dec. 1941), 43–4.

LEVENSON, MICHAEL. *A Geneology of Modernism: A Study of English Literary Doctrine 1908-1922.* Cambridge: Cambridge University Press, 1984.

LEVINE, GEORGE. *Darwin and the Novelists: Patterns of Science in Victorian Fiction.* Cambridge, Mass.: Harvard University Press, 1988.

LÉVI-STRAUSS, CLAUDE. *Structural Anthropology* (2 vols.), trans. Monique Layton. Harmondsworth: Penguin, 1978.

LOGAN, J. D. 'The Witchery of Woman's Smile: A Study in Popular Aesthetics.' *The Canadian Magazine* 39 (October 1912).

LOTHE, JAKOB. 'Repetition and Narrative Method: Hardy, Conrad, Faulkner', in Jeremy Hawthorn (ed.), *Narrative: From Malory to Motion Pictures.* London: Edward Arnold, 1985.

——. *Conrad's Narrative Method.* Oxford: Clarendon Press, 1989.

LUCAS, E. V. 'Concerning Tea.' *Cornhill Magazine*, January 1897, 72–9.

LUTOSŁAWSKI, WINCENTY. 'A Visit to Conrad in 1897'. *Blue Peter* 10 (December 1930), 638–40.

LYND, ROBERT. 'Mr. Conrad's Fame.' *New Statesman* 4 July 1914.

LYTTON, LADY CONSTANCE, and WARTON, JANE. *Prisons and Prisoners: Some Personal Experiences of a Suffragette.* London: Heinemann, 1914.

MACARTHUR, JAMES. 'New Books: Romance in Malaya.' *Bookman* August–September 1895, 39–41.

MCCRACKEN, SCOTT, 'Postmodernism, a *Chance* to Reread?', in Scott McCracken and Sally Ledger (eds.), *Cultural Politics at the Fin de Siècle.* Cambridge: Cambridge University Press, 1995.

MCDONALD, PETER D. *British Literary Culture and Publishing Practice 1880-1914.* Cambridge: Cambridge University Press, 1997.

MÉGROZ, R. L. *Joseph Conrad's Mind and Method: A Study of Personality in Art.* London: Faber and Faber, 1931.

MEREDITH, GEORGE. *Diana of the Crossways.* 1885. New York: Book League of America, 1931.

MERLEAU-PONTY, MAURICE. *The Phenomenology of Perception*, trans. Colin Smith. London: Routledge and Kegan Paul, 1962.

MEYER, BERNARD C. *Joseph Conrad: A Psychoanalytic Biography.* Princeton: Princeton University Press, 1967.

MEYERS, JEFFREY. *Joseph Conrad: A Biography.* London: John Murray, 1991.

MICKIEWICZ, ADAM. *The Romantic.* 1822. trans. W. H. Auden, in Czesław Miłosz, *The History of Polish Literature.* 1969. Berkeley: University of California Press, 1983.

——. *Konrad Wallenrod*, trans. George Rapall Noyes and others. Berkeley: University of California Press, 1925.

——. *Forefathers' Eve, Part III.* 1832. In Harold B. Segel (ed. and trans). *Polish Romantic Drama.* Ithaca, NY: Cornell University Press, 1977.

MILLER, JANE. Introduction, *Chance.* London: Hogarth Press, 1984.

MILLER, J. HILLIS. 'Joseph Conrad', in *Poets of Reality: Six Twentieth-Century Writers.* Cambridge, Mass.: Belknap Press of Harvard University Press, 1966.

MILLER, J. HILLIS. *Fiction and Repetition: Seven English Novels.* Oxford: Blackwell, 1982.

MILLER, JANE. *Seductions: Studies in Reading and Culture.* London: Virago, 1990.

MIŁOSZ, CZESŁAW. 'Joseph Conrad in Polish Eyes'. *Atlantic Monthly* 200:5 (1957), 219–28.

MOFFAT, WENDY. 'Domestic Violence: The Simple Tale within *The Secret Agent.*' *English Literature in Transition 1880–1920* 37:4 (1994), 465–89.

MOI, TORIL. *Sexual/Textual Politics: Feminist Literary Theory.* London: Methuen, 1985.

MONGIA, PADMINI. 'Empire, Narrative and the Feminine in *Lord Jim* and *Heart of Darkness*, in Keith Carabine, Owen Knowles, and Wiesław Krajka (eds.), *Contexts for Conrad.* Boulder, Colo.: East European Monographs, 1993, 135–50.

——. ' "Ghosts of the Gothic": Spectral Women and Colonized Spaces in *Lord Jim*', in Andrew Michael Roberts (ed.), *Conrad and Gender.* Amsterdam: Rodopi, 1993.

MONMONIER, MARK. *Maps With the News.* Chicago: University of Chicago Press, 1989.

MONTAGUE, C. E. Review. *The Manchester Guardian*, 15 January 1914, 6.

MOORE, GENE (ed.). *Conrad's Cities: Essays for Hans van Marle.* Amsterdam: Rodopi, 1992.

——. 'In Defense of *Suspense.*' *Conradiana* 25:2 (1993), 99–114.

——. 'The Colonial Context of Anti-Semitism: Poradowska's *Yaga* and the Thys Libel Case.' *The Conradian* 18:2 (1993), 25–36.

MOORE, HENRY CHARLES. *Noble Deeds of the World's Heroines.* London: The Religious Tract Society, 1913.

MORF, GUSTAV. *The Polish Heritage of Joseph Conrad.* London: Sampson, Low, Marston, 1930.

MORGAN, ROSEANNE. *Women and Sexuality in the Novels of Thomas Hardy*. London and New York: Routledge, 1988.

MORRELL, LADY OTTOLINE. *Ottoline: The Earlier Memoirs of Lady Ottoline Morrell*, ed. Robert Gathorne-Hardy. London: Faber and Faber, 1963.

MOSER, THOMAS. *Joseph Conrad: Achievement and Decline*. Cambridge, Mass.: Harvard University Press, 1957.

MOTT, FRANK LUTHER. *A History of American Magazines* (6 vols.). Cambridge. Mass.: Harvard University Press, 1957.

MULVEY, LAURA. *Visual and Other Pleasures*. Basingstoke and London: Macmillan, 1989.

MUNRO, C. K. *At Mrs Beam's*. 1921. *Great Modern British Plays*, ed. J. W. Marriot. London: Harrap, 1929.

MURSIA, UGO. *Scritti Conradiani*, ed. Mario Curelli. Milano: Mursia, 1983.

——. 'Notes on Conrad's Italian Novel: *Suspense*', trans. Mario Curelli, in Gene Moore (ed.), *Conrad's Cities: Essays for Hans van Marle*. Amsterdam: Rodopi, 1992

NADELHAFT, RUTH. *Joseph Conrad: A Feminist Reading*. Hemel Hempstead: Harvester Wheatsheaf, 1991.

NAJDER, ZDZISŁAW (ed.). *Conrad's Polish Background: Letters to and from Polish Friends*, trans. Halina Carroll. London: Oxford University Press, 1964.

——. (ed.). *Congo Diary and Other Uncollected Pieces*. Garden City, NY: Doubleday, 1978.

——. *Joseph Conrad: A Chronicle*. Cambridge: Cambridge University Press, 1983.

——. (ed.). *Conrad Under Familial Eyes*, trans. Halina Carroll-Najder. Cambridge: Cambridge University Press, 1983.

—— Introduction. *A Personal Record*. Oxford: Oxford University Press, 1988.

NOCHLIN, LINDA. 'Women, Art, and Power', in *Women, Art, and Power and Other Essays*. London: Thames and Hudson, 1989.

OATES, JOYCE CAROL. *Contraries: Essays*. New York: Oxford University Press, 1981.

O'HANLON, REDMOND. *Joseph Conrad and Charles Darwin: The Influence of Scientific Thought on Conrad's Fiction*. Edinburgh: Salamander Press, 1984.

OLIPHANT, MARGARET. *Annals of a Publishing House: William Blackwood and His Sons* (3 vols.). Edinburgh and London: William Blackwood, 1897.

——. 'The Anti-Marriage League'. *Blackwood's Magazine*, January 1896, 135–49.

OREL, HAROLD. *Popular Fiction in England 1914–1918.* Lexington: The University Press of Kentucky, 1992.

ORWELL, GEORGE. *The Collected Essays, Journalism and Letters,* vol. 4. Harmondsworth: Penguin, 1970.

ORZESZKOWA, ELIZA, *An Obscure Apostle,* trans. C. S. de Soissons. London: Greening, 1899.

PANOFSKY, ERWIN. *Renaissance and Renascences in Western Art.* 1960. London: Paladin, 1970.

———. *Perspective as Symbolic Form,* trans. Christopher S. Wood. New York: Zone Books, 1991.

PANKHURST, EMMELINE. 'The Importance of the Vote'. Suffragist Pamphlet. London, 24 March 1908.

PANKHURST, SYLVIA. *The Suffragette Movement.* 1931. London: Virago, 1977.

PARRY, BENITA. *Conrad and Imperialism: Ideological Boundaries and Visionary Frontiers.* London: Macmillan, 1983.

PATER, WALTER. *Appreciations, with an Essay on Style.* London: Macmillan, 1889.

PATMORE, COVENTRY. *Principle in Art: Religio Poetae and Other Essays.* 1889. London: Duckworth, 1913.

PAYN, JAMES. Review. *Illustrated London News,* 5 February 1898.

PECORA, VINCENT. '*Heart of Darkness* and the Phenomenology of Voice.' *Journal of Literary History* 52 (1985), 993–1006.

PETTERSON, TORSTEN. *Consciousness and Time: A Study in the Philosophy and Narrative Technique of Joseph Conrad.* Abo: Abo akademi, 1982.

PLEYER, WILLIAM GROSVENOR. *The History of American Journalism.* Boston: Houghton Mifflin, 1927.

PONSARD, M. F. 'La Première Representation de *Lucrèce*'. *Revue des Deux Mondes* 155 (1 September 1899), 168–86.

POOVEY, MARY. *Uneven Developments: The Ideological Work of Gender in Mid-Victorian England.* Chicago: University of Chicago Press, 1988.

PORADOWSKA, MARGUERITE. *Yaga* in *Revue des Deux Mondes* 82 (1 and 15 August 1887).

———. *Demoiselle Micia. Revue des Deux Mondes* 90 (1 and 15 December 1888) and 91 (1 January 1889).

———. *Popes et popadias. Revue des Deux Mondes* 114 (15 November and 1 December 1892).

———. *Marylka. Revue des Deux Mondes* 127 (15 February 1895) and 128 (1 and 15 March 1895).

———. *Pour Noémi. Revue des Deux Mondes* 154 (15 August 1899) and 155 (1 September 1895).

PYKETT, LYN. *The 'Improper' Feminine: the Women's Sensation Novel and the New Woman's Writing*. London and New York: Routledge, 1992.

QUILLER-COUCH, A. T. Review. *Pall Mall Magazine*, March 1898, 428.

RADWAY, JANICE. *Reading the Romance: Women, Patriarchy, and Popular Literature*. Chapel Hill: University of North Carolina Press, 1984.

RAUCHBAUER, OTTO. *The Edith Oenone Somerville Archive in Drishane*. Dublin: Irish Manuscripts Commission, 1995.

RAY, MARTIN (ed.). *Joseph Conrad: Interviews and Recollections*. London: Macmillan, 1990.

REILLY, JIM. *Shadowtime: History and Representation in Hardy, Conrad and George Eliot*. London and New York: Routledge, 1993.

RESSLER, STEVE. *Joseph Conrad: Consciousness and Integrity*. New York: New York University Press, 1988.

RETINGER, J. H. *Conrad and His Contemporaries, Souvenirs*. London: Minerva, 1941.

REYNOLDS, SIR JOSHUA. *Discourses on Art*, ed. Robert R. Wark. San Marino, Calif.: Huntingdon Library, 1959.

RICOEUR, PAUL. *Oneself As Another*. trans. Kathleen Blamey. Chicago and London: University of Chicago Press, 1992.

ROBERTS, ANDREW MICHAEL. 'The Gaze and the Dummy: Sexual Politics in *The Arrow of Gold*', in Keith Carabine (ed.), *Joseph Conrad: Critical Assessments*, iii. Robertsbridge, East Sussex: Helm Information, 1992.

——. (ed.). *Conrad and Gender*. Amsterdam: Rodopi, 1993.

——. 'Secret Agents and Secret Objects: Action, Passivity, and Gender in *Chance*,' in Andrew Michael Roberts (ed.), *Conrad and Gender*. Amsterdam: Rodopi, 1993.

——. (ed.). *Joseph Conrad*. London and New York: Longman, 1998.

ROSE, JACQUELINE. 'Sexuality and Vision', in Hal Foster (ed.,) *Vision and Visuality: Discussions in Contemporary Culture*. Seattle: Bay Press, 1988.

ROUSSEL, ROYAL. *The Metaphysics of Darkness: A Study in the Unity and Development of Conrad's Fiction*. Baltimore and London: Johns Hopkins University Press, 1971.

SADLEIR, MICHAEL. 'Joseph Conrad'. *Dictionary of National Biography 1922–1930*, ed. J. R. H. Weaver. London: Oxford University Press, 1937.

SAID, EDWARD. *Joseph Conrad and the Fiction of Autobiography*. Cambridge, Mass.: Harvard University Press, 1966.

——. *The World, the Text and the Critic*. London: Faber and Faber, 1984.

SCHWARZ, DANIEL R. *Conrad: Almayer's Folly to Under Western Eyes.* London: Macmillan, 1980.

——. *Conrad: The Later Fiction.* London: Macmillan, 1982.

SCOTT, BONNIE KIME. *The Gender of Modernism: A Critical Anthology.* Bloomington: Indiana University Press, 1990.

SEDGWICK, EVE KOSOFSKY. *Between Men: English Literature and Male Homosocial Desire.* New York: Columbia University Press, 1985.

SHERRY, NORMAN. *Conrad's Eastern World.* Cambridge: Cambridge University Press, 1966.

SHERRY, NORMAN. *Conrad's Western World.* Cambridge: Cambridge University Press, 1971.

——. *Conrad and His World.* London: Thames and Hudson, 1972.

——. (ed.). *Conrad: The Critical Heritage.* London and Boston: Routledge and Kegan Paul, 1973.

——. (ed.). *Joseph Conrad: A Commemoration.* London: Macmillan, 1976.

SHELDEN, MICHAEL. *Graham Greene: The Man Within.* London: Heinemann, 1994.

SHOWALTER, ELAINE. *A Literature of their Own: From Charlotte Brontë to Doris Lessing.* 1977. London: Virago, 1982.

——. *The Female Malady: Women and Madness and English Culture 1830–1980.* London: Virago, 1988.

SIEGLE, ROBERT. 'The Two Texts of *Chance.*' *Conradiana* 16:2 (1984), 83–101.

SŁOWACKI, JULIUSZ. *Collected Works,* ed. Antoni Malecki. Lwów, 1866.

——. *Fantazy,* in Harold B. Segel (ed. and trans). *Polish Romantic Drama.* Ithaca, NY: Cornell University Press, 1977.

SMILES, SAMUEL. *Thrift.* London: John Murray, 1897.

SMITH, DAVID (ed.). *Joseph Conrad's Under Western Eyes.* Hamden: Archon Books, 1991.

SNEDDON, ROBERT W. 'A Grand Woman'. *Pictorial Review,* September 1923.

STAPE, JOHN H. 'An Allusion to an Eastern Tale in the "Author's Note" to *Chance.*' *L'Époque Conradienne* (1988), 69–70.

——. (ed.). *The Cambridge Companion to Joseph Conrad.* Cambridge: Cambridge University Press, 1996.

——. and KNOWLES, OWEN (eds.). *A Portrait in Letters: Correspondence To and About Conrad.* Amsterdam: Rodopi, 1996.

STEVENS, RAY. Review of *The Collected Letters of Joseph Conrad.* *English Literature in Transition 1880–1920* 35 (1992).

STOTT, REBECCA. *The Fabrication of the Late Victorian "femme fatale": The Kiss of Death.* Basingstoke: Macmillan, 1992.

STRACHEY, RAY. *The Cause.* 1928. London: Virago, 1978.

STRAUS, NINA PELIKAN. 'The Exclusion of the Intended from Secret Sharing in Conrad's *Heart of Darkness*'. *Novel* 20:2 (1987) 123–37.

SULLIVAN, ALVIN (ed.). *British Literary Magazines: The Victorian and Edwardian Age, 1837–1913.* Westport, Conn., and London: Greenwood Press, 1984.

SYMONS, ARTHUR. *Studies in Two Literatures.* 1897. New York: Garland Publishing, 1977.

——. *Notes on Joseph Conrad with Some Unpublished Letters.* London: Myers, 1925.

TANNER, TONY. ' "Gnawed Bones" and "Artless Tales": Eating and Narrative in Conrad', in Norman Sherry (ed.), *Joseph Conrad: A Commemoration.* London: Macmillan, 1976.

——. 'Joseph Conrad and the Last Gentleman.' *Critical Quarterly* 28 (1986), 109–42.

TAYLOR, JENNY. *In the Secret Theatre of Home: Wilkie Collins, Sensation Narrative, and Nineteenth-Century Psychology.* London: Routledge, 1992.

TEETS, BRUCE (ed.). *Joseph Conrad: An Annotated Bibliography.* New York and London: Garland, 1990.

TENNANT, ROGER. *Joseph Conrad: A Biography.* New York: Atheneum, 1981.

THOMPSON, GORDON W. 'Conrad's Women', *Nineteenth-Century Fiction* 32:4 (1978) 442–63.

THOMSON, GEORGE. 'Conrad's Later Fiction.' *English Literature in Transition* 12:4 (1969).

THORBURN, DAVID. *Conrad's Romanticism.* New Haven and London: Yale University Press, 1974.

TICKNER, LISA. *The Spectacle of Women: Imagery of the Suffrage Campaign 1907–14.* London: Chatto and Windus, 1987.

TOMASELLI, SYLVANA, and PORTER, ROY (eds.). *Rape: An Historical and Social Enquiry.* Oxford: Blackwell, 1986.

TRILLING, LIONEL. 'On the Modern Element in Modern Literature', *Partisan Review* 28:1 (1961) 9–35.

TROTTER, DAVID. *The English Novel in History.* London: Routledge, 1993.

Unsigned Article. 'Joseph Conrad'. *T.P.'s Weekly* 22 January 1904, 113.

Unsigned Article. 'Women's Code of Honour.' *Living Age* 271 (23 December 1911), 762.

Unsigned Article. 'Conrad's New Novel, "Victory—An Island Story".' *Munsey's Magazine* 53 (January 1915), 906.

Unsigned Review. *Daily News* 25 April 1895, 6.

Unsigned Review. 'Fiction: *Almayer's Folly.' Literary World* 27 (18 May 1895), 155.

Unsigned Review. *Daily Mail*, 7 December 1897, 3.

Unsigned Review. *Literature*, 26 March 1898.

Unsigned Review. *Glasgow Evening News*, 30 April 1903, 2.

Unsigned Review. *Daily Telegraph*, 9 November 1904, 4.

Unsigned Review. *Nation*, 17 July 1920, 503–4.

WATT, GEORGE. *The Fallen Woman in the Nineteenth-Century English Novel*. London and Canberra: Croom Helm, 1984.

WATT, IAN. 'Joseph Conrad: Alienation and Commitment', in Hugh Sykes Davies and George Watson (eds.), *The English Mind: Studies in the English Moralists Presented to Basil Willey*. Cambridge: Cambridge University Press, 1964.

WATT, IAN. 'Conrad, James, and *Chance*', in Maynard Mack and Ian Gregor (eds.), *Imagined Worlds: Essays on Some English Novels and Novelists in Honour of John Butt*. London: Methuen, 1968, 301–22.

——. *Conrad in the Nineteenth Century*. Berkeley: University of California, 1979.

WATTS, CEDRIC (ed.). *Joseph Conrad's Letters to Cunninghame-Graham*. Cambridge: Cambridge University Press, 1969.

——. *A Preface to Conrad*. 1982. London: Longman, 1993.

——. *The Deceptive Text: An Introduction to Covert Plots*. Brighton: Harvester Press, 1984.

——. Introduction. *Lord Jim*. Harmondsworth: Penguin, 1986.

——. *Joseph Conrad: A Literary Life*. Basingstoke and London: Macmillan, 1989.

WELLS, H. G. Review. *The Saturday Review*, 16 May 1896, 509–10.

——. *Ann Veronica*. London: Heinemann, 1909.

WHARTON, EDITH. *The House of Mirth*. 1905. New York: Berkeley Books, 1981.

WHITE, ANDREA. *Joseph Conrad and the Adventure Tradition: Constructing and Deconstructing the Imperial Subject*. Cambridge: Cambridge University Press, 1993.

WILEY, PAUL. *Conrad's Measure of Man*. Madison: University of Wisconsin Press, 1954.

WILLARD, GRACE. 'Conrad the Man.' *New York Evening Post Literary Review*, 9 August 1924, 952.

WILLIAMS, NEVILLE. *Powder and Paint: A History of the English-woman's Toilet*. London: Longman's, Green, 1957.

WILLISON, IAN, GOULD, WARWICK, CHERNAIK, WARREN (eds.). *Modernist Writers and the Marketplace*. Basingstoke: Macmillan, 1996.

WILLY, TODD. 'The Conquest of the Commodore: Conrad's Rigging of "The Nigger" for the Henley Regatta.' *Conradiana* 17:3 (1985), 163–82.

WILSON, ROBERT. *Conrad's Mythology.* Troy, NY: Whitston, 1987.

WITOSZEK, NINA. *The Theatre of Recollection: A Cultural Study of the Modern Dramatic Tradition in Ireland and Poland.* Stockholm: University of Stockholm, 1988.

WOOLF, VIRGINIA. *The Common Reader.* London: Hogarth Press, 1925.

WOLLAEGER, MARK A. *Joseph Conrad and the Fictions of Skepticism.* Stanford: Stanford University Press, 1990.

WOOD, MRS HENRY. *East Lynne.* 1861. London: Ward, Lock, 1910.

YOSHIDA, TETSUO. 'Joseph Conrad's Napoleonic Fiction.' *Studies in English Language and Literature* (Kyushu University) 33 (January 1983), 65–94.

ZANGWILL, ISRAEL. 'The Sword and the Spirit.' Suffragist Pamphlet. London, November 1910.

Index